Brian Hart

with Mario Rinvolucri, Herbert Puchta & Jeff S

English in Mind

Second edition

Teacher's Resource
Book 1A

CAMBRIDGE
UNIVERSITY PRESS

CAMBRIDGE UNIVERSITY PRESS
Cambridge, New York, Melbourne, Madrid, Cape Town,
Singapore, São Paulo, Delhi, Mexico City

Cambridge University Press
The Edinburgh Building, Cambridge CB2 8RU, UK

www.cambridge.org
Information on this title: www.cambridge.org/9780521183185

First published 2004
Second edition 2010
3rd printing 2013

Printed in Dubai by Oriental Press

A catalogue record for this publication is available from the British Library

ISBN 978-0-521-18318-5 Teacher's Resource Book 1A and 1B
ISBN 978-0-521-18326-0 Combo 1A with DVD-ROM
ISBN 978-0-521-18327-7 Combo 1B with DVD-ROM
ISBN 978-0-521-18319-2 Audio CDs 1A and 1B
ISBN 978-0-521-18320-8 Testmaker Audio CD/CD-ROM 1A and 1B
ISBN 978-0-521-15374-4 DVD (PAL) 1
ISBN 978-0-521-12377-8 DVD (NTSC) 1
ISBN 978-0-521-17681-1 Classware DVD-ROM 1

Contents

Introduction

'If you can teach teenagers, you can teach anyone.' Michael Grinder

Teaching teenagers is an interesting and challenging task. A group of adolescents can be highly motivated, cooperative and fun to teach on one day, and the next day the whole group or individual students might turn out to be truly 'difficult' – the teacher might, for example, be faced with discipline problems, disruptive or provocative behaviour, a lack of motivation, or unwillingness on the students' part to do homework assigned to them.

The roots of these problems frequently lie in the fact that adolescents are going through a period of significant changes in their lives. The key challenge in the transition period between being a child and becoming an adult is the adolescent's struggle for identity – a process that requires the development of a distinct sense of who they are. A consequence of this process is that adolescents can feel threatened, and at the same time experience overwhelming emotions. They frequently try to compensate for the perceived threats with extremely rude behaviour, and try to 'hide' their emotions behind a wall of extreme outward conformity. The more individual students manage to look, talk, act and behave like the other members of their peer group, the less threatened and insecure they feel.

Insights into the causes underlying the problems might help us to understand better the complex situation our students are in. However, such insights do not automatically lead to more success in teaching. We need to react to the challenges in a professional way[1]. This includes the need to:

- select content and organise the students' learning according to their psychological needs;
- create a positive learning atmosphere;
- cater for differences in students' learning styles and intelligence(s), and facilitate the development of our students' study skills.

English in Mind second edition has been written taking all these points into account. They have significantly influenced the choice of texts, artwork and design, the structure of the units, the typology of exercises, and the means by which students' study skills are facilitated and extended.

The importance of the content for success

There are a number of reasons why the choice of the right content has a crucial influence over success or failure in the teaching of adolescents. Teachers frequently observe that teenagers are reluctant to 'talk about themselves'. This has to do with the adolescent's need for psychological security. Consequently, the 'further away' from their own world the content of the teaching is, the more motivating and stimulating it will be for the students. The preference for psychologically remote content goes hand in hand with a fascination with extremes and realistic details. Furthermore, students love identifying with heroes and heroines, because these idols are perceived to embody the qualities needed in order to survive in a threatening world: qualities such as courage, genius, creativity and love. In the foreign language class, students can become fascinated with stories about heroes and heroines to which they can ascribe such qualities. *English in Mind* treats students as young adults, offering them a range of interesting topics and a balance between educational value and teenage interest and fun.

As Kieran Egan[1] stresses, learning in the adolescent classroom can be successfully organised by starting with something far from the students' experience, but also connected to it by some quality with which they can associate. This process of starting far from the students makes it easier for the students to become interested in the topic, and also enables the teacher finally to relate the content to the students' own world.

A positive learning atmosphere

The creation of a positive learning atmosphere largely depends on the rapport between teacher and students, and the one which students have among themselves. It requires the teacher to be a genuine, empathetic listener, and to have a number of other psychological skills. *English in Mind* supports the teacher's task of creating positive learning experiences through: clear tasks; a large number of carefully designed exercises; regular opportunities for the students to check their own work; and a learning process designed to guarantee that the students will learn to express themselves both in speaking and in writing.

Learning styles and multiple intelligences

There is significant evidence that students will be better motivated, and learn more successfully, if differences in learning styles and intelligences are taken into account in the teaching-learning process.[2] The development of a number of activities in *English in Mind* have been influenced by such insights, and students find frequent study tips that show them how they can better utilise their own resources.[3]

The methodology used in *English in Mind*

Skills: *English in Mind* uses a communicative, multi-skills approach to develop the students' foreign language abilities in an interesting and motivational way. A wide range of interesting text types is used to present authentic use of language, including magazine and newspaper clippings, interviews, narratives, songs and engaging photostories.

---

1 An excellent analysis of teenage development and consequences for our teaching in general can be found in Kieran Egan: *Romantic Understanding*, Routledge and Kegan Paul, New York and London, 1990. This book has had a significant influence on the thinking behind *English in Mind*, and the development of the concept of the course.

2 See for example Eric Jensen: *Brain-Based Learning and Teaching*, Turning Point Publishing, Del Mar, CA, USA, 1995, on learning styles. An overview of the theory of multiple intelligences can be found in Howard Gardner: *Multiple Intelligences: The Theory in Practice*, Basic Books, New York 1993.

3 See Marion Williams and Robert L. Burden: *Psychology for Language Teachers*, Cambridge University Press, 1997 (pp. 143–162), on how the learner deals with the process of learning.

Grammar: *English in Mind* is based on a strong grammatical syllabus and takes into account students' mixed abilities by dealing with grammar in a carefully graded way, and offering additional teaching support.

Vocabulary: *English in Mind* offers a systematic vocabulary syllabus, including important lexical chunks for conversation and extension of the vocabulary in a bank at the back of the book.

Culture: *English in Mind* gives students insights into a number of important cross-cultural and intercultural themes. Significant cultural features of English-speaking countries are presented, and students are involved in actively reflecting on the similarities and differences between other cultures and their own.

Consolidation: Check your progress revision pages give teachers a clear picture of their students' progress and make students aware of what they have learned.

Projects give students the opportunity to use new language in a less controlled context and allows for learner independence.

Teacher support: *English in Mind* is clearly structured and easy to teach. The Teacher's Resource Book offers step-by-step lesson notes, background information on content, culture and language, additional teaching ideas and the tapescripts, photocopiable materials for further practice and extra lessons, taking into consideration the needs of mixed-ability groups by providing extra material for fast finishers or students who need more support, as well as entry tests.

Student support: *English in Mind* offers systematic support to students through: Study help sections and Skills tips; classroom language; guidance in units to help with the development of classroom discourse and the students' writing; lists of irregular verbs and phonetics (at the back of the Student's Book); and a Grammar reference (at the back of the Workbook).

English in Mind: components

Each level of the *English in Mind* series contains the following components:

- A and B Combos with accompanying DVD-ROMs
- Audio CDs
- Teacher's Resource Book
- Testmaker Audio CD/CD-ROM
- DVD
- Classware DVD-ROM
- Website resources

The Combo

Each Combo consists of eight Student's Book units as well as the corresponding Workbook pages.

The Student's Book

Combos 1A and 1B have Welcome units at the beginning. This is to allow teachers to revise, reasonably quickly, some of the key areas of language which students covered in the previous level of *English in Mind* or in their previous learning. An alternative use of the Welcome unit might be as diagnostic exercises, allowing teachers to gauge the strengths and weaknesses of their particular group of students before continuing with the material.

The units have the basic following structure, although with occasional minor variations depending on the flow of an individual unit:

- an opening **reading** text
- a **grammar** page, often including pronunciation
- two pages of **vocabulary** and **skills** work
- either a **photostory** or a **Culture in mind** text, followed by **writing skills** work and extra speaking

The **reading texts** aim to engage and motivate the students with interesting and relevant content, and to provide contextualised examples of target grammar and lexis. The texts have 'lead-in' tasks and are followed by comprehension tasks of various kinds. All the opening texts are also recorded on the Class Audio CDs, which allows teachers to follow the initial reading with a 'read and listen' phase, giving the students the invaluable opportunity of connecting the written word with the spoken version, which is especially useful for auditory learners. Alternatively, with stronger classes, teachers may decide to do one of the exercises as a listening task, with books closed.

Grammar follows the initial reading. The emphasis is on active involvement in the learning process. Examples from the texts are isolated and used as a basis for tasks, which focus on both concept and form of the target grammar area. Students are encouraged to find other examples and work out rules for themselves. Occasionally there are also **Look!** boxes which highlight an important connected issue concerning the grammar area. This is followed by a number of graded exercises, both receptive and productive, which allow students to begin to employ the target language in different contexts and to produce realistic language. Next, there is usually a speaking activity, aiming at further personalisation of the language.

Each unit has at least one **Vocabulary** section, with specific word fields. Again, examples from the initial text are focused on, and a lexical set is developed, with exercises for students to put the vocabulary into use. Vocabulary is frequently recycled in later texts in the unit (e.g. photostories or Culture in mind texts), and also in later units

Pronunciation is included in every unit. There are exercises on common phoneme problems such as /ɪ/ in *sit* vs. /iː/ in *seat*, as well as aspects of stress (within words, and across sentences) and elision. Vital areas such as the use of schwa /ə/ are dealt with on more than one occasion, and often in relation to a grammar area, for example, the pronunciation of 'than' when comparatives are taught.

Language skills are present in every unit. There is always at least one **listening skills** activity, with listening texts of various genres; at least one (but usually several) **speaking skills** activity for fluency development. **Reading skills** are taught through the opening texts and also later texts in some units, as well as the Culture in mind sections. There is always a **writing skills** task, towards the end of each unit.

The final two pages of each unit have either a **photostory** or a **Culture in mind** text. The **photostories** are conversations between teenagers in everyday situations, allowing students to read and listen for interest and also to experience the use of common everyday language expressions. These Everyday English expressions are worked on in exercises following the dialogue. The photostories are expanded with videostories on the DVD/DVD-ROM, where students can follow the progress of the characters through a term at school. The **Culture in mind** texts are reading texts which provide further reading practice, and an opportunity for students to develop their knowledge and understanding of the world at large and in particular the English-speaking world. They include a wide variety of stimulating topics: school clubs in Britain, remembering heroes from all over the world, how teenagers earn money, teen talk in Britain, fortune telling, reggae music and a heroic footballer player.

Towards the end of each unit there is a **writing skills** task. These are an opportunity for students to further their control of language and to experiment in the production of tasks in a variety of genres (e.g. letters, emails, reports, etc.). There are model texts for the students to aid their own writing, and exercises providing guidance in terms of content and organisation. Through the completion of the writing tasks, students, if they wish, can also build up a bank of materials, or 'portfolio', during their period of learning: this can be very useful to them as the source of a sense of clear progress and as a means of self-assessment. A 'portfolio' of work can also be shown to other people (exam bodies, parents, even future employers) as evidence of achievement in language learning. Many of the writing tasks also provide useful and relevant practice for examinations such as Cambridge ESOL PET or Trinity Integrated Skills Examinations.

At the end of every other unit there is an extra speaking section, titled 'Last but not least' where students are given the opportunity for freer practice of the grammar and vocabulary that they have learnt in the unit.

There is a **Check your progress** section after every two units. Here the teacher will find exercises in the Grammar and Vocabulary that were presented in the previous two units. The purpose of these (as opposed to the more formal tests offered on the Testmaker CD-ROM) is for teachers and students alike to check quickly the learning and progress made during the two units just covered; they can be done in class or at home. Every exercise has a marking scheme, and students can use the marks they gain to do some simple self-assessment of their progress (a light 'task' is offered for this).

Beyond the units themselves, *English in Mind* offers at the end of the Student's Book a further set of materials for teachers and students. These consist of:

- **Vocabulary bank**: extension of vocabulary from the units in the main body of the Student's Book for students to build on their vocabulary. This section is attractively illustrated and the words are taught either through definitions or pictures. This section is particularly useful for those students who want to learn more.

- **Get it right!** This section is based on the Cambridge Learner Corpus and concentrates on typical errors that students often make at this level. These errors are dealt with through a variety of exercises and activities which correspond with the grammar studied in the units in the

Student's Book. They allow students to focus on the errors they make and give them the opportunity to correct them.

- **Projects:** activities which students can do in pairs or groups (or even individually if desired), for students to put the language they have so far learned into practical and enjoyable use. They are especially useful for mixed-ability classes, as they allow students to work at their own pace. The projects produced could also be part of the 'portfolio' of material mentioned earlier.

  A presentation about a well-known person, can be done after student's have finished the first five units of Combo 1A. It concentrates on the grammar, vocabulary and topics of these five units.

  A class survey, fits in after students have finished Unit 8 of Combo 1A.

  A poster about the future, should be done once student's have finished Unit 5 of Combo 1B, and finally,

  A talk on an event that happened this year, is an enjoyable way for students to round off Combo 1B.

- An **irregular verb** list for students to refer to when they need.

- A listing of **phonetic symbols**, again for student reference.

The DVD-ROM

The Student's Book includes a DVD-ROM which contains the listening material for the Workbook (listening texts and pronunciation exercises) in MP3 format and a range of carefully graded grammar and vocabulary exercises to provide further practice of the language presented in each unit. It also contains the 'Team Spirit' videostories corresponding to the photostories in the Student's Books. These complement the photostories by dealing with the same themes and reflecting the same values, but they contain separate stories and scenes to them. They may take place before, at the same time as or after the photostories. There are four exercises for each videostory on the DVD-ROM, including a 'videoke' one in which students record their voices onto a short section of the videostory and can then play it back, either solo or as a pair with a friend. This provides a fun, sociable element, but also good practice of spoken English. The DVD-ROM also includes games for students to practise in an enjoyable and motivating way.

The Workbook

The Workbook is a resource for both teachers and students, providing further practice in the language and skills covered in the Student's Book. It is organised unit-by-unit, following the Student's Book. Each Workbook unit has six pages, and the following contents:

Remember and check: this initial exercise encourages students to remember the content of the initial reading text in the Student's Book unit.

Exercises: an extensive range of supporting exercises in the grammatical, lexical and phonological areas of the Student's Book unit, following the progression of the unit, so that teachers can use the exercises either during or at the end of the Student's Book unit.

Everyday English and **Culture in mind**: extra exercises on these sections in alternating units, as in the Student's Book.

Study help: these sections follow a syllabus of study skills areas, to develop the students' capacities as independent and successful learners. After a brief description of the skill, there are exercises for the students to begin to practise it.

Skills in mind page: these pages contain a separate skills development syllabus, which normally focuses on two main skill areas in each unit. There is also a skill tip relating to the main skill area, which the students can immediately put into action when doing the skills task(s).

Unit check page: this is a one-page check of knowledge of the key language of the unit, integrating both grammar and vocabulary in the three exercise types. The exercise types are: a) a cloze text to be completed using items given in a box; b) a sentence-level multiple choice exercise; c) sentences to be completed with given vocabulary items.

At the end of the Workbook, there is a **Grammar reference** section. Here, there are explanations of the main grammar topics of each unit, with examples. It can be used for reference by students at home, or the teacher might wish to refer to it in class if the students appreciate grammatical explanations.

The audio for the Workbook is available on the Audio CDs as well as on the Combo DVD-ROM in MP3 format.

The Teacher's Resource Book

The Teacher's Resource Book covers the content for both A and B Combos, and contains:

- clear, simple, practical teaching **notes** on each unit and how to implement the exercises as effectively as possible
- complete **tapescripts** for all listening activities
- complete **answers** to all exercises (grammar, vocabulary, comprehension questions, etc.)
- **optional further activities**, for stronger or weaker classes, to facilitate the use of the material in mixed-ability classes
- **background notes** relating to the information content (where appropriate) of reading texts and Culture in mind pages
- **language notes** relating to grammatical areas, to assist less-experienced teachers who might have concerns about the target language and how it operates (these can also be used to refer to the Workbook Grammar reference section)
- a complete **answer key** and **tapescripts** for the **Workbook**.
- A **'Memo from Mario'** page at the end of each unit of teaching notes and ideas for further exploitation of the material in the Student's Book written by the well-known methodologist Mario Rinvolucri.
- four **entry tests** which have been designed with two purposes. They can be used purely as diagnostic entry tests, or teachers can also use them for remedial work before beginning the Welcome unit in Combo 1A or after completing it.
- **photocopiable communication** activities: one page for each unit reflecting the core grammar and/or vocabulary of the unit. The Communication Activities recycle the key grammar and/or vocabulary in each unit. They are designed to activate the new language in a communicative context. They cover a range of fun and motivating activity types: board games; quizzes; information gap activities; descriptions; 'Find someone who … ', etc.

- **photocopiable extra grammar exercises**: extra exercises for each unit, reflecting the key grammar areas of the unit. The Grammar Practice Exercises cover specific areas of the key grammar from each unit. They are intended for fast finishers or students who need extra practice.
- **teaching notes** for the Photocopiable Communication Activities which contain clear step-by-step instructions for all the activities. In addition, there are answers for the Communication Activities, where relevant, and answers for all of the Grammar Practice Exercises.

Other resources

Testmaker Audio CD/CD-ROM: This allows you to create and edit your own texts, choosing from unit tests, which can be combined in unit pairs to match the course syllabus, or end-of-year tests. The tests offer 'standard' and 'more challenging' levels of testing, and can be created in A and B versions to avoid the sharing of answers. The listening test recordings are provided in audio CD format.

DVD: This contains both the 'Team Spirit' videostories and the complete 'EiMTV' material from the original edition.

Classware DVD-ROM: This contains the Student's Book in digital format to project on a whiteboard or via a computer with projector. You can enlarge parts of the page for a clearer focus. The 'Team Spirit' videostories and class listenings are also included, together with scripts.

Web resources: In addition to information about the series, the *English in Mind* website contains downloadable pages of further activities and exercises for students as well as interactive activities for students and wordlists with multiple translations. It can be found at this part of the Cambridge University Press website:

www.cambridge.org/elt/englishinmind

Introductory note from Mario Rinvolucri

As you read through the Teacher's Resource Book you will, at the end of each unit, find small contributions of mine that offer you alternative ways of practising a structure, of dealing with a text or of revising words.

- I want to stress that the ideas presented are simply alternatives to the ways of working proposed to you by the authors. I strongly recommend that you try the authors' way first.
- When you teach the book through for the second or third time you may be ready then to try something a bit different. The authors and I believe that options are important but options are not useful if they confuse you.
- Maybe you could think of my contributions as a sort of sauce with a slightly different flavour to be tried for variety's sake.

Mario Rinvolucri, Pilgrims, UK, guest methodologist.

Speaking & Functions	Listening	Reading	Writing
Talking about school Talking about hobbies Expressing likes and dislikes	An interview about a hobby	Article: An unusual hobby Culture in mind: School clubs	Email about your hobbies and interests
Talking about housework Last but not least: arranging to meet and making plans	Radio interview with a volunteer in Namibia	Article: Helping at a hospital Photostory: Let's give him a hand	Email about organising a party
Talking about the past Talking about when/where people were born	Presentation of 'my hero'	Article: Erin Brockovich Culture in mind: Remembering heroes	Three paragraphs about your hero
Asking about the past Retelling a story Last but not least: Alibi – a game	Television story Song: *You've Got A Friend In Me*	Article: The ping pong friendship that changed the world Photostory: Not a nice thing to say	Diary entry or email about an enjoyable weekend
Talking about obligations Describing job requirements Talking about people and their jobs	Talking about success Descriptions of future jobs	Article: What does 'success' mean? Article: Following a dream Culture in mind: Teenagers: earning money	Description of a job
Talking about food and fitness Last but not least: talking about food and places to eat	School canteen dialogue	Article: A long and healthy life Photostory: A double ice cream …	Paragraph about food and fitness
Comparing things Talking about learning English	Interviews about language learning An interview with David Crystal	Article: Speaking in many tongues Culture in mind: Teen talk	Description or email about language learning

1 Welcome

This unit is designed to serve as a review, giving students the opportunity to revise and practise language they already know, and it is also a tool for teachers to find out how much students know already and which areas students may need to do more work on before continuing with the course.

A PEOPLE

1 Greetings and introductions

a ▶ **CD1 T1** Students read through the words in the box and the gapped dialogue. Go through the example, if necessary. Students complete the exercise. Students can compare answers in pairs. Play the recording for students to listen and check, pausing the recording as necessary.

TAPESCRIPT

Liz: Hi. My name's Liz.

Monica: Hello, Liz. I'm Monica.

Liz: Nice to meet you. Excuse me a moment. Hi, Jack. How are you?

Jack: I'm fine, thanks. How about you?

Liz: I'm OK, thanks. Monica, this is my friend, Jack.

Monica: Nice to meet you, Jack.

Jack: Nice to meet you too, Monica.

> **Answers**
> 2 I'm 3 fine 4 you 5 this 6 Nice

b In groups of three, students act out the dialogue in Exercise 1a. Students can change the names and invent new names for themselves, if they want. Monitor and help as necessary. Ask stronger groups to act out their dialogue in front of the class.

✳ OPTIONAL ACTIVITY

If students are meeting for the first time, you may like to expand Exercise 1b. Separate the class into two groups and give students two minutes to practise the dialogue with as many people as possible in the other group. When time is up, have a team competition with students naming students in the other group and scoring one point for each correct answer.

LOOK!

Go through the examples in the Look! box with students and remind them of subject pronoun and possessive adjective changes. If necessary, elicit the

other subject pronouns and possessive adjectives from them and write them on the board:

I – my	you – your	he – his
she – her	it – its	we – our
you – your	they – their	

2 The verb *be*

a Go through the pictures with students and remind them when *'re* is used (it's the contracted form of *are*). Students complete the exercise. They may use short forms where possible. Check answers.

> **Answers**
> 2 'm/am 3 'm not/am not; I'm/I am 4 's/is
> 5 's not/ is not/ isn't; 's/is 6 're not/aren't/
> are not; 're/are

┌─ **Language note** ─┐
Point out to students that it is possible to say *He's/ She's/It's not* instead of *He/She/It isn't; You're/ We're/They're not* instead of *You/We/They aren't* e.g. *He's not Spanish. They're not Japanese.* This is particularly common in spoken English.
└──────────────┘

b ▶ **CD1 T2** Students read through the dialogue. Check any problems. Remind them to use short forms where possible. Students complete the exercise and compare answers in pairs. Play the recording for students to check or change their answers. Play the recording again, pausing as necessary.

TAPESCRIPT

Jack: Hi. My name's Jack, and this is Monica. She's from Italy.

Marek: Nice to meet you. I'm Marek, and those two people are my friends, Barbara and Adam. Are you from Rome, Monica?

Monica: No, I'm from Milan. Where are you from?

Marek: We're from Poland. Adam and I are from Warsaw and Barbara's from Gdansk. Are you on holiday in Cambridge?

Monica: No, I'm not. I'm a student at a language school here. Are you all students?

Marek: Yes, we are. We're at a language school too.

> **Answers**
> 2 is 3 's/is 4 'm/am 5 are 6 Are 7 'm/am
> 8 are 9 're/are 10 are 11 's/is 12 Are
> 13 'm/am 14 Are 15 are 16 're/are

c In pairs, students ask and answer questions orally about the people in Exercise 2b.

Possessive adjectives

Books closed. Write the subject pronouns (*I, you,* etc.) on the board and then the first possessive adjective (*my*). Elicit the others from students. Students open their books at page 7 and read the instructions and the email in Exercise 3. Students complete the exercise and compare answers in pairs. Check answers as a class.

Answers
2 your 3 Your 4 my 5 Their 6 her 7 his
8 Our 9 His 10 your

> **Language note**
> Although *it/its* are used for animals, *he/his* and *she/her* can be used for animals if you know their gender (as in Exercise 3, question 9).

 ## have / has got

Warm up

As an introduction to this exercise for weaker classes, ask students to describe what they have in their pockets or bags. Elicit the form *I have got* ... (give an example of your own if students find this difficult) and expand by asking students if they can remember what was in a student's bag. Elicit *He has got* ... Write the different forms of *have got* on the board and elicit the short forms, negatives and inversion in questions. Ask a few questions of your own to make sure students understand this verb, e.g.
T: *Elisa, have you got any brothers or sisters?*
S1: *Yes, I've got ...*

> **Language note**
> Students may produce questions like *How many brothers have you?*, so they may find it helpful to think about how they say these things in their own language and note the differences.

a ▶ **CD1 T3** Read through the instructions and the questions with students. Elicit the words they are likely to be listening for to answer the questions (numbers). Play the recording. Check answers, playing and pausing the recording again as necessary.

TAPESCRIPT

Monica: Have you got a big family, Marek?

Marek: No, there's just me and my mother and my brother, Milos.

Monica: So you haven't got any sisters?

Marek: No, I haven't.

Monica: How old is your brother?

Marek: Milos? He's nineteen. He's at university now. He's a really good-looking guy. He's tall and he's got fair hair and green eyes.

Monica: He sounds great.

Marek: What about you? Have you got any brothers and sisters?

Monica: Yeah, I've got two little sisters. There's Silvia – she's twelve. And then there's Lisa – she's nine.

Marek: Have they got black hair, like you?

Monica: Yes, we've all got black hair. Silvia's got brown eyes, too, but Lisa's eyes are blue – they're amazing!

Answers
1 One brother, no sisters.
2 Two sisters, no brothers.

b ▶ **CD1 T3** Look at the table with students and make sure they understand what they have to do. Elicit some different possible colours for hair and eyes. Play the recording for students to complete their tables. Check answers. Play the recording again, pausing as necessary for students to clarify any problems.

Answers
Milos: 19; fair; green
Silvia: 12; black; brown
Lisa: 9; black; blue

c Go through the example with students, showing them how each line must be followed to find out who has/hasn't got things. Students complete the exercise. Check answers.

Answers
2 My parents have got green eyes.
3 My aunt and uncle haven't got a cat.
4 My friend's brother has got a red nose.
5 Sid's father hasn't got a car.
6 My grandfather has got grey hair.

★ OPTIONAL ACTIVITY

Write the following questions on the board.
1 Have you got a pet?
2 Have you got a bicycle?
3 Have your parents got a car?
4 Has your family got a flat or a house?
5 Has your flat/house got a garden?

In pairs, students ask and answer the questions noting down their partner's answers. Monitor and make sure pairs are taking turns to ask and answer and are using the correct question and verb forms. Note down any repeated mistakes to go through as a class later. You may like to practise this form further by asking students to write a short paragraph about their partner. Ask a few students to read out their sentences to the class. Are there any interesting pieces of information for further discussion?

Divide the class into pairs and ask students to draw a picture of their partner (you should get some humorous results!). Tell students they are going to interview their partner in order to write a paragraph under the drawing. In open class, elicit some questions and write them on the board. In pairs, students interview each other and write a short paragraph about their partner. These can be placed on the walls of the classroom (or passed around the class) for students to look at. You could ask them to find people that they have something in common with and report back to the class.

B ROOMS AND HOMES

1 Colours

a Ask students to write the name of each colour. Monitor and check spelling.

> **Answers**
> 2 black 3 brown 4 pink 5 grey 6 red
> 7 green 8 yellow 9 blue 10 orange

b Read through all the colours and check students know them all. Explain that students must find things in the classroom for each colour. In small groups, students complete the exercise. To make this more fun, you can set a time limit and the group who can match things to the most colours is the winner.

Call out a student's name and a classroom object; the student has to give you the colour of that object. Continue like this until you are sure students are confident with the colour adjectives.

2 Rooms and furniture

a Elicit as many rooms in a house as you can and write them on the board. Students then look at pictures A–F. Go through the example with them. Students complete the exercise.

If weaker students have problems labelling the rooms, give them further clues, e.g.
You cook food in the ... kitchen.
You eat in the ... dining room.
You sleep in the ... bedroom.
You watch TV in the ... living room.
You have a bath in the ... bathroom.

Students compare answers in pairs before a whole class check.

> **Answers**
> B kitchen C dining room D bedroom
> E living room F bathroom

b Students read through the furniture vocabulary in the box. Check any problems. Go through the example with them, explaining that they must match the words in the box to the labelled items in each picture. Students complete the exercise. Check answers.

> **Answers**
> 2 fridge 3 cooker 4 sink 5 window
> 6 table 7 chair 8 bed 9 cupboard 10 sofa
> 11 armchair 12 shower 13 toilet 14 bath

Mime an action in one of the rooms in Exercise 2, e.g. *cooking in the kitchen* and ask students: *Where am I? / Which room am I in?* Students guess using the phrases *In the kitchen/bathroom*, etc. until they get the correct answer. In small groups, students mime the other rooms and the other members of the group guess which room they're in.

3 There is / There are

a Write the following sentences on the board.
There is a table in my kitchen.
There are three chairs in my living room.

Read the sentences with students. Ask them if the nouns in each sentence are singular or plural, elicit the answers and then ask students to look at the expressions used with each. Make sure students understand that *There is / There's ...* is for singular and *There are ...* is for plural.

Students read through sentences 1–5. Go through the first item with them as an example. Ask them to look at the noun and decide if it is singular or plural (singular) and elicit that *There's ...* should be used. Students complete the exercise. Check answers.

> **Answers**
> 2 There are 3 There are 4 There are
> 5 There's a

b Students look at the picture in their books for 30 seconds. With books closed, in pairs, students make as many sentences as they can about the picture. They can do this orally or by writing their sentences down. Monitor and check they are using *There's / There are* and nouns correctly. To make this more fun, you can set a time limit and the pair with the most correct sentences is the winner!

4 Prepositions of place

a Read through the instructions and the prepositions in the box with students. Check students understand all the prepositions by giving them a few examples using things in the classroom, e.g.

My desk is between the board and the door. Your dictionary is in your bag. etc. In pairs, students now make sentences about items in the picture. They can use *There is / There are* expressions with the prepositions or they can concentrate only on using the prepositions. Monitor and check they are using the prepositions correctly. Review any problems at the end of the exercise.

> **Example answers**
> There's a cat in the box. / The cat is in the box.
> The TV is next to the door.
> The windows are behind the sofa.
> There's a picture between the windows.
> The books are on the table.
> There's an umbrella on the rug.

b Students draw a plan of their own house/flat. Give an example of the type of detail required by drawing a plan of your own house/flat on the board. Go through the example sentences in the book with the whole class. In pairs, students describe their house to their partner. Encourage students to explain in detail, using *there is/are*, prepositions of place, colours and the vocabulary of rooms and furniture. Circulate to help with any vocabulary questions.

C ACTIVITIES

1 Activity verbs

Read through the verbs in the box with students, checking pronunciation. You can mime some of these to help students understand, if necessary. Students then look at pictures 1–12. Go through the example with them. Students complete the exercise. They can compare answers in pairs before a whole class check.

> **Answers**
> 2 read 3 close 4 jump 5 cry 6 open
> 7 smile 8 listen 9 shout 10 run 11 write
> 12 swim

2 Imperatives

Read the instructions as a class and do the first item as an example, if necessary. Remind students to match the pictures with the verbs and decide if they need a positive or a negative imperative. Students complete the exercise. Check answers.

> **Answers**
> 2 Close the window! 3 Smile! 4 Don't jump!
> 5 Listen! 6 Don't shout!

★ OPTIONAL ACTIVITY

Whole class. This gives further practice in positive imperatives. The aim of this activity is for students to follow your commands (using the verbs in Exercise 1) if you say *Teacher says ...* followed by an imperative. If you say an imperative only without *Teacher says ...* in front of it, students should NOT follow your instructions. Any student who follows an instruction which has been said without *Teacher says ...* is out of the game, e.g.
T: *Teacher says smile* (students should all smile). *Teacher says jump* (students should all jump). *Cry* (students should not cry).

After a few verbs, ask for student volunteers to come out and take the role of the teacher.

3 Adverbs of frequency

Warm up

Books closed. Introduce the idea of frequency by asking students what they do at the weekends. Ask the following questions and make a list of the activities on the board: *Do you go to the cinema / play football / watch TV / visit your grandparents / walk the dog / go swimming*, etc. Students will probably answer *Yes* or *No* at this stage, but leave the list of activities on the board to return to later.

a Students put the adverbs in the correct place in the diagram.

> **Answers**
> 1 always 2 usually 3 often 4 sometimes
> 5 hardly ever 6 never

Return to the activities on the board and ask students to tell you which of them they always/usually/often/sometimes/hardly ever/never do at the weekend. Ensure they use the correct word order in their answers.

LOOK!

Read through the examples in the Look! box with students. Offer some more examples of your own to clarify the rule.

b Read through the sentences with students and check understanding. Students complete the sentences so that they are true for them.

> **Answers**
> Students' own answers

Language note

When using *always* and *usually*, students often make the following mistakes:
I always play football.
I usually visit my grandmother.

Point out to students that, in many cases, they need to say when events take place:
I always play football <u>on Sundays</u>.
I usually visit my grandmother <u>at the weekend</u>.

c Divide the class into pairs and ask them to compare answers with a partner before listening to some example sentences in open class.

4 Object pronouns

To introduce this section write the following table on the board (do not write the object pronouns at this stage):

Subject	Possessive pronoun	Object pronoun
I	My	*Me*
You	Your	*You*
He	His	*Him*
She	Her	*Her*
We	Our	*Us*
They	their	*Them*

Elicit the object pronouns by writing the words *He likes ...* on the board and ask students to complete the table.

Ask students to complete the sentences using the object pronouns. Check answers.

Answers
2 me 3 her 4 him 5 you 6 us

5 *can/can't* for ability

Warm up

To introduce the language in this exercise, write the following sentences on the board:
I can swim.
I can't speak French.

Point out the positive and negative forms and elicit the question form from students.

Ask students some questions of your own to check understanding, e.g.
T: Elisa, can you swim?
S1: Yes, I can. / No, I can't.
T: Milos, can you speak French?
S2: Yes, I can. / No, I can't.

a ▶ **CD1 T4** Read the instructions and ask students to look at the first two columns of the table (Marek and Liz) only. Remind them of the marking system. Play the recording, pausing after the first answer to check students understand what they have to do.

Play the recording for students to complete the exercise. Check answers. Play the recording again, pausing as necessary for students to clarify any problem answers.

TAPESCRIPT

Liz: Jack and Monica are at the swimming pool. Do you want to go there too?

Marek: No, not really. I can't swim!

Liz: Really?

Marek: Yeah, really. But I'd like to learn. Maybe you can teach me.

Liz: No, I don't think so. I can swim but not very well. You're good at music, aren't you?

Marek: Well, yeah, I can sing – I really like singing. And I can play the piano and the guitar.

Liz: I can't play any musical instruments. We've got a piano at home but I can't play it. And I can't sing, either. When I sing at home, my brother shouts at me.

Marek: Don't listen to him! Anyway, you're really good at art. You can paint and draw – I love your pictures.

Liz: Can you paint?

Marek: Oh, I can paint a bit, but not very well.

Answers
Marek: swim ✗; sing ✓✓; play the piano ✓✓; paint ✓
Liz: swim ✓; sing ✗; play the piano ✗ ; paint ✓✓

b Go through the example with students, reminding them to look carefully at how they have marked the table. Pay attention to the use of *but*. As students write sentences, monitor to check they are using forms correctly. Check some in open class.

Example answers
Marek can sing very well, but Liz can't.
Marek can play the piano very well, but Liz can't.
Marek can paint, but not very well. Liz can paint very well.

c Students now think about the activities in the table and complete the third column about themselves.

d In pairs, students ask and answer questions and complete the last column of the table about their partner. Ask one pair to demonstrate the example to the rest of the class. Students continue asking and answering until they have completed their table. Monitor and check students are using the correct forms and that they are taking it in turns to ask and answer. Ask some students to report back to the class what they found out about their partner.

D IN TOWN AND SHOPPING

1 Places

Read through the items in the box with students, making sure they understand them all. Go through the example, if necessary. Students complete the exercise. Check answers.

Answers
B 6 C 5 D 2 E 4 F 1 G 8 H 7

2 *There is/are* (negative and questions) + *a/an/any*

Make sure students understand when to use *a/an/any* in negatives and questions. Elicit a few questions and answers from students about their town to demonstrate this point, e.g.
T: Alex, is there a cinema in (name of students' town)?
S1: Yes, there is.
S1: Bertha, are there any supermarkets in (name of students' town)?
S2: Yes, there are.

a Students read through items 1–4 and a–d. Do the first item with them as an example, if necessary. Remind students they should look carefully at the verbs in items 1–4 and the nouns in a–d to see if they are singular or plural. Students complete the exercise. Check answers.

Answers
2 b 3 d 4 a

b Read through the instructions with students and do the first question as an example if necessary. Students complete the sentences. Monitor and check students are using the forms correctly. Feedback in open class, writing answers on the board where necessary to draw attention to the use of the article or *any*.

Answers
2 Is there / is. 3 Is there / there is.
4 Are there / there aren't.

c Students read through sentences 1–4. Do the first item with them as an example, if necessary. Remind them to look at the verb and the noun carefully before they choose *a* or *any*. Students complete the exercise. Check answers.

Answers
2 a 3 a 4 any

d Weaker classes: As an introduction to this activity, students may be interested to hear some sentences about the place you lived when you were a child. Write some sentences on the board to help give students ideas for their own sentences.

Stronger classes: Encourage students to ask you questions about the place you lived as a child.

Give students two minutes to write as many sentences as they can about the place they live. In pairs, students compare sentences before listening to a few examples in open class.

3 Times

Read through the sentences with students and ask them to say them out loud. If students have difficulty telling the time in English, you may like to ask questions about when things happen, e.g. *What time does school start? What time do you get up?*

Answers
2 The café opens at nine fifteen and closes at nine o'clock.
3 The disco opens at ten o'clock and closes at one thirty.
4 The train leaves at seven twenty and arrives at nine thirty-five.
5 The film starts at seven forty-five and finishes at nine thirty.
6 The bookshop opens at ten o'clock and closes at six o'clock. On Saturdays the bookshop closes at twelve fifteen.

✱ OPTIONAL ACTIVITY

For further practice you could write the following items on the board and ask students to make sentences: 7.35; 5.15; 6.00; 8.20; 11.45; 4.30; 2.50.

Divide the class into pairs and tell them to write times for their partners to say out loud, scoring one point for each correct sentence.

4 Clothes

a Books closed. Elicit as many clothes as students know and write them on the board.

Students open their books at page 13 and read the instructions for Exercise 4a. Go through the example with them. They write in as many of the words as they can and then write the other letters in the correct order and match the words to the pictures to complete the exercise. Weaker students can work in pairs. Students complete the exercise. Check answers. Check any pronunciation problems at this point.

b Go through the examples with students, reminding them of the singular and plural forms of the verb *be*. Students can complete this exercise in pairs or you can call out the items from Exercise 4a and ask students to respond.

> **Language note**
>
> It may be useful to point out to students that colours come after the verb *be* in English. We say: *It's a blue shirt.* NOT ~~*It's a shirt blue*~~.

c Go through the example questions and answers with students. In pairs, students ask and answer about their favourite clothes.

(5) Money and prices

If you can, bring in some examples of US dollars, British pounds and euros to show students before you begin this exercise.

a In open class, match the words and symbols. To check understanding ask students where each currency is used.

LOOK! 🔍

Go through the information in the Look! box with students, making sure they understand how to say the written prices correctly.

b ▶ **CD1 T5** Students read through the list of prices. Remind them what the sign is for each currency. Play the recording for students to hear how the prices are pronounced. Go round the class asking students to say the prices out loud. Correct any errors in pronunciation.

TAPESCRIPT/ANSWERS

1 Twelve pounds
2 Twenty-five euros
3 One hundred and twenty-five dollars
4 Eleven dollars twenty-five
5 Seventeen euros fifty
6 Fifteen pounds ninety-nine

c In pairs, students now go through the items in Exercise 4a and say the prices. With weaker students, you may want to call out an item and a student's name and the student has to say the price, so that you can check that everyone is saying the prices correctly.

d In pairs, students ask and answer about the items in Exercise 4a. Ask one pair to demonstrate the example dialogue. Monitor and check students are using the correct question forms and that they are taking turns to ask and answer.

2 Free time

Unit overview

TOPIC: Hobbies and interests, school subjects

TEXTS

Reading and listening: a text about an unusual hobby
Listening: to a teenager talking about his hobby
Reading: a text about after-school clubs and activities
Writing: an email to an e-pal

SPEAKING AND FUNCTIONS

Talking about hobbies
Expressing likes and dislikes
An interview about school

LANGUAGE

Grammar: Present simple (positive and negative); *like + -ing*; Present simple (questions and short answers)
Vocabulary: Hobbies and interests, school subjects
Pronunciation: /n/ (*man*) and /ŋ/ (*song*)

1 Read and listen

Warm up

Refer students to the photos. Ask them what the girl is doing (looking after bees) and if they are afraid of bees. Do not discuss what Claire's hobby is at this point since this will be done in Exercise 1a.

a Pre-teach any vocabulary (*volleyball, beekeeping, hives*) or stronger students can use a dictionary to check the meanings. Ask students to read the two questions and predict the answers. Then students read the text quickly and find the answers to check their predictions. Remind students that they don't have to understand every word in the text to answer the questions. Check answers.

> **Answers**
> She's 15. Her hobby is beekeeping.

b ▶ **CD1 T6** Students read through the list of questions and check any vocabulary problems. Go through the first item as an example, if necessary. Play the recording for students to listen and read the text at the same time. Students complete the exercise and compare answers in pairs. Play the recording again, pausing as necessary for students to check or change their answers.

TAPESCRIPT
See the reading text on page 14 of the Student's Book.

> **Answers**
> 1 She's from Wales.
> 2 Her friends play volleyball and go to the cinema; they like swimming and dancing. But Claire doesn't.
> 3 They are scared of the bees.
> 4 She loves reading about bees.
> 5 Because she wants to buy more bee hives.

> ✴ **OPTIONAL ACTIVITY**
>
> Ask students if they are afraid of bees, spiders or any other creatures. They can tell the class how they feel when they see or feel the creature, what they do and what they say. Students may want to tell a story about the creature. This may be better done in L1 at this stage, since it requires the use of past tenses.

2 Grammar

✴ Present simple (positive and negative)

a Books closed. Write an example sentence of your own on the board, e.g. *I come from Scotland. She doesn't come from Scotland.* In pairs, students think of another similar sentence. Write a few of their sentences on the board.

Students now open their books at page 15 and read through the examples from the reading text. Ask them what they notice about the verbs in each sentence (two end in -s). Ask them which verbs end in -s and elicit that they are the third person (*he/she/it*) forms.

Students complete the rule with the information they have. Check answers.

> **Answers**
> you; they; -s

> ✴ **OPTIONAL ACTIVITY**
>
> If further practice with third person forms is needed, write the base forms from these examples on the board: *come, go, get, take.* Call out students' names and ask them to use each base form in a sentence about a friend.

There are certain third person singular spelling rules which it may be useful to explain to students once it is clear they understand the present simple. As follows:

- Verbs ending in -sh, -ch, -x, -ss, -o, add -es (e.g. *wash – washes; watch – watches; fix – fixes; kiss – kisses; go – goes*).

- Verbs ending in -y, change the -y to -i and add –es (e.g. *fly – flies; study – studies*).

Stronger classes: Ask them to give another example of each of these verbs in English.

Weaker classes: They can choose one of the sentences from the Look! box and produce a sentence about themselves.

Grammar notebook

Students should use a grammar notebook and note down the spelling rules. Some students may find it useful to write down the base forms and the -ing forms.

b Go through the first sentence as an example with students. Ask them why the answer to question 1 is *loves* and not *love* (because Sara is third person singular). Alternatively, you can write the first sentence on the board with two answer options, e.g. *Sara love/loves films.* Elicit the correct verb form and ask a student to come out and cross out the wrong form on the board. Students complete the exercise. Check answers.

Answers
2 hate 3 take 4 teaches 5 flies 6 reads 7 go

✳ OPTIONAL ACTIVITY

If you feel students need further practice of the present simple positive form, you can call out the first person of a verb (e.g. *I get up*) and ask a student to call out the next person. Continue like this with positive forms until you are sure students understand.

c Ask students to read through the words in the box first. Check they understand each item. Weaker students may find it more useful to match the words in the box with the pictures first. Explain to students what the verbs *like*, *love* and *hate* mean by giving examples of your own (e.g. *I like English. I love school. I hate Maths.*). Make faces to express each one as you say them. Go through the example with students, pointing out the third person verb and the boy in the picture.

Answers
2 I like bananas.
3 She loves ice cream.
4 They like cats.
5 She hates winter.
6 We love football.

d Students read through the examples on the page. They can look back at the text on page 14 to see the sentences in context, if necessary. Ask them what they notice about the verbs in these sentences compared to the verbs in the sentences in Exercise 2a. (These verbs use the negative auxiliaries *don't/doesn't* and the base form doesn't change.) Give students another example of your own if necessary (e.g. *I don't teach French.*). Ask some stronger students to give an example of their own.

Write *don't/doesn't* on the board and elicit the full forms *do not / does not*. Students fill in the table. Check answers.

Answers
don't; doesn't

Language notes

1 Explain to students that it is more common to use short forms when we speak and full forms when we write. Full forms tend to be more formal.

2 Students may produce statements like *She not like … / She not likes … .* Explain that English uses the auxiliary verb *do/does* in present simple negative statements. Ask students if the same or a similar thing occurs in their own language.

e Go through the first item as a class, reminding students that *like* becomes *don't like* in the negative. Remind students to use short forms. Students complete the exercise. Check answers.

Answers
2 We don't eat a lot of meat at home.
3 My parents speak French.
4 I don't know his phone number.
5 My brother gets up late at the weekend.
6 My father doesn't drive to work.

✳ OPTIONAL ACTIVITY

If you feel students need more practice, call out base forms and ask students for the positive or negative form of it in a person of your choice (e.g. *I, he, you*).

f Check students understand all the sentences. Go through the first item with students as an example, making sure students realise that they must make the sentences negative. Students complete the exercise. They can compare answers in pairs before a whole class check.

Answers
2 I don't get up early on Sunday.
3 My sister doesn't watch a lot of TV.
4 I don't buy my CDs in that shop.
5 You don't know the answer.

Vocabulary

✳ Hobbies and interests

a ▶ **CD1 T7** Students look at the pictures. Go through the first item with students as an example. In pairs, students complete the exercise. Play the recording, stopping to check their answers. Now play the recording again, pausing it for students to repeat the words.

TAPESCRIPT/ANSWERS

A 3 swimming
B 7 listening to music
C 6 dancing
D 5 playing computer games
E 1 going to the cinema
F 2 reading
G 9 running
H 4 painting
I 8 playing the guitar

b Ask students to look at the table. Give an example of your own from the table to check students understand what to do (e.g. *My brother plays computer games*). Explain that you have chosen a person, a verb in the correct form and an activity and that this sentence is true about your brother. In pairs, students make sentences and tell their partner. Monitor, making sure students are using the correct verbs for each person.

Vocabulary bank

Refer students to the vocabulary bank on page 63. Read through the words and phrases in open class and check understanding. For further practice, divide the class into pairs and ask students to ask each other questions starting with *How often do you … ?* (e.g. *How often do you go for walks?*). Circulate and help as necessary. Listen to some of their ideas in open class as feedback.

Vocabulary notebook

In their vocabulary notebooks, students start a section called *Hobbies and interests*. They should note down any new vocabulary from this section and should add any new words as they come across them.

✳ OPTIONAL ACTIVITY

See if students can think of one hobby for each letter of the alphabet.

Grammar

✳ like + -ing

a Go through the examples from the reading text with students. Ask them what they notice about the verbs in bold (they all end in *-ing*). Then ask them to look at the verbs which go before the *-ing* forms (*loves/enjoy/like/hate*).

Students complete the rule with the information they have worked out.

> **Answer**
> *-ing*

Check students have understood the rule by giving them an example of your own, e.g. *I like teaching English.* Ask one or two students to give examples of their own using *like/love/enjoy/hate*.

LOOK! 🔍

Read through the information in the Look! box with students and explain that there are certain spelling rules when we add *-ing* to a verb in English:

1   If a verb ends in *-e*, we drop the *-e* before adding *-ing* (e.g. *dance – dancing; smile – smiling*).

2   If a verb ends in a vowel + a consonant, double the final consonant before adding *-ing* (e.g. *swim – swimming; run – running*).

Language notes

It may only be appropriate to give your students rules 1 and 2 (from the Look! box) at the moment but note the further rules 3–5 below.

3   Verbs ending in *-y*, *-x* and *-w*, add *-ing* (e.g. *play – playing; fix – fixing; show – showing*).

4   If a verb has two or more syllables and ends in a vowel + a consonant, and if the stress is on the final syllable, double the final consonant and add *-ing* (e.g. *begin – beginning*).

5   If a verb has two or more syllables and ends in a vowel + a consonant, but the stress is not on the last syllable, add *-ing* (e.g. *listen – listening*).

b Check students understand the verbs in the box. Go through the example with students. Students complete the exercise. Check answers.

> **Answers**
> 2 playing 3 riding 4 running 5 talking 6 going

✳ OPTIONAL ACTIVITY

Stronger classes: Ask students to decide which *-ing* spelling rule applies to each verb.

Weaker classes: Put the infinitives of the verbs in Exercise 4 on the board and ask students to see what patterns they can see when *-ing* is added to each.

Speak

a Remind students of the hobbies mentioned in Exercise 3 (*going to the cinema, reading, swimming, painting, playing computer games, dancing, listening to music, playing the guitar, running*).

Give students an example of your own with one of the verbs (e.g. *I love going to the cinema.*). In pairs, students make statements and note down what their partner says. Students should try to use each verb at least once.

b Students report what their partner said to a different partner. Ask some stronger students to tell the class about their partner.

6 Listen

a ▶ **CD1 T8** Explain that students are going to hear a teenager talking about his hobby. Students must decide which of the pictures shows his hobby (picture 2). Play the recording. Check answers.

Weaker classes: This recording could be played through once and then paused after each section, allowing students time to note down their answers. Remind students they need to be listening for the key words they see in the table in their book and any *like/love/hate* words.

b ▶ **CD1 T8** Read through the sentences with students and check understanding. Explain that students must decide if the sentences are true or false. Play the recording again. Students compare answers with a partner before feedback in open class.

TAPESCRIPT

Interviewer: Mark, you've got an unusual hobby.

Mark: Yes, I'm a magician.

Interviewer: Do your friends and family know about it?

Mark: Yes, they do. They like watching my tricks at home. And they sometimes come to my shows.

Interviewer: Oh, how often do you give a show?

Mark: Once a month, at the youth club. It's great. I love showing my new tricks.

Interviewer: How do you learn new tricks?

Mark: I talk to other magicians. I read books about magic tricks, and I have some DVDs. It's easy to get information about magic tricks. But it's not easy to learn them!

Interviewer: So does it take a long time to learn a new trick?

Mark: Yes, it does. I practise three times a week, on Monday, Tuesday and Wednesday. Sometimes I hate practising, but of course it's important to do it.

Interviewer: Do you tell your friends how the tricks work?

Mark: No, of course not. Magicians never do that! I don't tell my friends, and I don't tell my brother.

Interviewer: Your brother? Does he want to become a magician too?

Mark: No, he doesn't. He only wants to know how the tricks work!

Answers
1 T 2 F 3 F 4 F

7 Pronunciation

See notes on page 64.

8 Grammar

✱ Present simple (questions and short answers)

Warm up

Books closed. Write the following sentences on the board.

Yes, I do.
No, I don't.

Ask students to give you as many questions as possible for which these sentences are the answers. You may like to give some examples of your own to get students started. As students give answers, write some examples on the board and point out the inversion of auxiliary verb and subject in questions. Pay close attention to ensure correct word order and intonation as you elicit.

a Books open. Read through the sentences with students and check understanding. Ask students to complete the table using the correct form of the auxiliary verb. Feedback in open class.

Answers
Do; don't; Does; does; does

b Look at the example with students and point out that they must complete the sentences with auxiliary verbs and positive or negative answers. Students complete sentences and check answers with a partner before feedback in open class. Circulate and monitor to check that students are on track.

Answers
2 Do 3 Do 4 Does
B responses are students' own short answers

Culture in mind

9 Read and listen

If you set the background information as a homework research task, ask the students to tell the class what they found out.

> **BACKGROUND INFORMATION**
>
> **National Curriculum:** Introduced into England, Wales and Northern Ireland for students aged 5 to 16 in state schools in 1988, this ensures that certain basic material and subjects are covered by all pupils.

Warm up

Ask students what their favourite subjects are at school. Help with translations if they do not know the English words. Ask them which subjects they don't like.

a Tell students they are going to read a text about three girls who go to school in England. Introduce the idea of a curriculum (the subjects taught in the school) and extra-curricular activities. Ask them to read the text quickly to find the different subjects and clubs. Tell them not to worry about understanding every word, but to focus on the task. Check the answers.

> **Example answers**
>
> 1 English, Maths, History, Geography, PE, ICT (Information and Communication Technology), French, Spanish, Biology, Chemistry, Physics, Music, Technology, Drama
> 2 horse-riding, gymnastics, theatre, school orchestra, pottery, sailing

b Look at the pictures with students. Students decide which of them are subjects and which are clubs. Check answers.

> **Answers**
>
> subjects: D, E, F, H, J
> clubs: B, C, G, I

c ▶ **CD1 T11** Students read the text again and listen. They decide if the sentences are true or false. Allow students to ask questions about difficult vocabulary at this stage. Students compare answers with a partner before feedback in open class. If the sentence is false ask students to say why.

> **Answers**
>
> 1 T 2 F (they study two or three languages)
> 3 F (some of the clubs meet at lunchtime) 4 T
> 5 T 6 F (some of the clubs get help from parents) 7 F (all of them are free) 8 F (Sarah hopes they will start a photography club soon)

d In pairs or small groups, students discuss the question. Circulate and help with vocabulary as required. As this is a free practice activity, encourage students to focus on fluency and not worry if they make a mistake. In open class, ask some pairs for their ideas and write them on the board.

10 Write

a Explain to students that they are going to read an email from a new e-pal. Before they reply, they must read it quickly and answer the question.

> **Answers**
>
> sports, painting, taking photographs, riding her bike, watching sport on TV, listening to music, going to the cinema

b This can be set for homework. Ask students to read the email again and find examples of each of the four points.

Tell students that there are no set rules when writing an email, but that they should follow the email in the book as a good example of how to give information. Point out that the information is separated into three paragraphs. You may like to elicit a few further ideas for starting emails. (Opening lines: *Hello!/Dear ...*)

- Paragraph 1: Elicit the kind of information this gives (introduction, name, age, nationality).
- Paragraph 2: Elicit what information this gives (details of hobbies she likes).
- Paragraph 3: Elicit what information this gives (about her best friend and her favourite actor).
- Closing lines: Elicit other ways of ending an informal email or letter (e.g. *Love, / Keep in touch, / Hope to hear from you soon.*).

Students plan and prepare their reply. They can bring their emails into class the next day for checking.

11 Speak

a In pairs, students think of five questions to ask Sarah. With weaker classes, you may like to ask students to write down questions in order to check accuracy and then allow them to read their questions.

b Students act out an interview. It is a good idea to ask and answer a couple of questions yourself to give an example of the type of answers expected. Invite different pairs to act out their dialogue for the class.

Memo from Mario

Free time

Sentence completion competition

▶ This exercise is designed to follow the work on 'An unusual hobby' (page 14) that the authors prescribe. It could also be used as a review activity later in the course.

▶ Put the students into groups of three. Tell them to close their books. Explain that you will read them the text 'An unusual hobby', sentence by sentence but that you will stop one word before the end of each sentence.

▶ They shout out the missing word. The first student in each group to shout out the word correctly gets a point. Each student records how many points he/she has won. If there is a dead-heat, both or all three students get a point.

▶ Do your first reading ending each sentence with an upward intonation on the second-to-last word. e.g. 'An unusual ...'

▶ The student with most points in each group now opens the book on page 14 but sits so the other two cannot read or see the text.

▶ This student takes over the teacher's role and reads each sentence with the last word omitted for the other two students to fill in.

▶ Round off the exercise yourself, reading the sentences, but this time leaving off the last two or three words for the students to supply.

RATIONALE

Learning words and short lexical chunks is something good language learners tend to do a lot on their own. Learning by heart is central to most of the major educational traditions in the world, though it is currently less popular in Western educational systems.

Mild competition seems to be something teenagers thrive on.

Acknowledgement

This activity is a modification of a technique Robert O'Neill used in the 1970s.

Unit overview

TOPIC: Helping other people

TEXTS

Reading and listening: a text about a student doing voluntary work in Namibia in his gap year
Listening: an interview with a student doing voluntary work in Namibia
Writing: an email about organising a party

SPEAKING AND FUNCTIONS

Talking about housework and helping in the home
Talking about future arrangements and plans

LANGUAGE

Grammar: Present continuous for activities happening now; present simple vs. present continuous
Vocabulary: housework
Pronunciation: /ɜː/ (w<u>or</u>ld)
Everyday English: *It's not my problem; though; Come on!; That's right; See?; So what?*

1 Read and Listen

If you set the background information as a homework research task, ask the students to tell the class what they found out.

BACKGROUND INFORMATION

Gap year is used to describe the year that some students take out of education between secondary school and university at age 18. Popular gap year activities are travelling abroad or gaining work experience, which may be voluntary or paid.

Canterbury is a city (population c. 43,000) in the south east of England. The city contains many historic buildings including a cathedral and a castle.

Namibia (population c. 1,821,000) is a country in southern Africa on the Atlantic Coast. It shares borders with Angola and Zambia to the north, Botswana to the east and South Africa to the south. It gained independence from South Africa in 1990 and its capital city is Windhoek. The majority of Namibia is desert and it has very low population density (2.5 people per square kilometre).

Okavango Delta is in Botswana and is the world's largest inland delta. It floods for six months of every year and is known for its wildlife.

Botswana (population c. 1,640,000) is a country in southern Africa bordered by South Africa to the south, Zambia to the north, Namibia to the west and Zimbabwe to the north east. It gained independence from Great Britain in 1966. Botswana's successful economy is dominated by industry, tourism and mining (especially diamonds).

Warm up

Books closed. Write the title of the unit on the board and ask students what they understand by it.

a Books closed. In open class introduce the term *volunteer work*, and ask students if they can think of any work that people do for free in order to help other people. You should allow students to make their explanation in L1 if necessary. Write some of their ideas on the board.

b Books open. Ask students to look at the photos and answer the questions. Students read the text quickly to check their ideas. Tell them not to try to understand every word but to focus on answering the questions and getting a general idea of what the text is about.

> **Answers**
> Mike is 19; he is helping sick people in Namibia, Africa.

c ▶ **CD1 T12**   Check that students understand the sentences. You may want to pre-teach the following key words: *conservation, mobile hospital*. Play the recording while students read. Pause as necessary to check understanding and clarify any difficulties. Students answer the questions and compare answers with a partner before feedback. Ask students to correct false sentences.

TAPESCRIPT

See the reading text on page 20 of the Student's Book.

> **Answers**
> 1 T
> 2 F – He wants to become a teacher.
> 3 F – Money is not the reason he is there.
> 4 T
> 5 F – He wants to travel.

d Read through the questions with the class and check understanding. In open class, listen to some of their suggestions. Working individually, students think of their answers and make a note of them. Monitor to check progress and help with vocabulary as necessary. Organise students into pairs or small groups to discuss their ideas. Get feedback from some individuals and write the most interesting ideas on the board. With weaker classes let students read their answers. Stronger classes might try to remember their sentences without referring to their notes.

2 Grammar

✱ Present continuous for activities happening now

a Books closed. Write on the board *I'm writing on the board.* Then underline the first person of the verb *be* positive form and elicit the other persons from students and put them on the board. Follow the same procedure for the negative and the question and short answers forms. Remind students that we do not repeat the *-ing* form in the short answers. Now write the following on the board: *We use the present continuous to talk about something that is happening now / every day.* Ask students to identify which alternative is correct and ask a student to come out and cross out the wrong one on the board.

Students open their books at page 21 and read through the three examples from the text. If necessary, students can refer back to the text on page 20 to see the sentences in context.

Then they can read through the Rule box and complete the gaps.

> **Answers**
> 1 continuous   2 to be

Ask a few questions of your own to check understanding: *Am I swimming now? Is it raining at the moment? Are you watching TV now?* etc.

Weaker classes: At this point, you could ask them to go back through the text on page 20 and find more examples of the present continuous tense (*... but now he's living in Namibia; I'm working with the doctors and nurses here ... ; I'm staying here for two months; I'm living in a small house; I'm enjoying my life; I'm learning a lot.*)

Then they read through the grammar table and complete the gaps. Check answers.

> **Answers**
> Positive: are
> Negative: isn't
> Questions: Am; Are; Is
> Short answers: are; aren't; is; isn't

b Go through the first item with students and ask them why the answer is *'s taking* (because it is third person singular subject) and ask them what the base form of the verb is (*take*) and what spelling change has taken place (drop the *-e* and add *-ing*). Students now complete the exercise; remind them to use short forms where possible. Check answers.

> **Answers**
> 2 're watching / are watching
> 3 aren't listening / are not listening
> 4 'm doing / am doing
> 5 Are; watching
> 6 Is; having

c Ask students to read through the verbs in the box and look at the pictures.

Do the first item with them as an example, if necessary. Students now complete the exercise. Remind them to look carefully at the context of each picture and decide if they need a positive or negative verb form. Check answers.

> **Answers**
> 2 's watching / is watching the television
> 3 are listening to music
> 4 'm not enjoying / am not enjoying this programme
> 5 're winning / are winning
> 6 's not doing / is not doing her homework

✱ OPTIONAL ACTIVITY

To check students have understood the form correctly, ask them questions about the pictures in Exercise 2c, e.g.

Picture 1: *What is your grandfather doing? / Is your grandfather reading a book?*

Picture 2: *Is Ellie playing a computer game? / What's Ellie doing?*

3 Pronunciation

See notes on page 64.

4 Grammar

✱ Present simple vs. present continuous

a Ask students if they can remember when they use the present simple (for habits and routines) and when they use the present continuous (for activities happening now). Read through the examples of both tenses as a class, pointing out the time expressions used with each tense. Ask students to explain why each tense is used. Go through the first item in the exercise with students to check they understand. Ask students to think about their choice of verb each time and to look out for the time expressions used, since this will help them choose the verb they need. Check answers, asking students to explain their choice of verb.

> **Answers**
> 2 's wearing 3 It's raining 4 It rains
> 5 's cooking 6 cooks 7 He never listens

LOOK!

Explain to students that there are some verbs in English which are hardly ever used in the present continuous tense. Read through the examples in the Look! box with students. Ask them if the same thing happens with these verbs in their language.

Grammar notebook

Students can copy the notes from the Look! box into their grammar notebooks and perhaps add some information about the verbs and how this works in their own language.

b Write the headings *Present simple* and *Present continuous* on the board. Read through the time expressions in the box with students.

Weaker classes: Ask them to look back at the example sentences in Exercise 4a and find as many of the expressions in the box as they can (*at the moment, today*). Ask them which tenses they are used with and put the words under the correct heading on the board. Now go through the examples in Exercise 4b and students can then complete the exercise.

Stronger classes: Go through the examples in Exercise 4b and ask students to complete the exercise.

In pairs, students compare answers and give feedback. Write their answers on the board or ask one or two students to come out and write the answers under the correct heading.

> **Answers**
> Present simple: usually, every weekend, never, every evening, twice a year
> Present continuous: at the moment, this afternoon, right now, today, this week

Grammar notebook

Students can copy these time expressions into their grammar notebooks and write an example of their own for each expression.

c Go through the first item with students as an example, focusing on the time expressions to help them work out which tense to use. Check students understand the term *surfing the net*. Remind them to use short forms where possible and to check the spelling rules for the present continuous if they need to. Students complete the exercise. Check answers, asking students to explain their choice of verb.

> **Answers**
> 1 walks; 's going / is going
> 2 have; 're learning / are learning
> 3 's surfing / is surfing; wants
> 4 know; don't remember
> 5 aren't dancing / are not dancing; don't like / do not like
> 6 does ... mean; don't understand

5 Listen

a ▶ **CD1 T15** Ask students to describe what is happening in each of the photographs. With weaker classes you may like to write the three options on the board. Tell them that they are going to listen to an interview with Mike Coleman, the volunteer in Namibia from Exercise 1. Play the recording while students answer the question. Check answers.

TAPESCRIPT

Interviewer: Good morning, and welcome to Radio Kent. This morning we're talking about volunteer work. On our phone line, we have Mike Coleman, from Canterbury. Right now he's in Namibia. Morning, Mike.

Mike: Hi Carol.

Interviewer: What are you doing there in Namibia?

Mike: I'm working as a volunteer in a hospital. I'm here for two months. I help the doctors and nurses – you know, I carry things and get things for them, talk to the patients – that kind of thing.

Interviewer: And what are you doing right now?

Mike: I'm having breakfast. We always have breakfast at about eight o'clock, then we go to the hospital.

Interviewer: Do you make your own breakfast?

Mike: Yes, we do. And lunch and dinner too!

Six of us live here together and we do all our own housework.

Interviewer: Really?

Mike: Yes – we do all the cooking and cleaning. We wash our own clothes too – there's no washing machine here! So we do the washing by hand.

Interviewer: Do you like that?

Mike: No, not much! In fact, I hate it! I prefer tidying up. I sometimes clean windows and floors at the hospital too, so I'm good at it now.

Interviewer: OK Mike. And tell us – do you like being there in Namibia?

Mike: Oh yes – I love it. I'm having a great time. I'm working with wonderful people and I'm learning a lot.

Interviewer: That's great, Mike. Thanks for your time and good luck in your work.

Mike: It's my pleasure. Thanks. Have a good day.

Interviewer: You too. Bye now.

Answer
Picture 3

b ▶ **CD1 T15** Read through the sentences with students. Point out the use of the present simple in sentences 1–4 to describe habitual, repeated actions and the use of the present continuous in sentence 5 to describe an action happening at the time of speaking. Play the recording. Students listen and decide if sentences are true or false. During feedback, ask students what they heard on the recording to make them choose their answers.

Answers
1 T 2 T 3 F (They do their own washing as they don't have a washing machine.) 4 T 5 F (He is working with wonderful people.)

LOOK! ○━

Students may be confused by the difference between *doing the washing-up* and *doing the washing*. Look at the examples and explanations in the Look! box with students.

Encourage them to translate the sentences, as they may use different verbs in their own language. Ask a stronger student to put each phrase into a sentence to check understanding.

6 Vocabulary

✱ Housework

▶ **CD1 T16** Read through expressions 1–7 with students and check they understand them all. Go through an example with students. Students complete the exercise. They can compare answers

in pairs before listening to the recording. Play the recording for students to check their answers. Play the recording again, so students can repeat the words.

TAPESCRIPT/ANSWERS
A 6: tidy up / tidy a room
B 2: do the ironing
C 4: do the shopping
D 7: clean the windows
E 1: do the cooking
F 3: do the washing
G 5: do the washing-up / wash up

Vocabulary bank

Refer students to the vocabulary bank on page 63. Read through the words and phrases in open class and check understanding.

Vocabulary notebook

Students should start a section in their vocabulary notes called *Housework*. They should copy down the expressions from Exercise 6 and the Look! box. If necessary, they can translate them into their own language. Ask students if they know any more housework expressions they could add to the list.

✱ **OPTIONAL ACTIVITY** ┤

What am I doing?

In small groups, students each choose an activity and take turns to mime it to the rest of the group. The others have to guess what he/she is doing. Set a time limit of about 20 seconds for the students to guess. The person who guesses correctly has the next turn. This can also be done as a whole class activity.

7 Speak

a Go through the example questions with students. Ask a few students the questions and check they use the correct tense when answering. Divide students into small groups to ask and answer questions about housework. Groups could appoint a secretary who notes down the results under each name. Ask for group feedback. Are there any general trends? Do boys do more / less / the same as girls? Put any interesting points on the board for further discussion.

✱ **OPTIONAL ACTIVITY** ┤

Groups can give feedback. Put the results on the board and students can draw up a class graph to show how work is distributed.

b Read through the questions and the example with students. Point out the use of adverbs of frequency and the present simple tense. In pairs, students discuss the questions. Ask for feedback and put any interesting points on the board for further discussion.

Photostory: Let's give him a hand

8 Read and listen

Warm up

Introduce the characters to students. They are two boys, Joel and Pete, and two girls, Jess and Debbie, from the same school. Tell students the characters will appear regularly later in the book.

Look at the first picture with students. Ask students where the children are (in the street) and what they might be talking about (the man trying to push his car). Ask students if they have ever been in a car that broke down. What did they do?

a **CD1 T17** Read the questions with students and ask them to look at the photos. Play the recording for students to read and listen to find the answers.

TAPESCRIPT

See the text on page 24 of the Student's Book.

Answers
Jess, Joel and Pete help the man push his car. Debbie doesn't help because she thinks the man should push his own car.

b Go through the first item with students as an example. Ask students to match the beginnings and endings to make a summary of the story. Allow students to go back through the dialogue if they can't remember what happened.

Answers
2 a 3 f 4 e 5 b 6 d

✱ OPTIONAL ACTIVITY

In groups, students can act out the dialogue from the photo story.

9 Everyday English

a Read through the expressions from the dialogue with students. Do the first item as an example. Ask students if they can remember (without looking back) who said this (Debbie). Students complete the exercise, only looking back at the dialogue if they need to. Check answers.

Answers
1 Debbie 2 Pete 3 Joel 4 Pete 5 Debbie
6 Jess

b Ask students to read through the dialogue and check they understand it. Check any vocabulary problems. Go through the first item as an example. Students complete the exercise and compare answers in pairs before a whole class check.

Answers
2 Come on! 3 See 4 though 5 So what?
6 it's not my problem

Vocabulary notebook

Students should start a section called *Everyday English* in their vocabulary notebooks and note down these expressions.

Discussion box

Weaker classes: Students can choose one question to discuss.

Stronger classes: In pairs or small groups, students go through the questions in the box and discuss them.

Monitor and help as necessary, encouraging students to express themselves in English and to use any vocabulary they have learned from the text. Ask pairs or groups to feedback to the class and discuss any interesting points further.

10 Improvisation

Divide the class into pairs. Tell students they are going to create a dialogue between Debbie and the car driver from the photostory. Read through the instructions with students. Give students two minutes to plan their dialogue. Circulate and help with vocabulary as necessary. Encourage students to use expressions from Exercise 9. Students practise their dialogue in pairs. Listen to some of the best dialogues in open class.

11 Team Spirit

a Look at the photo with students and ask them to describe what is happening and to guess what the teacher is going to say. Listen to some of their ideas in open class.

Answers
Students' own answers

b Ask students to match the words and definitions. Allow them to use a dictionary if necessary. Students check their answers with a partner before feedback in open class. Watch Episode 1 of the DVD.

Answers
2 f 3 e 4 b 5 c 6 a

12 Write

Warm up

Ask students how often they send or receive emails. Who do they write to? What do they write about?

a Students read through the email quickly. Check any vocabulary problems. In pairs, students answer the questions. Remind them to use the present continuous tense in their answers. Feedback in open class.

> **Answers**
> 1 The event is Maggie's sister's 18th birthday party. It is happening that evening.
> 2 There are about 50 people coming.
> 3 Maggie's mother and father are preparing food in the kitchen. Her sister Gill and brother Alex are putting up a big tent and some lights in the garden. Some of her sister's friends are putting out the tables and chairs.

b Remind students of the differences between writing an email and a letter (Unit 2). Elicit/Give the following information about emails and write it on the board:

- Opening: Include **To, From, Subject**.
- Greeting: Informal expressions like *Hi!* or *Hello!*
- Content: Does not have to be split into paragraphs as in a letter and can be very informal.
- Signing off: Does not need full sentences, can just have your name.

Students now choose one of the events and plan their emails. Students can prepare this in class and write the email for homework.

13 Last but not least: more speaking

a ▶ **CD1 T18** Ask students to complete the dialogue using the words in the box. Remind them that as Monique and Tanya are talking about activities happening at the time of speaking, they use the present continuous tense. Play the recording for students to check their answers, pausing if necessary for clarification.

TAPESCRIPT
Monique: Hi, Tanya. It's Monique speaking.
Tanya: Oh, hi, Monique. How are you?
Monique: Fine, thanks, and you?
Tanya: Yeah, I'm OK. A bit busy right now.
Monique: Busy? What are you doing?
Tanya: Well, I'm helping my brother with his maths homework, but I'm also tidying my room ...
Monique: What else?
Tanya: I'm thinking about what I can get James for his birthday.
Monique: You know what, Tanya? Let's meet in Parker Square in half an hour and go to the shops together. We can look for a present for James there.

Tanya: Sorry, Monique, I can't.
Monique: No? What a pity! Why's that?
Tanya: I'm also studying for my English test, too. It's tomorrow!
Monique: Oh no!

> **Answers**
> 1 doing   2 helping   3 tidying   4 thinking
> 5 studying

b In pairs, students change the dialogue to make it relevant to them. Circulate and help with vocabulary if necessary. Students act out the dialogue in pairs. Stronger groups should try to do this without reading it out, but weaker classes may benefit from looking at the text for help. Listen to some of the dialogues in open class.

Check your progress

1 Grammar

a 2 lives   3 Do; like   4 play   5 doesn't like
6 gives   7 Does; work; does   8 Do; write; don't
9 don't get up

b 2 works; is working   3 am reading; don't read
4 don't watch; are watching   5 Do; swim; are swimming   6 Is; helping; isn't; is having

2 Vocabulary

a 2 Drama   3 Maths   4 English   5 Science
6 History   7 French   8 Geography   9 Technology
10 Chemistry

b Hobbies and interests: dancing, playing the guitar

Housework: doing the ironing, cleaning the windows, tidying up

and students' own answers

How did you do?

Check that students are marking their scores. Collect these in and check them as necessary and discuss any further work needed with specific students.

Memo from Mario

Helping other people

First letter and last letter dictation

▶ Ask the students to close their books. Explain to them that you are going to dictate one of the paragraphs from the text 'Helping at a hospital' (page 20). Tell them that they are to write down the <u>first</u> and <u>last</u> letter of each word, leaving the appropriate number of spaces in between. So, if you dictate 'a' they write down 'a'.
if you dictate 'an' they write down 'an'
if you dictate 'the' they write down ' t __ e'
if you dictate 'year' they write down 'y __ __ r', etc.

▶ Give the students clear examples by having one person come to the board and write down or type so it appears on the IWB, the first three or four words of the paragraph you are going to dictate.
e.g. E _ _ _ _ y   y _ _ _ r   m _ _ _ y   y _ _ _ _ g

▶ Dictate the paragraph slowly, as leaving out letters is harder for some students than writing the words in full. In the early part of the dictation remind the students to only write first and last letters.

▶ When the dictation is done, ask the students to work in pairs and fill in the missing letters.

▶ When the students have completed the task, ask them to open their books and correct or complete anything that needs it.

> **RATIONALE**
>
> Very auditorily acute students will remember much of the passage in your voice.
>
> More visually gifted people will, both at the omission phase and the reconstruction phase, see the word on their inner mental screen. Visualising the sequence of letters in words can help with spelling in a language like English with its erratic sound-spelling correspondences.
>
> I would suggest that this exercise is a powerful aid to spelling.

> **VARIATION**
>
> There are some language groups which tend not to pronounce the endings of English words. This makes them hard to understand. Speakers of Brazilian Portuguese and of Thai drop English word endings a lot. To help such groups, dictate texts to them and ask them to only write down the last three letters of each word. After the re-construction phase ask them to read the passage aloud focusing on and 'foregrounding' the endings of the words.

Acknowledgement

The kernel idea for this technique comes from *On Love and Psychological Exercises*, A.R. Orage, Sam Weisner, New York, 1996.

Who's your hero?

Unit overview

TOPIC: Heroes

TEXTS

Reading and listening: a text about Erin Brockovich
Listening: a student's presentation about his hero
Reading: a text about memorials and ways of remembering heroes
Writing: a text about a hero

SPEAKING AND FUNCTIONS

Talking about where people were born

LANGUAGE

Grammar: Past simple: *be* and regular verbs (positive and negative); *was born / were born*;
Vocabulary: multi-word verbs, memory words
Pronunciation: *was* and *were* /ɒ/, /ɜː/, /ə/

1 Read and listen

If you set the background information as a homework research task ask students to tell the rest of the class what they found out.

BACKGROUND INFORMATION

Erin Brockovich (born 28 June 1960) is an American legal clerk and activist, made famous by the film *Erin Brockovich* (2000) directed by Steven Soderbergh and starring Julia Roberts and Albert Finney, both of whom won Oscars.

Pacific Gas and Electric is the utility that provides gas and electricity to most of northern California. It employs 20,000 people and had a revenue of over $13 billion in 2007.

Hinkley is a small community (population c. 1,915) in the Mojave Desert in northern California.

Warm up

You could give your students background information in L1 about the topic of pollution and ways people are affected by it and try to prevent it. Ask students to tell you about the kind of pollution there is in their town and what is being done about it.

a To encourage students to use headings and non-linguistic clues such as pictures to get information before reading, ask them to look at the photos and title and read the instructions.

Weaker classes: You may want to pre-teach vocabulary in the text such as *law company, law case, sick* and *chromium* before students read the text.

Stronger classes: Encourage students to guess the meaning of unknown vocabulary while reading.

Listen to some of their suggestions before students read the text quickly to check their ideas. Did anyone in the class get the answer? (She is a 'hero' because she helped lots of sick people and won a law case against a big company.)

b ► **CD1 T19**   Read through questions 1–6 with the class. Play the recording while students read and listen. Students answer the questions and compare answers with a partner before feedback. Play the recording again, pausing as necessary to clarify any problems.

TAPESCRIPT

See the reading text on page 28 of the Student's Book.

> **Answers**
> 1 Her job was to organise papers.
> 2 Because she realised there were lots of papers about very sick people in Hinkley.
> 3 They lived near a big Pacific Gas and Electric factory.
> 4 That they were sick because of the chromium in their drinking water.
> 5 $333 million ($500,000 each)
> 6 She has her own company and she gives talks all over the world.

c   In pairs or small groups, students discuss the question. Ask students to report back to the rest of the class.

2 Grammar

✳ Past simple: *be*

a   Write the following sentence on the board: *Erin Brockovich was born in Kansas*. Ask students if this is in the past or the present (past). Now ask students to look back at the text on page 28 and find more examples of the past simple of the verb *be*. Ask them if they can work out how to form the past tense. Elicit the positive forms and write them on the board under the heading *Positive*.

> **Answers**
> was thirty / was in a car accident / was to organise papers / there were lots of papers / there was a chemical / people were sick / people were ill / there were 600 / that was $333 million / there was a film / the film was very successful

b Write the table headings on the board.

Weaker classes: You may like to complete the table in open class, giving examples of each form to students and asking questions to elicit further examples.

Stronger classes: Ask students to look at the examples they found in Exercise 2a and see if they can complete the rest of the table. Check understanding by asking them when they use *was* (singular, except *you* form) and when they use *were* (all plural forms and *you* form).

> **Answers**
> Negative: wasn't; weren't
> Question: Was; Were
> Short answer: was; wasn't; were; weren't

c Go through the first sentence with students, asking them why the answer is *was* and not *were* (because Erin (she) = a third person singular subject). Students complete the exercise. Check answers.

> **Answers**
> 2 were 3 wasn't 4 was 5 weren't

d Complete the first question with students, reminding them of the word order for questions with the verb *be*. Students complete the exercise. Check answers.

> **Answers**
> 2 Was 3 Were 4 Was 5 Were 6 Was

e Go through the example dialogue with students, pointing out that if an answer is negative then they must provide the correct answer as well. If an answer is positive, they must try to provide more information to back up their answers. In pairs, students now ask and answer the questions in Exercise 2d.

> **Answers**
> 2 No, it wasn't. Her job was to organise papers.
> 3 Yes, there were. Erin started to look for more information about Hinkley.
> 4 No, it wasn't. There was chromium in the water.
> 5 Yes, they were. They were sick because of the chromium.
> 6 Yes, it was. The film was very successful.

Grammar notebook

Make sure students copy the completed table from Exercise 2b into their grammar notebooks and write a few examples of their own.

 Pronunciation

See notes on page 64.

 Grammar

✱ *was born / were born*

Books closed. Write the following information on the board: *Name, Year of birth, Place of birth.* Now complete the information about yourself (the information can be real or invented). Point to *Year of birth* and repeat *In + year.* Now ask students: *When were you born? Where were you born?* Make sure they are answering using *In + year* and *In + place.*

Students open their books at page 29 and look at the two example sentences about Erin Brockovich. Ask them to fill in the gaps with the year and the place. Check answers.

> **Answers**
> Students' own answers

> **Language note**
> Explain to students that in English, when we say a year before the year 2000, we split it into two parts (1999 = *nineteen ninety-nine*). For the years 2000–2009 we say the number (2001 = *two thousand and one*) and after 2010 we say it as two parts again (2012 = *twenty twelve*). It may be useful for students to compare how they say this in their own language.

 Speak

a In pairs, students ask their partner when and where they were born. Remind students they need to use *in + year* and *in + place* to answer the questions. Ask a few students to give feedback to the class.

b In the same pairs, students now ask and answer about family members. Go through the example dialogue first, reminding students to use *was/were* as appropriate for the subject of their question.

6 Grammar

✱ Past simple: regular verbs

a Tell students that the text on page 28 contained a number of verbs used in the past simple. Ask if they can remember any without looking back at the text. Look at the example with students and point out that by adding *-ed*, we express the past simple form of a *regular* verb. Write the base forms of the verbs in this exercise on the board. Students now locate the other verbs in the text and write down the past simple. Check answers.

> **Answers**
> married, helped, started, realised, visited, lived, believed, planned, ordered

b Ask students to read through the rule. Go through the first part with them as an example. Students complete the rule. Check answers.

> **Answers**
> -ed; -d; consonant; i; -ed

c Go through the first item as an example. Students then complete the exercise. Allow them to compare answers with a partner before checking in open class.

> **Answers**
> 2 ordered 3 wanted; agreed 4 tried; answered
> 5 visited 6 stopped; helped

d Put the example on the board. Ask students to find the past simple negative form (*didn't agree*) and ask them what they notice about it (the auxiliary verb *did + not* is used). Ask them what they notice about the verb following the auxiliary part + *not* (it does not have *-ed*). Give them an example of your own (*I didn't cook yesterday*). Now ask a few students to give you an example of something they didn't do yesterday to check they have understood the form. Students now complete the negative part of the box.

> **Answer**
> didn't

e Ask students to read through the verbs in the box and look at the pictures, then go through the example. Students complete the exercise. Check answers. Go through any problems at this point with the positive and negative forms.

> **Answers**
> 2 stayed; didn't like 3 rained; didn't play
> 4 didn't watch; studied 5 tidied; didn't clean
> 6 talked; didn't say.

Grammar notebook

Remind students to copy down the spelling rules for regular past simple verbs and to note down some examples for each rule. They can also note down the form of the past simple regular positive and negative forms.

 Listen

If you set the background information as a homework research task ask students to tell the rest of the class what they found out.

> **BACKGROUND INFORMATION**
> **Dorothy Stang** (7 July 1931–12 February 2005) was an American-born nun who campaigned for the poor and the environment, particularly against the deforestation of the Amazon. She was murdered in 2005.

Warm up

Ask students to look at the photos and elicit the meaning of hero (someone you admire greatly). Ask them why they think Dorothy Stang is Pete's hero.

a Read the instructions aloud with the class. In pairs, students take a short while to discuss the questions and try to answer them.

b ▶ **CD1 T23** Tell students they are going to listen to a presentation about Dorothy Stang and that they should listen for information to complete sentences 1–6. Play the recording while students complete the sentences. If necessary play the recording again during feedback.

TAPESCRIPT

Teacher: OK, so Pete is going to give us his presentation today. So, Pete, can you come up here please, to the front of the class? Who is your presentation about, Pete?

Pete: Erm, it's about someone called Dorothy Stang. She was an American woman who lived in Brazil.

Teacher: OK, Pete, tell us all about her and why she's your hero.

Pete: Right, OK. Well, Dorothy Stang was born in 1931. She was born in a place called Dayton in Ohio in the USA. One day she decided to change her life. She wanted to help poor people somewhere. So in 1966 she went to live and work in Brazil, in a state called Pará ...

Teacher: Where in Brazil is that, Pete?

Pete: It's in the north. Part of the Amazon forest is there, erm, it's right up in the north of Brazil.

Teacher: Good, thanks. Go on.

Pete: Right, so, she lived in a town called Anapú and in the 1970s she started to work with small farmers there. She tried to protect the forest – she had lots of enemies, people who didn't like her and wanted to kill her.

Girl: Why?

Pete: Well, a lot of people wanted to cut down the trees, they wanted money for the wood, but it was illegal and Dorothy was one of the people who tried to stop it.

Girl: Oh, right.

Pete: Anyway, Dorothy was sure people wanted to kill her. But she always said: 'I don't want to run away, I want to stay here and save the people and the trees.' So she stayed, she didn't leave Anapú. And in 2004, she was 'Woman of the Year' in Pará state.

But one day in 2005, erm it was the 12th of February in fact, 2005, she was on her way to a meeting, there were two farmers with her, and two men walked up to her and they pulled out a gun and they killed her.

Boy: What about the two farmers? Did they kill them too?

Pete: No, they escaped, and they helped the police to find the two killers. They're in prison now. So, Dorothy Stang is my hero. She worked all her life to help people and to protect the forest, and she died for that. I think she was great.

Girl: Where can we find out more about her?

Pete: Erm, well, they made a film about her in 2008. It's called *They Killed Sister Dorothy.* Or you can look on the Internet. There are quite a few ...

> **Answers**
> 1 1931 2 1966 3 north 4 2004
> 5 12th February 6 prison

 Students discuss the question in pairs or as a class. Listen to some of their ideas in open class as feedback.

8 Vocabulary
✳ Multi-word verbs

This is an introduction to multi-word verbs. All the example verbs in the Student's Book are literal – the meaning of the verb is reflected in the verbs themselves.

a Refer students to the examples and check they understand the meaning of the verbs. Ask them if they can think of any other verbs that use *up* or *down*.

Stronger classes: Set a time limit and put students in pairs to think of verbs.

Weaker classes: Ask the whole class to think of verbs and write them on the board.

Check answers.

> **Example answers**
> **Verbs with** *up*: put up (e.g. a picture), sit up, get/ stand up, move up, look up, turn up (volume)
> **Verbs with** *down*: sit down, walk/drive/go down (e.g. the street/hill/road), put down, count down, look down, turn down (volume), stand down, set down (e.g. bus, train, etc.)

b ▶ CD1 T24 Go through the example with the whole class. Students now complete the exercise. Students can compare answers in pairs. Then play the recording for students to check their answers. Pause as necessary. Once students have checked their answers, play the recording again for students to repeat the verbs.

TAPESCRIPT/ANSWERS

A 2: Pick it up, please!

B 6: Come down!

C 7: Get out!

D 5: Take it off!

E 1: Climb up!

F 8: Put it down!

G 4: Get in!

H 3: Put them on!

c Go through the example with students. Explain to students that the verbs may not be exactly the same, as in the example (*climb/come*). Students then match the opposites. Students can compare answers with a partner. Check answers.

> **Answers**
> pick up – put down
> put on – take off
> get in – get out

d Give an example of your own for the verb *climb up*, then ask for an example situation for *come down*. In pairs, students think of situations for the other verbs. Check answers.

Vocabulary bank

Refer students to the vocabulary bank on page 64. Read through the words and phrases in open class and check understanding. For further practice, ask students to write sentences including one of the verbs.

Vocabulary notebook

Encourage students to start a new section *Multi-word verbs* in their notebook and add the words from the box. They may find it useful to note down translations.

Culture in mind

9 Read and listen

If you set the background information as a homework research task ask students to tell the rest of the class what they found out.

> **BACKGROUND INFORMATION**
>
> **Simón Bolívar** (24 July 1783 – 17 December 1830) was a military commander who was one of the most important leaders of Spanish America's struggle for independence.
>
> **Mount Rushmore** is a 19-metre-high granite sculpture by Gutzon Borglum in South Dakota, USA. It depicts the heads of former US presidents George Washington, Thomas Jefferson, Theodore Roosevelt and Abraham Lincoln. It was carved between 1927 and 1941 and now attracts approximately two million visitors a year.
>
> **Monument to the People's Heroes**, a 37.94-metre-high obelisk in Beijing, is a national monument of the People's Republic of China.
>
> **Beijing** (formerly Peking) is the capital of the People's Republic of China. It is China's second largest city and has a population of c. 17,430,000. Beijing hosted the Olympic Games in 2008.

Eternal Flame at the Tomb of the Unknown Soldier. There are many sites dedicated to the soldiers killed in major wars. The two most famous tombs of the unknown soldier in Europe are at Westminster Abbey in London, created in 1920, and the one beneath the Arch of Triumph in Paris, created in 1921. This tomb honours the unknown dead of the First World War and an eternal flame is kept burning in their memory. A ceremony is held there every 11 November on the anniversary of the armistice signed between France and Germany in 1918.

Dr Martin Luther King, Jr. (15 January 1929 – 4 April 1968) was an American clergyman, activist and prominent leader in the African-American civil rights movement. He received the Nobel Peace Prize in 1964 for his work to end racial segregation. He was assassinated in Memphis, Tennessee.

Lady Diana Spencer (1 July 1961 – 31 August 1997) was the first wife of Charles, Prince of Wales and mother to his two sons Princes William and Harry. Married to Charles in July 1981, they were divorced in 1993. Diana remained a popular celebrity until her death in a car accident in Paris.

Diana, Princess of Wales Memorial Fountain is located in Hyde Park, London. It was opened in July 2004 to commemorate the life of Diana.

Liverpool is a city in north western England (population c. 444,500). Liverpool was a very wealthy port in the nineteenth century, but became poor after heavy bombing in the Second World War and industries leaving the area. It is now being regenerated. It is the home of the Beatles and has named its airport *John Lennon International*.

John Lennon (9 October 1940 – 8 December 1980) was an English rock musician, most famous as one of the Beatles. Working with Paul McCartney he wrote many classic pop songs including *Come Together*, *Hey Jude* and *Strawberry Fields Forever*. Lennon was brought up in Liverpool, but later moved to New York with his wife, the Japanese artist Yoko Ono. He was shot dead outside his apartment block in 1980.

Brazil (population c. 189,987,291 in 2007) is a country in South America. It is the world's fifth largest country and the tenth largest economy. The capital Brasilia was founded as recently as 1956 and is a world reference for urban planning and architecture. Portuguese is the official language of Brazil and the country is recognised as the best football nation, having won the World Cup on five occasions.

Tom Jobim Antonio Carlos "Tom" Jobim (25 January 1927 – 8 December 1994) was a Brazilian musician and songwriter, famous for creating the bossa nova style of music.

The Hollywood Walk of Fame is a pavement in Los Angeles, California, USA which is embedded with more than 2,000 stars containing the names of famous film stars.

Warm up

Ask students which people or places in their country are famous all over the world. Ask them to think about living people as well as people from the past. Allow students to explain their ideas in L1 where appropriate.

a Look at the photos with students and in open class, ask them where they think the photos were taken. Listen to some of their ideas but do not comment at this stage.

b ▶ **CD1 T25** Students read quickly to find out where the pictures were taken. You may like to pre-teach some or all of the following difficult words: *statues; independence; human rights; messages; car accident; handprints; footprints; autographs; concrete.* Check answers.

Answers
Eternal Flame at the Tomb of the Unknown Soldier in Paris, France; Diana, Princess of Wales Memorial Fountain in London, UK; statue of Simon Bolivar in Caracas, Venezuela; Mount Rushmore in South Dakota, USA; the Monument of the People's heroes in Beijing, China.

c Check that students understand the meaning of the items in the list. They read the text again to find the answers. Let students check their answers in pairs before asking for feedback.

Example Answers
1 politicians, soldiers, film stars, sport stars and musicians
2 The statues of Bolívar in South America; Mount Rushmore
3 In January
4 The Diana, Princess of Wales Memorial Fountain; John Lennon Airport; Tom Jobim Airport
5 An area in Hollywood where you can see the handprints, footprints and autographs of film stars in the concrete.

d Read through the questions with students. Check understanding. Put students into small groups and ask them to compare lists. Ask a representative from each group to give feedback and encourage further class discussion on interesting points.

10 Vocabulary

✷ Memory words

Read through the words in the box with students to check understanding. Spend some time in open class deciding which type of words they are (adjective, noun or verb). Then look through the sentences with students and encourage them to guess which type of word goes in the gap.

Check answers in open class.

Answers
2 remember 3 memory 4 forget
5 memorial 6 forgetful 7 unforgettable

Vocabulary notebook

Encourage students to start a new section *Memories* in their notebook and add the words from the box. They may find it useful to note down translations.

11 Write

a Students read the text silently and match the paragraphs and the questions. Check answers.

Answers
a 2 b 3 c 1

b Ask students to think of people they admire. You could elicit students' heroes as a whole class, or students could work in pairs.

Weaker students: They can work in pairs to choose a hero to write about, make a plan together and complete the writing task for homework.

It will help students organise their work if they use Dave's text as a model, and answer the three questions, in the same order.

If the task is set for homework, their information can be used to prepare the poster in Exercise 12 and give the presentation.

12 Speak

To help them make their posters, refer students back to Pete's presentation poster on page 31. They only need to include a few short pieces of information about their hero and if they have them, a photo or picture of their hero.

Students each give a two-minute presentation. Weaker students, who have worked in pairs, can give a joint presentation.

Memo from Mario

Who's your hero?

Role play families

▶ Get the students to shout out family words such as…

son, daughter, mother, father, uncle, aunt, grandfather, grandmother, step-mother, step-father, uncle, aunt, cousin, etc.

▶ Have a student with good handwriting at the board copying them down or typing them so they appear on the IWB. If students shout out the word in their mother tongue first, ask the scribe to put the mother tongue and English words up on the board together.

▶ Get the class to work on any words the scribe has spelt wrongly. Let students volunteer the spellings they think are correct. Edge them towards the correct spellings.

▶ Check that all the family words are understood by the students and delete any words in their mother tongue left on the board.

▶ Organise the students into groups of six to eight. Tell them that each group is a family. They have to decide who is the daughter, son, father, mother and so on.

▶ Once this is established ask each student to:

say their family role.	*I am …*
decide on their age.	*I am …*
say when they were born.	*I was born in … (year)*

▶ Get the students to drill these three facts round their group so that they all know the facts about the others in their group.

▶ To round off the exercise, randomly pick students round the class and ask them to give the three 'facts' about themselves in role and about one of their classmates, again in role.

> **RATIONALE**
> Linguistic: the '*I was born*' is one that students typically still get wrong at an intermediate level and so it is worth giving them plenty of practice in getting it right.
>
> Group-dynamic: Even in this drill-like activity the symbolic building of a family has a strong group-binding effect.

VARIATION FOR OTHER LEVELS

At intermediate level I have used family role-playing as a free activity. In a class of 30 students there are six family groups and six students stay on the side, observing, as the groups allocate themselves family roles and develop these roles for five-ten minutes.

The six students then become 'candidates for adoption', one for each group.

The 'adoptees' introduce themselves as do the family members.

Each student then writes a private diary page about their feelings during the role play that nobody sees but them.

Acknowledgement

I learnt this technique from Soili Hameleen from Finland.

5 Making friends

Unit overview

TOPIC: Making friends

TEXTS

Reading and listening: a text about the friendship between two table tennis players

Listening: a story about four people in a TV programme

Listening: a song by Randy Newman: *You've got a friend in me*

Writing: a diary entry or an email to a friend about last weekend

SPEAKING AND FUNCTIONS

Talking about past activities
Talking about how long ago things happened
An interrogation game

LANGUAGE

Grammar: Past simple (regular and irregular verbs, questions and short answers)

Vocabulary: Past time expressions, sports

Pronunciation: Word stress

Everyday English: *What about?; to be honest; On the other hand; I didn't mean to; Never mind*

1 Read and listen

Warm up

Write the title of the unit on the board and ask students how they make friends and why friends are important. Listen to some of their suggestions in open class.

a This is an opportunity to revise sports vocabulary. Ask students to give you names of sports and make a list on the board.

b Tell students they are going to read a text about a friendship between two sportsmen. Students read the text to answer the questions. Tell them it is not important to understand every word at this stage. Check answers.

Answers
Chinese and American; table tennis

c ▶ **CD1 T26** Read through the instructions with the students. Before listening, you may like to pre-teach some difficult vocabulary, especially with weaker classes: *to each other; came up to; silk scarf; translator; peace flag; relationship*. With stronger

classes you may prefer to encourage them to guess the meaning of new words from the context. Play the recording while they read and listen to answer the questions. After the first listening, let students compare their answers with a partner. Check answers. If necessary, play the recording again, pausing to clarify any problems.

TAPESCRIPT

See the reading text on page 34 of the Student's Book.

Answers
A 3 B 1 C 5 D 4 E 2

d Read through the sentences to check understanding. Give students time to read through the text carefully and answer the questions. Students compare answers with a partner before feedback.

Answers
1 Because of the political situation between the two countries (the Cold War).
2 Because he had missed the US team bus.
3 Because he didn't have anything with him to give.
4 Because it was big news to see a Chinese and an American athlete together.

e In pairs, students discuss the question. Listen to some of their ideas in open class as feedback.

2 Grammar

✳ Past simple: regular and irregular verbs

a Write the following base forms on the board in jumbled order: *play, arrive, want, get, give, go*. Ask students to read through the sentences in 1 and 2. Ask them what they notice about the verbs in 1 and what they can remember from Unit 4 (these verbs are all regular past simple). Ask them to match the past simple forms with their base forms on the board. Now ask students to look at the sentences in 2 and see if they can match the verbs with their base forms. Ask them what they notice about these verbs (they are not regular: the verbs in 2 are irregular past simple).

b Students read through the list of verbs in the box. Go through the examples in the table with them. Students complete the exercise. Check answers.

To check students' understanding at this point,
you can call out a few base forms of regular and
irregular past simple verbs and ask students to
call out the past simple form.

c Encourage students to read through the whole
text first to try to get the general meaning. Go
through the first example and elicit that the verb
be is irregular. Students complete the exercise.
Check answers.

✳ OPTIONAL ACTIVITY

Stronger classes: Write the infinitives of the
verbs in the summary in Exercise 2c on the board,
in jumbled order. Read the summary aloud, with
students' books closed. When you come to a gap
in the text make a sound, such as 'beep', to indicate
where the gap is and continue the sentence.
Students supply you with the missing verbs from
the list on the board, but in the past simple. With
smaller classes, this could be done as a game in
teams, with points awarded for the correct verb
form and spelling.

Grammar notebook

Students should note down the regular and
irregular verbs from this unit in their grammar
notebooks.

✳ Past simple: questions

d Put the following present simple question on
the board:
Do | you | go | to the cinema | every week?

Quickly revise how to form present simple
questions. Below the present simple question,
add the following past simple question:
Did | you | go | to the cinema | last night?

Ask students what they notice about the two
questions and elicit that the auxiliary verb is
different and the time reference is different. Now
ask one or two students the past simple question
from the board and elicit the short answers. If
necessary, ask a few more past simple questions
with different time references (e.g. *Did you see the
football match yesterday? Did you go to the park
last weekend? Did you see Maria last night?* etc.).
Students read through the examples in their books
and complete the table. Check answers.

e Students order the words to make past simple
questions. Do the first item as an example, if
necessary. Students complete the exercise.
Check answers.

❸ Speak

In pairs, students now ask and answer the questions
in Exercise 2e. Go through the example dialogue
with a student. Students complete the exercise.
Ask a few students to demonstrate their questions
and answers to the class.

❹ Vocabulary

✳ Past time expressions

a Give students a few examples of your own using
the time expressions, e.g. *I went to the bank
yesterday morning. I saw a film last Saturday. I left
home an hour ago.* Now ask a few students to give
you some examples. Read through all of the time
expressions with students and ask them how they
would say these things in their own language. Are
there any similarities or differences? Ask students
to think of words to fill the spaces and write
correct answers on the board.

Language notes

1   Students may notice that a different tense is
    used with these expressions in their language.
    Discuss this with them.

2   Some students may want to say *the last week
    / ago one hour* because of the way their own
    language works. Monitor students carefully
    when they are using these expressions and
    give them some extra practice if necessary.

3   Check the pronunciation of *ago* /əˈgəʊ/.

4   Explain that these time expressions can be used
    at the beginning or at the end of sentences.

b Do the first item as an example with information about yourself. Students complete the exercise. Students can compare answers in pairs. Ask for feedback and discuss any interesting facts.

Alternatively, students can write three pieces of false information and three pieces of true information about themselves. They can then work in pairs and read their sentences to each other for the partner to guess which is the false information.

c Students read through the statements. Go through the example with students, reminding students that *ago* always goes at the end of the time expression. Students now complete the exercise. Check answers in pairs.

> **Answers**
> 2 four days ago 3 an hour ago
> 4 two months ago 5 five hours ago

5 Speak

Remind students of the past simple questions from Exercise 2e. If necessary, write a past simple question on the board again and elicit where the *Wh-* word goes, e.g.
... | did | you | go | last night?
Where | did | you | go | last night?

Remind them that the auxiliary goes before the person in questions. Now go through the example exchange with students, making sure they can see how to make the question from the prompt. Students ask and answer the questions.

> **Answers**
> When did you start school?
> When did you begin learning English?
> When did you arrive at school this morning?
> When did you first meet your best friend?
> (Students' own answers to the questions.)

> **Language note**
>
> Point out to students that the expression *this morning* is a past time expression in this context.

6 Vocabulary

✳ Sports

Warm up

Ask students if they practise any sports. If so, which? Do they play in a team or on their own? How often do they practise/play?

a  Elicit any sports which students already know and write the words on the board. Now ask students to look at the pictures in their books. Do the first item with them as an example

and then students complete the exercise. Play the recording for students to listen and check their answers. Play the recording again, pausing for students to repeat each word.

TAPESCRIPT/ANSWERS
A cycling
B swimming
C ice hockey
D basketball
E surfing
F skiing
G volleyball
H snowboarding
I skateboarding

b Do the first item as an example. Ask a student to give you the answer. (*Which sports are team sports? Basketball, volleyball, ice hockey.*) Students may wish to discuss other sports which are not always team sports but which can be, e.g. cycling, swimming, skiing. Students complete the exercise. In pairs or small groups, students answer the other questions.

> **Answers**
> 2 cycling, skateboarding
> 3 swimming, surfing
> 4 skiing, snowboarding, ice hockey
> 5 (Students' own answers)
> 6 (Students' own answers)
> 7 (Students' own answers)

Vocabulary bank

Refer students to the vocabulary bank on page 64. Read through the words and phrases in open class and check understanding. For further practice, divide the class into pairs for them to test each other by making short dialogues, e.g. *A: I want to play hockey. What do I need? B: A stick.*

Vocabulary notebook

Students should start a section called *Sports* and note down the vocabulary from this unit. They can add translations or illustrations if it will help them.

✳ OPTIONAL ACTIVITY

Stronger classes: This is a vocabulary extension activity. In pairs or small groups, students write down the names of the places where the sports in Exercise 6a are done.

> **Answers**
> 1 swimming: pool
> 2 surfing: sea
> 3 skiing: slopes; mountain; piste
> 4 cycling: track; cross-country
> 5 basketball: court
> 6 volleyball: court
> 7 ice hockey: rink/pitch
> 8 skateboarding: ramp
> 9 snowboarding: slope

7 Pronunciation

See notes on page 65.

8 Listen

Warm up

Books closed. Ask students which are their favourite television programmes and write some of their answers on the board. From the list, choose a drama series which the whole class has seen or heard about. Elicit the names of characters in the programme and ask students to work in pairs and describe what happened in the last episode that they saw. As a class, students explain the story.

[a] Books open. Tell students they are going to hear a conversation in which a boy and a girl talk about a television programme. Students look at the pictures and read the names of the characters.

[b] ▶ CD1 T29 Look at the pictures with students. Ask individual students to give a description of each picture. Ask what they think the relationship is between the characters. In pairs, students put the pictures in order to tell a story. Play the recording while students listen and order the pictures. Let students compare their answers before listening to the recording again, pausing to check answers.

TAPESCRIPT

Boy: Did you see *Friends Forever* last night?

Girl: No, I didn't. I didn't watch TV yesterday. What was it about?

Boy: Well, there were these two boys, Dan and Nick. They were really good friends, you know. And they played in the same football team. And one day, their team had a very important match.

Girl: Uh huh. And what happened?

Boy: Well, it wasn't a great start for Dan and Nick's team. At half time the score was 3:0 to the other team. But then Dan and Nick both started to play really well, and they scored two goals each, and their team won 4:3. It was fantastic, and the fans were really excited.

Girl: Right.

Boy: So, the next issue of their school magazine had an article with a big photo of Dan and Nick, and the headline said, 'Friends score double!'

Girl: So?

Boy: Well, Nick's father, Mr Winter, read the article. And he saw that Dan's family name was Stern, and he wasn't very happy.

Girl: Hang on a minute. I don't get it. When Nick's father found out about Dan's family name, he wasn't happy?

Boy: That's right. Because he saw that Dan was Dan Stern. And Nick's dad, Mr Winter and Dan's dad, Mr Stern, were businessmen. And they were in the same business. And they just didn't like each other at all.

Girl: Oh, right. So then what happened?

Boy: Well, Nick's dad talked to him and said he couldn't be friends with Dan, and they argued, and Nick said 'No, Dan's my friend', you know?

Girl: Right.

Boy: Well, Dan and Nick were great. Nick phoned Dan, and the two boys said 'Our friendship is more important than our dads' businesses.' And they stayed friends.

Girl: Good for them. What about their fathers, though?

Boy: Well, one day, their fathers both went to a match. And Nick and Dan each scored a goal in that match too. After the match, the two fathers spoke ...

Girl: ... and became friends too?

Boy: Well, no, not really friends, I mean, but at least they spoke to each other ... the programme stopped there so it wasn't really very clear if they became real friends or not after that, but ....

Answers
A 4 B 1 C 8 D 3 E 5 F 6 G 2 H 7

✳ **OPTIONAL ACTIVITY**

In pairs, students continue the story. Encourage them to make notes of their ideas and to use their imaginations. When students have a coherent ending to their story, divide the class into different pairs and ask students to tell their stories to their new partners. Try to ensure that students tell their whole story without interruptions. Listen to some of the best ideas in open class.

9 Listen: a song

If you set the background information as a homework research task ask students to tell the rest of the class what they found out.

BACKGROUND INFORMATION
Randy Newman (Randall Stuart "Randy" Newman) (born 28 November 1943) is an Academy award winning singer-songwriter, composer and pianist who is notable for his satirical pop songs, e.g. *Short People*, *I Love LA* and for his many film scores, e.g. *Toy Story* (which includes the song *You've Got A Friend In Me*), *Monsters Inc.* and *Cars*.

a Tell the students they are going to listen to a song called *You've Got A Friend In Me*. Read through the phrases in the box and check understanding of *smarter* and *stick together*. Ask students to read the words of the song and put the phrases into the correct places. Circulate to check students are on track, but don't offer any help at this stage.

TAPESCRIPT
See the text on page 37 of the Student's Book.

b ▶ CD1 T30 Play the recording while students check their answers to Exercise 9a. Students compare answers with a partner before open class feedback. You may like to play the song again and encourage students to sing the words.

> **Answers**
> 1 from your nice warm bed
> 2 I've got them too
> 3 We stick together
> 4 a little smarter than I am

Photostory: Not a nice thing to say

10 Read and listen

Warm up
Ask students to look at the photostory and tell you who the characters are (Joel, Pete, Jess and Debbie). What can they remember about Debbie, the character from Unit 2? (Debbie didn't want to help the man by pushing his car, but the others did.) Students look at the title of the story and try to predict what is going to happen.

a ▶ CD1 T31 Read through the instructions and the questions with students. Play the recording for students to read and listen. Check answers.

> **Answers**
> Pete is unhappy with Debbie.

TAPESCRIPT
See the text on page 38 of the Student's Book.

b Ask students to read through the sentences and check understanding. Go through the example with them. Students complete the sentences with the names of the characters. Allow them to look back at the story if necessary. Check answers.

> **Answers**
> 2 Debbie 3 Pete 4 Joel 5 Debbie 6 Jess
> 7 Debbie 8 Jess

11 Everyday English

a Students must decide who said these expressions from the photostory. Do the first one as an example if necessary.

> **Answers**
> 1 Pete 2 Jess 3 Debbie 4 Pete 5 Jess 6 Jess

b Read through the dialogues with students and check they understand. Ask students to use the expressions in Exercise 11a to complete the gaps. Students complete the exercise. In pairs, students compare answers before a whole class check.

> **Answers**
> 2 What about 3 to be honest
> 4 on the other hand 5 I didn't mean to
> 6 Never mind

Vocabulary notebook
Students should now note down the expressions in their vocabulary notebooks. Encourage them to use translations or explanations to help them remember each one.

Discussion box
Weaker classes: Students can choose one question to discuss.

Stronger classes: In pairs or small groups, students go through the questions in the box and discuss them.

Monitor and help as necessary, encouraging students to express themselves in English and to use any vocabulary they have learned from the text. Ask pairs or groups to feedback to the class and discuss any interesting points further.

12 Improvisation
Divide the class into pairs. Tell students they are going to create a dialogue between Debbie and her mum. Read through the instructions with students. Give students two minutes to plan their dialogue. Circulate and help with vocabulary as necessary. Encourage students to use expressions from Exercise 11. Students practise their dialogue in pairs. Listen to some of the best dialogues in open class.

13 Team Spirit ● DVD 1 Episode 2
a Look at the photo with students and read through the questions. Divide the class into pairs and ask them to discuss how they think the people feel. Listen to some of their ideas in open class.

b Read through the instructions with students. Ask students to work in pairs and write a short story to explain why they wanted to meet and what happened. You may like to encourage students to plan their story first and spend some time thinking about the organisation of their story before writing. Tell students that one way to structure a story is to answer four *Wh-* questions: *Who* (was there)? *Where* (were they)? *What* (happened)? *Why* (didn't Pete come)? Circulate and help with vocabulary as necessary.

c If there is time, listen to the students' stories in open class. You may like to pin stories around the classroom and ask students to circulate and read them, then vote on which was the best. Watch Episode 2 and find out what happened. Did anyone guess correctly?

14 Write

a If students choose this task, they should look back at the picture story on page 37 and recall the story they told in Exercise 8c. They write a diary entry as if they were Dan from the story.

b If students choose this task, they should read the questions and the email from Alison. They write a similar email to a friend about a weekend or a day that they enjoyed.

It will help students organise their work if they use Alison's email as a model, and answer the three questions, in the same order.

15 Last but not least: more speaking

Warm up

Your approach to this game will depend on the sensitivity of your class. It can be played with two students making up a story about what they did last Saturday, but can be more effective if you invent a scenario, for example, there was a robbery at the school between 4 and 7 last Saturday, even that one of the teachers was murdered! In any case, it is good to introduce the concept of alibis, inventing stories and cross examination before the activity.

a Explain that in this game, two students have to invent a story about what they were doing at a certain time in the past. After a given time, the students are asked questions by the rest of the class and must come up with the same story. Choose two students and ask them to prepare a story. While they are doing this the rest of the class can be writing down questions to ask them during the interrogation. Alternatively, you could put the whole class in pairs and get them to invent a story each. This will give more pairs the opportunity to be questioned later.

b Student A is questioned by the rest of the class. Student B must not hear the questions and answers, so it is best if he/she leaves the room. Ensure students answer all questions and that they are using the past simple tense correctly in questions and answers.

c Student B is questioned. Students should ask identical questions and try to find differences between the two stories. If you have asked all students to invent stories and questioned each pair, the pair with the most differences in their stories is the guilty party!

Check your progress

1 Grammar

a 2 were 3 was 4 was 5 Was 6 wasn't 7 were

b 1 saw; didn't win 2 became; won; was 3 won
4 jumped; stopped; said 5 went; didn't enjoy
6 did; say; didn't say 7 Did; see; didn't see; saw
8 did; go; went; didn't go

2 Vocabulary

a 2 up 3 down 4 on 5 off

b 1 snowboarding 2 basketball 3 cycling
4 swimming 5 skiing 6 hockey 7 surfing
[Mystery word: Olympics]

How did you do?

Check that students are marking their scores. Collect these in and check them as necessary and discuss any further work needed with specific students.

Memo from Mario

Making friends

Rubbing out and remembering

▶ This exercise can be done to introduce the song, *You've got a friend in me* (page 37) or equally well as revision.

▶ Choose a student (Student A) to write or type. Dictate the song to Student A from line 11 through to the end (nine lines). The student writes it on the board or types it so it appears on the IWB.

▶ Ask Student A to read the text twice to the class. (Don't forget to thank the student and ask him/her to go back to his place!) If you are introducing the song check that all the meanings are clear to everybody. If this is a monolingual class then maybe a quick mother tongue translation will be required.

▶ Ask another student (Student B) to come to the front and delete three words, each from a different line of the song. Ask Student B to pick another classmate (Student C) who then has to read the text, **including the deleted words**. Then, ask Student C to designate another 'class leader' (Student D) and then go back to his/her seat. Make it clear that all books must be closed and that writing is not allowed.

▶ The new leader (Student D) deletes three more words, each from a different line and so on with other students.

As more and more holes develop in the text, get the whole group to help whoever is reading at a given moment. This is a naturally collaborative exercise.

Round the activity off by asking the original secretary student (Student A), to put the missing words back with the help of the group.

> **RATIONALE**
>
> Despite marvellous audio technology the coursebook cannot help belonging to the visual world.
>
> I feel it is useful to do whatever we can to make work from the coursebook as auditory as possible, since the auditory version of language is the primary one. As a species we only started writing and reading language 10,000 short years ago.
>
> This 'rub-out' technique trains the students' use of their ears and their auditory memory.

> **VARIATION FOR OTHER LEVELS**
>
> The technique is particularly good with a strongly rhythmical text like a song, a well- made speech or a poem. *'Friends, Romans, Countrymen, lend me your ears ...'* would be a good advanced level example.

Note

All the way through this activity the students are the protagonists. You are in the wings.

Enjoy the effect of new leader-rubbers-out picking the next leader-victim!

Acknowledgement

As far as I know the first written reference to this technique came in one of the 1963 issues of the *English Language Teaching Journal*

6 Successful people

Unit overview

TOPIC: Successful people, jobs and duties

TEXTS

Reading and listening: a text about four successful people
Reading: a text about a Formula 1 racing driver
Reading: a text about how teenagers earn money
Writing: a text about somebody else's job

SPEAKING AND FUNCTIONS

Talking about the housework students have to do at home
Talking about ambitions and future job plans
Talking about the advantages and disadvantages of a job

LANGUAGE

Grammar: *have to / don't have to*
Vocabulary: Jobs; work and money
Pronunciation: /f/ sound in *have to*

1 Read and listen

If you set the background information as a homework research task ask students to tell the rest of the class what they found out.

BACKGROUND INFORMATION

Jeff Bezos Jeffrey Preston Bezos (born 12 January 1964) is the founder of the online retail giant amazon. com. Amazon was central in the growth in popularity of online shopping. In 2008 Bezos' personal wealth was estimated at US$8.2 billion.

Oprah Winfrey (born 29 January 1954) is famous for her talk show *The Oprah Winfrey Show* which is the highest-rated talk show in the history of television. The richest African-American in history, she has used her fame to help the poor and disadvantaged of the world.

Ana Ivanovic (born 6 November 1987) is a former world no.1 Serbian tennis player. In 2008, she won the French Open and was runner-up in the Australian Open. She is also a UNICEF National Ambassador for Serbia.

Johnny Depp (born 9 June 1963) is an American actor, known for his portrayal of strange, eccentric characters in films such as *Pirates of the Caribbean*, *Edward Scissorhands* and *Charlie and the Chocolate Factory*.

Warm up

Ask students to look at the pictures, say what they know about the people and what they think the people have in common. (They are all famous/talented/successful/wealthy.)

a Ask students to read through jobs 1–4. Go through the first one with students as an example, if necessary. Students match the people and the jobs. Check answers.

> ### Answers
> A 3 B 4 C 1 D 2

Elicit the meaning of *successful* (*achieving highly*). Ask students to read the text quickly once and tell you what the topic is.

b In open class discuss the similarities and differences between the people.

> ### Answers
> **Differences:** Some are men, some are women. They come from different countries, have different interests and professions.
> **Similarities:** They are successful, rich and talented.

c Ask students to read the text quickly and focus on the meanings of success. Tell them not to worry if they don't understand every word at this stage. Feedback in open class after students have compared answers with a partner.

> ### Possible answers
> being rich; being famous and recognised by everybody; being very, very good at something; being happy

d Ask students to read through the list. Check understanding. Explain any problem items in L1 if necessary or ask stronger students to look up anything they don't know in a dictionary. Students work on their own to answer the question, then compare answers with a partner. Ask for class feedback and find out what most of the class ticked as requirements for success.

✳ OPTIONAL ACTIVITY

Stronger classes: In small groups, students discuss each of these things and then rank them in order of importance for success.

Weaker classes: They could classify these in order in L1 and discuss them in L1.

Ask for feedback and discuss any interesting points.

e ▶ **CD1 T32** Read the instructions with the class. Elicit the words and phrases they think they may hear; refer students back to the list in Exercise 1d.

Weaker classes: Ask them to copy down the items from Exercise 1d and then tick the ones mentioned.

Stronger classes: Can make notes without using Exercise 1d.

Play the recording. Students note down the ideas about what makes a successful person.

Find out if the ideas mentioned are the same or different to most of the class's ideas. Ask students to report their ideas to the rest of the class.

TAPESCRIPT

Presenter: What does 'successful' mean? Is it money? Is it being famous? We asked teenagers what they thought. Here are some of the answers we got.

Speaker 1: I think money is very important. I think you have to be rich. You can't say 'I'm successful' if you don't have lots of money. Well, I don't think so anyway. And most successful people <u>are</u> rich, because they're very good at what they do, so other people pay them lots of money. Like film stars, for example.

Speaker 2: You don't have to be famous to be successful. You have to be good at something that you enjoy doing – that's all.

Speaker 3: What does 'successful' mean? It means ... well, I think a person is successful if they're very famous. You're successful if you can't go out of your house without people shouting your name out!

Speaker 4: Well, I'm sure you don't have to be intelligent to be successful! That's if you think being rich and famous is the same as being successful. There are lots of rich, famous people who aren't very intelligent at all.

Speaker 5: I think you have to have the respect of other people. Erm, you know ... other people who say you're good at what you do. And I think you have to be good at what you do – that's success, I think. Yeah – you have to enjoy your work and be good at it.

Speaker 6: It's not money, I don't think, and it's not being famous or things like that. I think you're successful if you're happy in your life, if you sleep easily at night, if you're doing the things you want to do.

> **Answers**
> 1 having lots of money 2 being good at what you do 3 being famous 4 being intelligent 5 being respected 6 being happy

f Students work in pairs and discuss the question. They should agree on someone they want to talk about and discuss why that person is successful.

✳ OPTIONAL ACTIVITY

Who am I?

In small groups (or as a whole class), students take turns to choose a character from Exercise 1. The others have to guess who they are by asking present simple questions, e.g.

S2: Do you play tennis?
S1: No.

The person who has chosen the character can only answer using *Yes* or *No*. The person who guesses correctly can choose next. If the person answers using words other than *Yes* or *No*, they must tell the rest of the group who they chose. Then the next person can choose.

② Grammar
✳ *have to / don't have to*

a Read the examples with the class. Give an example of your own if necessary, e.g. *I have to be in school at 8.00 every day.* Students complete the rule, comparing in pairs before a whole class check. After completing the rule, students complete the table. Check answers. To check understanding, ask a few students some questions about themselves, e.g. *Do you have to wear a school uniform? Do you have to do homework every day?*

> **Answers**
> Positive: has to
> Negative: don't; doesn't
> Question: Do; Does
> Short answer: do; don't; does; doesn't
> Rule: have to / has to; don't have to / doesn't have to

b Students read through the sentences. Go through the first item with them as an example if necessary. You can ask them why the answer is *have to* and not *has to* to check they are using the correct form. Students complete the sentences. Check answers.

> **Answers**
> 2 has to 3 doesn't have to 4 don't have to
> 5 have to 6 don't have to

③ Pronunciation

See notes on page 65.

④ Speak

a Students look at the pictures. Check they understand all the words. Do the first item as an example if necessary. Students tick the things that they have to do at home and cross the ones they don't have to do.

b In pairs, students ask and answer about what they have to do. Go through the example dialogue with them, reminding them of the questions and short answer form. Find out how many have to do each type of housework listed. Ask *Who has to help in the garden? How many people in the class have to do their own cooking?* If there are any interesting results these can be discussed further in open class.

⑤ Vocabulary
✱ Jobs

a ▶ CD1 T34 Ask students to read through the list of jobs, making sure they know the meanings of the words. If necessary ask them questions to check understanding, e.g. *Which person flies a plane? Serves drinks on a plane?* In pairs, students match the jobs to the pictures. Check answers. Play the recording for students to check or change their answers. Play it again for students to repeat each word.

TAPESCRIPT/ANSWERS

A	8: pilot	G	6: flight attendant
B	12: architect	H	11: teacher
C	1: engineer	I	7: lawyer
D	10: firefighter	J	4: vet
E	2: shop assistant	K	9: dentist
F	3: nurse	L	5: doctor

> **Language notes**
>
> 1   Students may need some extra practice in the pronunciation of engineer /endʒɪˈnɪər/.
>
> 2   You may want to remind students that we always use articles to talk about jobs in English. We say *She is a lawyer.* NOT ~~She is lawyer.~~

b Students write the names of three other jobs they are interested in. They can look them up in a dictionary or check with you.

Set a time limit for this and once students have finished, ask for feedback and write any interesting/ unusual jobs on the board.

In small groups, students can discuss why they are interested in the jobs they chose.

c ▶ CD1 T35 Explain that they are going to hear four teenagers talking about jobs. Go through the list of jobs with them and elicit some of the words/phrases they think they may hear when they listen. Write them on the board. Play the recording while students listen and match the people with the jobs. Check answers. Play the recording again if necessary, pausing for students to check answers.

TAPESCRIPT

Luke: My uncle's a vet and in the holidays I often help him. It's great for me because I really love animals. Of course I know that you have to study hard and for a long time to be a vet, but that's my dream and I'm sure I can do it.

Rose: I want to work in IT – information technology. You have to be really good to get the best jobs, and then you can earn a lot of money, but that's not my real interest. I just love computer programming and I want to do more and more.

Sam: My dream is to play professionally. I know I have to practise a lot, so I joined a club and I practise almost every day, and play matches at the weekend. One day I want to be as good as Rafael Nadal or Roger Federer!

Judith: Well, a lot of my friends want to be flight attendants, and I know why – you get to travel to lots of great places! And that's what I want to do too – but I don't want to travel as a flight attendant, I want to be the pilot flying the plane! There are lots of women pilots, and I want to be one of them.

> **Answers**
> 1 Luke: vet
> 2 Rose: computer programmer
> 3 Sam: tennis player
> 4 Judith: pilot

Vocabulary bank

Refer students to the vocabulary bank on page 65. Read through the words and phrases in open class and check understanding. For further practice of vocabulary, divide the class into small groups and ask them to discuss how they feel about each one, e.g. *Would you like to work at home? Why/why not?* When they have all had a chance to give their opinions, have a discussion in open class.

Vocabulary notebook

Remind students to go to their vocabulary notebooks and make a mind map or list of the words for jobs in Exercise 5a, and to add the words they have just looked up in Exercise 5b.

⑥ Speak

a ▶ CD1 T36 Ask students to read through the list of words and the gapped dialogue. Check they understand everything.

Stronger classes: They can look at the words and phrases and predict some of the content of the conversation they are going to hear.

Weaker classes: Go through the first item with students as an example, if necessary. Remind students to look at the context round a space to help them work out which words go in. Students complete the exercise and compare answers in pairs.

Play the recording, pausing as necessary, for students to check or change answers.

TAPESCRIPT

Jenny: What do you want to be when you leave school?

Mark: I want to be a pilot.

Jenny: Really? What do you have to do for that?

Mark: You have to get good school results and you have to be good at Maths and Physics. And you have to speak English really well. What about you? What do you want to do?

Jenny: I'm not sure, but I think I'd like to be a vet.

Answers
1 leave school 2 be a pilot 3 have to do
4 get good school results 5 Maths and Physics
6 speak English 7 not sure 8 I'd like

b Remind students what Jenny said she wanted to be in the dialogue in Exercise 6a (a vet). Refer students back to the dialogue and focus on the questions Jenny asked Mark. In pairs, students now read the phrases in the box and continue the dialogue. Remind them that Mark will be asking the questions and Jenny will be answering them. Ask some pairs to act out their dialogues in front of the class.

Example answers
Mark: Really? What do you have to do for that?
Jenny: Well, you have to get good results and you have to be good at Biology. And you have to study for five years.
Mark: That sounds like hard work! Do you have to do anything else?
Jenny: Well, of course, you have to like animals!

✳ OPTIONAL ACTIVITY

Students can memorise the whole dialogue from Exercise 6a and act it out with a partner.

c In pairs, students ask and answer about jobs they want to do. Remind them of the sort of questions Jenny and Mark asked in Exercises 6a and b. Monitor and check that students change roles so that each person has a turn to talk about his/her job. Ask for feedback from several students about themselves and their partners.

7 Read

If you set the background information as a homework research task ask students to tell the rest of the class what they found out.

BACKGROUND INFORMATION

Lewis Hamilton (born 7 January 1985) is a British Formula 1 racing driver who races for the McLaren Mercedes team and became the youngest ever Formula 1 World Champion in 2008.

Grenada is an island nation located in the south eastern Caribbean sea with an estimated population of 110,000. Its capital is St. George's.

Carl Lewis Frederick Carlton ("Carl") Lewis (born 1 July 1961) is a retired American sprinter and long jumper who won ten Olympic medals including nine golds, and ten World Championship medals, of which eight were golds. He set world records in the 100m, 4x100m, 4x200m, and his record in the indoor long jump has stood since 1984.

Formula 1 is the highest class of car racing, in which cars race at speeds of up to 360km/h. Each year the Formula 1 World Championship consists of 17 races, each of which is watched live on television by an average of 55 million people.

Go-kart racing is a sport in which small four-wheeled vehicles called karts or go-karts race round tracks.

Ron Dennis (born 1 June 1947) is the chairman of the McLaren group of companies and has been the team principal of the McLaren Mercedes Formula 1 team since 1981.

Michael Schumacher (born 3 January 1969) was a German Formula 1 racing driver who was World Champion seven times between 1994 and 2004, racing for the Ferrari team.

Kimi Röikkönen (born 17 October 1979) is a Finnish Formula 1 racing driver known as The Iceman for his calm, cool approach to races. He was World Championship runner-up in 2003 and 2005 before becoming World Champion in 2007.

Felipe Massa (born 25 April 1981) is a Brazilian Formula 1 racing driver who races for the Ferrari team. He began kart racing at the age of eight and has raced Formula 1 since 2002. In 2008, he was runner-up in the World Championship.

Warm up

Write *Formula 1* on the board and ask students if they have ever seen a race. Can they name any of the drivers or venues for the races? What do they think you have to be like to be a good driver? Listen to some of their ideas in open class.

a Ask students to look at the photos and to suggest ideas in answer to the questions. Don't comment on their answers at this stage. Students read the text quickly to check their ideas. Remind them to focus on the questions and not to worry if they don't understand every word. Check answers.

Answers

1 Lewis Hamilton 2 Formula 1 3 Because
Lewis Hamilton dreamt of being a Formula 1
driver from an early age and followed his dream.

b Read through the questions with students. Ask
them to read the text again to find answers to the
questions. Circulate and help with any questions
concerning vocabulary. Allow students to check
answers in pairs before feedback in open class.

Answers

1 When he was very young.
2 He started go-kart racing.
3 He told him that he wanted to drive McLaren
Formula 1 cars one day.
4 Because Lewis had won a go-kart
championship and Ron wanted to invite him
to join McLaren's 'Young Drivers' programme.
5 19
6 In his first six races, he came third in the first
race, second in the next four and then first.

c In open class, students discuss what they know
about Lewis Hamilton since 2008.

d Divide the class into groups of three. Read through
the instructions with students. Students choose
three people who became famous when they
were young and pool their knowledge about them.
Circulate and help with vocabulary as necessary.
When students have gathered enough information,
regroup them and ask them to explain their findings
to the new group.

Culture in mind

8 Read and listen

Warm up

Books closed. Ask students if they have ever earned
any money, either by helping their parents or by
working for somebody else. Is it common for young
people to have part-time jobs in their country?
Explain that in the United Kingdom it is common
for young people of 14 and over to have part-time
jobs to earn some extra cash. Ask students to guess
which type of jobs young people do and write
some of their ideas on the board.

a Students match the photos to the captions.
Check answers.

Answers

girl and baby: 3 boy and dogs: 4
boy with newspapers: 2 girl and elderly lady: 5

b ▶ CD1 T37 Ask students if they can see anything
that the jobs have in common. Then ask them to
read the text quickly and listen to check their ideas.

Answers

They are all jobs teenagers do to earn money;
they are all great ideas!

c Check students understand the questions and ask
them to read the text more carefully to find the
answers. Let them compare answers with a partner
before feedback in open class.

Answers

1 washing cars
2 dog-walking, delivering newspapers
3 delivering newspapers
4 helping elderly people, delivering newspapers
5 all jobs
6 dog-walking

d Students decide which of the jobs they would like
to do most and least. In pairs students compare lists
and discuss the pros and cons of each job. Encourage
them to give their reasons in full sentences. As
feedback, listen to some of their ideas in open class
and have a vote to find which job is most popular.

✱ OPTIONAL ACTIVITY

If students are interested in this topic, divide them
into small groups and ask them to decide on a way
of earning money in their free time. Students can
discuss which services they would offer, how much
they would charge and where they would find
work. Would they advertise in the newspaper, with
posters, get work through word of mouth? When
students have decided, ask them to present their
ideas to the rest of the class.

9 Vocabulary

✱ Work and money

Books closed. Write the words *Work and Money*
on the board and ask students to think of as many
words as possible connected to the topic. Listen
to their suggestions and write them on the board.
Elicit the words in the box and ask students what
type of word they are (verb, noun or adjective).

a Read through the words in the box and the
sentences and check understanding. Students
complete the sentences. Check answers.

Answers

2 save 3 earn 4 Saturday job 5 spend
6 pocket money 7 waste 8 full-time

b In pairs students discuss the differences between
the terms. Circulate to check students are on track
and help with vocabulary as necessary. Check
answers in open class.

10 Speak

a Refer students back to Exercise 5a on page 44 and review the jobs vocabulary. Ask them to choose a job they would like to do when they leave school. It could be one of the examples or any other of their choice. Ask students which job they have chosen and try to ensure that students are choosing a variety of different jobs to make Exercise 9c more interesting. You may even prefer to assign a different job to each student.

b Students make a list of good and 'not-so-good' things about the job. Encourage them to write at least three of each. You may like to give an example of your own to get them started, focusing on pay, hours, place of work, type of activity, colleagues, conditions, etc.

c Students give a short presentation on their job explaining why they would like to do it. Encourage other students to ask questions after each presentation. Make a note of any interesting vocabulary on the board.

11 Write

Students can do the preparation for this task in class, and complete the writing at home.

a Students read the questions. Then ask them to read through Hakan's paragraphs, checking any vocabulary problems. Students match the questions with the order of the paragraphs. Check answers.

b Students interview a friend in class or someone at home and write their paragraph for homework.

Weaker classes: They may need some more help with the structure of this. Remind them first to make notes on what the person says and then to expand their notes into full sentences within each paragraph. Remind them about what should be included in each paragraph:

Paragraph 1: What the person's job is, when they decided to do it and what they had to do to do it.

Paragraph 2: What the job involves and how long the person has to work each day/week.

Paragraph 3: What the person likes / doesn't like about their job.

Memo from Mario

Successful people

1 Words and phrases I like

► When students have completed the work around the 'Following a dream' text (page 45) suggested by the authors, offer them this vocabulary work.

► Tell each student to re-read the text and <u>underline</u> four or five words or phrases that they like, for whatever reason.

► Do the same yourself.

► Model the oral activity for them by telling them the words or phrases you have <u>underlined</u> and by explaining why you like the words.

► Call for volunteers to explain why they have <u>underlined</u> the words they have.

► Help them to find the words to express their reasons for liking words.

► One way of doing this is to go behind the student and 'reformulate' what they have tried to say. Be careful to reformulate in very simple language so the student realises that you have understood him/her accurately.

► Once you have helped five or six students in open class, ask people to work in pairs and explain their likings to a classmate.

> **RATIONALE**
>
> Words are not neutral signifiers for realities in the world. They are emotionally charged entities that affect people at an unconscious level. People like words for their auditory, musical quality. People like the sounds of the vowels and consonants in them. People like them for their look on the page. People like them for their meanings and for their associations. All of this affective stuff comes from the schemata we have within us and which we are mostly not aware of. If words were neutral this classical exercise would fall flat on its face.

Acknowledgement

This activity comes from Suggestopaedia and I learnt it from Lonny Gold.

2 Success stories

► In preparation, think back to a teenage success story of your own. Prepare to tell it to the class simply enough for them to get the gist.

► Tell your success story to your students.

► Put the students in groups of three and ask them to tell each other success stories of their own.

► The activity will normally start slowly and hesitantly and you need to be everywhere helping with vocabulary and grammar. There will certainly be some natural lapsing back into mother tongue when people just do not have enough resources in English.

► Ask for a volunteer to tell their success story to the whole class. Help this student with language and write up their story on the board or the IWB.

► Ask the class to copy down this text.

> **RATIONALE**
>
> In a unit about success at an international level it maybe makes sense to offer the students a chance to speak of their own, smaller successes.
>
> This is a linguistically risky exercise as it is asking students to say things they do not yet have the vocabulary for. It is, however, a good exercise as it demands that they find minimalist ways of saying complex things, which is a major communicational skill.
>
> Another plus in the exercise is that the model the students receive **is from you, the teacher** whom they know and relate to. Your voice, posture, look and the way you are is central to their learning of the language.

Exam tips

Priming the students with their own success stories is excellent preparation for exams, as speaking of successes buoys a person up and makes them walk tall. I ask my students to mentally take a couple of their own success stories into the examination hall with them. This calms their breathing, induces a good physiological state and makes them usefully full of themselves

Eat for life

Unit overview

TOPIC: Food and a healthy lifestyle

TEXTS
Reading and listening: a text about healthy eating
Listening: a dialogue in a restaurant
Writing: a paragraph about food and fitness

SPEAKING AND FUNCTIONS
Talking about a health quiz
Ordering food in a restaurant
Talking about restaurants and eating out

LANGUAGE
Grammar: Countable and uncountable nouns;
a/an some and *any, much* and *many*
Vocabulary: Food and drink
Everyday English: *I know what you mean; and stuff;
No problem; Absolutely!; as well; a couple of*

1 Read and listen

If you set the background information as a homework research task ask students to tell the rest of the class what they found out.

BACKGROUND INFORMATION

Okinawa is an area in southern Japan consisting of hundreds of islands in a chain over 1,000 km long. It is said to have the most beautiful beaches in Japan and enjoys temperatures above 20 degrees centigrade for most of the year. Due to the strategic position of the Okinawa islands, the United States have several large military bases there. The martial art Karate originated in Okinawa.

Mediterranean diet is a diet originating in Mediterranean countries like Greece, Italy and Spain, and consisting of plant foods, fresh fruit, olive oil, low to moderate amounts of milk, cheese, fish, chicken and wine, and low amounts of red meat. Total fat content is 25–35% and the diet is widely recognised as being a very healthy one.

a Ask students to think of things that can help people live a long time. Students note them down individually before comparing with a partner. Encourage them to think of things that you shouldn't do (smoke, drink alcohol excessively, etc.) as well as what you should do. You may like to give them a few ideas of your own to get them started.

Ask students to read the text quickly and see if their ideas are mentioned. Feedback in open class. If students are enjoying this topic, make a list on the board of things which are good or bad for you. Can students add any healthy/unhealthy foods to the list? Do they think that they have a healthy diet?

Answers
Believe in yourself; keep your mind active; think positively; love people and enjoy helping others; do some exercise every day; live an active and stress-free life; eat healthy carbohydrates; don't eat any bad fats; try not to use much oil in cooking.

b ▶ **CD1 T38** Read through the questions with students to check they understand them all. Now play the recording while students listen and read and find the answers to questions 1–4. Check answers.

TAPESCRIPT
See the text on page 48 of the Student's Book.

Answers
1 Your mind.
2 They do some exercise every day and they lead a stress-free life. They are positive and active. They eat very healthy food.
3 It contains many different vitamins and minerals and is good for your heart.
4 From olive oil and from fish.

c Ask students which member of their extended family (grandparents, uncles, aunts, etc.) has lived the longest. In small groups students compare the lifestyles of these people. Do they think the advice in the reading is always true or do they know of any people who have lived a very long time with an 'unhealthy' lifestyle? Circulate and help with vocabulary as necessary. Listen to some of their ideas in open class as feedback.

2 Vocabulary

✳ Food and drink

▶ **CD1 T39** With books closed, elicit as many food words from students as they know and write them on the board. Students now open their books and read through the food vocabulary in the box. Go through the first two examples with them as a class. Students then match the other items with the pictures. Students can compare answers in pairs.

Play the recording for students to check or change their answers. Play it again, for students to repeat each word. Check answers.

TAPESCRIPT/ANSWERS

A vegetables
B apples
C carrots
D rice
E mineral water
F eggs
G beans
H bread
I tomatoes
J sugar
K meat
L onions
M orange juice
N fruit

Language notes

1   Check students' pronunciation of these items, particularly: *vegetables* /ˈvedʒtəblz/, *onions* /ˈʌnjənz/, *tomatoes* /təˈmɑːtəuz/, *sugar* /ˈʃugə/.

2   Ask students if there are any words which are similar in their language.

✳ **OPTIONAL ACTIVITY**

I'm making a sandwich and ...

This game can be played by the whole class or in groups. One student starts the sentence and adds a food item, then the next student adds a new item and remembers the previous item, e.g.
S1: I'm making a sandwich and in it I'm putting onions.
S2: I'm making a sandwich and in it I'm putting onions and tomatoes.
S3: I'm making a sandwich and in it I'm putting onions, tomatoes and (adds another item).

The game continues in this way until someone forgets an item or gets an item wrong. When a student makes a mistake they are out of the game and the person who remembers the most items is the winner. Set a time limit for this game.

Vocabulary bank

Refer students to the vocabulary bank on page 65. Read through the words and phrases in open class and check understanding.

Vocabulary notebook

Students should start a section called *Food and drink* in their vocabulary notebooks. Students should copy these words down and add any more as they go along.

3 # Grammar

✳ Countable and uncountable nouns

a Books closed. Write *onion* on the board. Elicit the plural from students and write it beside the singular. Elicit one more example of a singular and plural and put them on the board under *onion/onions*. Now write *sugar* on the other side of the board and ask students if they can count it. Elicit another example of an uncountable noun (e.g. *bread*) and write it below sugar on the board. Then write the headings *Countable nouns* and *Uncountable nouns* above each column on the board.

Students now open their books at page 49 and read through the rule and the example sentences. Go through the first one with them as an example showing them which words to underline and which ones to circle. Students complete the exercise. Check answers.

Answers
2 They do some (exercise) every day.
3 Some <u>years</u> ago ...
4 The Okinawa women eat (fish) and green <u>vegetables</u>.

b Remind students of the information on the board from Exercise 3a and check they have understood the difference between countable and uncountable nouns. Go through the example with students. Students complete the exercise. Check answers. You can ask some students to come out and add their items to the list on the board.

Answers
Countable nouns: onions, eggs, apples, tomatoes, beans, carrots
Uncountable nouns: meat, water, rice, sugar, orange juice, bread

✳ **OPTIONAL ACTIVITY**

To check students have understood properly, call out the nouns from Exercise 2 and ask them to answer *Countable* or *Uncountable* when you call out the noun, e.g.
T: Paolo, apples.
Paolo: Countable.
T: Maria, bread.
Maria: Uncountable.

✳ *a/an* and *some*

c Using the lists on the board, ask students which word (*a/an* or *some*) we can put before *vegetable* (*a*) and *vegetables* (*some*). Ask students the same question with *bread* (only *some* can go before *bread*). Read through the rule with students, pointing out the example, and then ask students to try to complete the rule. Check answers.

d Go through the first item with students as an example if necessary. Focus on the noun after the gap and ask students to decide whether it is countable or uncountable. Remind them to do this in all the other items. Students complete the exercise. Check answers.

───── ✱ OPTIONAL ACTIVITY ─────

Stronger classes: They can write their own gapped *a/an/some* sentences for a partner to complete.

Weaker classes: If you feel they need further practice in this area, give them the following sentences to complete:
1 *I want ... tomatoes.*
2 *Eat ... pasta. It's good for you.*
3 *There is ... carrot in the kitchen.*
4 *Drink ... water! It's hot today.*
5 *Mark wants ... apple.*

✱ *much* and *many*

e Read through the examples with students. Ask them if the noun in each example is countable or uncountable (*countable: diseases, heart problems, meals; uncountable: oil, water*). Now point out the words before each of these nouns (*much/many*) and ask them to read the rule and try to complete it. Check answers.

f Go through the example with students. Elicit that *milk* is an uncountable noun, therefore *much* is used before it.

Weaker classes: Go through items 2–6 in the same way and circle the correct word. Once they have completed this part of the exercise, check answers. Then match item 1 with the answers in the second column. Try various wrong possibilities first to show students how there is only one correct answer.

Stronger classes: They can do parts 1 and 2 together.

Students complete the exercise. Check answers.

Grammar notebook
Students should note down all the new grammar points from this unit in their grammar notebooks and try to learn one rule each day for homework.

4 Speak

a Pre-teach any new vocabulary from the Health Quiz on page 50 (e.g. *average, burn calories*) and read through the questions with the class. Ask students to work in pairs to discuss the questions and guess which answer is correct in each case. Check answers with the whole class.

b Ask the example questions to different students and elicit different answers. Ask students to suggest some more questions. Students then ask each other their own questions about things in the quiz, while you monitor for errors. Get feedback with a few questions and answers from pairs at the end.

5 Pronunciation
See notes on page 65.

6 Listen

Warm up
Books closed. Ask students if they eat in a canteen at school. What type of food is served? Do they like it? Do they have dinner ladies and what are their duties? Listen to some of their ideas in open class.

a ▶ **CD1 T42** Books open. Look at the pictures and the menu with students. Students match the pictures with the items on the menu. Listen to the recording to check answers.

TAPESCRIPT/ANSWERS
A 4 fish; B 7 vegetarian curry and rice; C 8 yoghurt; D 2 vegetable soup; E 5 chicken and mushrooms; F 6 cheeseburger; G 9 ice cream; H 1 pasta with tomato sauce; I 10 cheese; J 3 mixed salad

b ▶ **CD1 T43** Tell students they are going to listen to a dialogue between two students and a dinner lady. Students listen and write down what Annie and Jack ask for. Play the recording again, pausing for clarification and to check answers.

TAPESCRIPT
Dinner lady: Next, please. Hello, dear. What would you like?

Annie: Hi. I'd like pasta to start, please.

Dinner lady: OK. And what else?

Annie: A cheeseburger with chips, please.

Dinner lady: OK – and what about dessert?

Annie: Erm, I'd like some yoghurt, please. Have you got strawberry?

Dinner lady: Of course. OK, then, here you are. Enjoy your meal.

Annie: Thanks. Bye.

Dinner lady: Hello, young man. What can I get for you?

Jack: Hi. OK, to start, I'd like a mixed salad, please.

Dinner lady: Would you like mayonnaise on it?

Jack: No thanks. Just some olive oil.

Dinner lady: OK. No problem.

Jack: And then erm ... grilled fish, please.

Dinner lady: OK. Anything with it?

Jack: Yes, I'd like some carrots.

Dinner lady: Sorry, we haven't got any carrots today. You can have green beans.

Jack: OK then.

Dinner lady: Do you want any dessert?

Jack: Yeah – some ice cream, please.

Dinner lady: Fine – there you go. Enjoy!

Jack: Thanks!

> **Answers**
> 1 pasta, cheeseburger with chips; strawberry yoghurt
> 2 mixed salad with olive oil; grilled fish with green beans (there are no carrots); ice cream

7 Grammar

✱ *some* and *any*

a Write the headings *Countable* and *Uncountable* on the board and elicit an example for each category and write it on the board. Now go through the examples with students. Ask them the following questions:

Sentence 1: Is the word yoghurt countable or uncountable? (uncountable) Is the verb positive or negative? (positive)

Sentence 2: Is the word carrots countable or uncountable, singular or plural? (plural countable) Is the verb positive or negative? (positive)

Which words are used before these words? (some)

Sentence 3: What do you notice about the verb in this sentence? (It's negative.)

What is the word before carrots? (any)

Now ask students to complete the rule. Check answers.

> **Answers**
> some; any

b Ask students to read through items 1–5 and check they understand them. Go through the example, eliciting the second answer from students. Ask them if the verb in the second part is positive or negative and which word they think they should use before they answer. Students complete the exercise. Check answers.

> **Answers**
> 1 any 2 any; some 3 some; any
> 4 some; any 5 some; some; any

8 Speak

a Divide the class into small groups and ask them to decide who has the healthier meal in Exercise 6b. Have a class vote to see which was healthier (Jack). You could also ask students which of the two meals they would prefer.

b Read through the instructions in open class. In pairs, students create dialogues similar to the listening in Exercise 6b before changing roles.

Weaker classes: Using the prompts, elicit a dialogue from students and write it on the board. Ask the class to repeat the questions, checking for intonation. Practise the dialogue with individuals, before dividing the class into pairs and letting them practise together. Leave the sample dialogue on the board for students to refer to.

Stronger classes: Let students create their own dialogues. Circulate and check intonation and pronunciation. Listen to a few examples as feedback.

Photostory: A double ice cream ...

9 Read and listen

Warm up

Ask students to look at the title of the photostory and the photos and to predict what they think this episode will be about (eating ice cream). You could also ask them who the characters are in this episode (Pete and Jess) and where they are (in a cafe after school).

a ▶ **CD1 T44** Read through the instructions with students and see if students can guess the answer to the question (they both order a double ice cream). Play the recording while students read. Check answers. Play the recording again, pausing as necessary for students to clarify any problems.

TAPESCRIPT
See the text on page 52 of the Student's Book.

b Read through items 1–7 with students and do the first one as an example if necessary. Students answer the questions. Check answers. Students can also correct the false statements.

10 Everyday English

a Read the expressions aloud with the class. Tell them to find them in the photostory and to try to match them with their meaning. Allow students to check answers with a partner before open class feedback.

b Students read the dialogue and then complete it with the expressions from Exercise 10a. Go through the first item as an example, if necessary. Check answers.

Vocabulary notebook

Encourage students to add these expressions to the *Everyday English* section in their vocabulary notebooks.

Discussion box

Weaker classes: Students can choose one question to discuss.

Stronger classes: In pairs or small groups, students go through the questions in the box and discuss them.

Monitor and help as necessary, encouraging students to express themselves in English and to use any vocabulary they have learned from the text. Ask pairs or groups to feedback to the class and discuss any interesting points further.

11 Improvisation

Divide the class into pairs. Tell students they are going to create a role play between Pete, Jess and Mrs Sanders. Read through the instructions with students. Give students two minutes to plan their dialogue. Circulate and help with vocabulary as necessary. Encourage students to use expressions from Exercise 10. Students practise their conversation in pairs. Listen to some of the best conversations in open class.

12 Team Spirit DVD 1 Episode 3

a Write the names *Jess*, *Debbie*, *Pete* and *Joel* on the board and in open class ask students to tell you as much as possible about each character.

b Read through the sentences and check the meaning of difficult vocabulary: *unhealthily; overweight; gross; rude*. Ask students to work in pairs and attempt to complete the gaps in the sentences using the names of the characters. Watch Episode 3 and check answers.

13 Write

Students can do the preparation for this task in class, and complete the writing at home.

Look at the example with students. Pay attention to the use of the present simple for habits/repeated actions and the use of *but* to express contrast. Using their notes from Exercise 12, students write a paragraph about one of their partners. In a future class, you may like to ask some students to read their paragraphs without mentioning the name of the students described. The rest of the class try to guess who the text refers to.

14 Last but not least: more speaking

Warm up

Books closed. Ask students how often they eat out and make a list of different places on the board.

a 1 Books open. Read through the questions with students. Ask them to make a list of places they eat out and decide which is their favourite and why. Students compare answers with a partner. Listen to some of their ideas in open class.

2 For this activity it is good to bring along some advertisements for restaurants for students to look at and use as examples. Look through the questions with students and listen to some of their ideas before asking them to work individually and note down their answers. Talk about your own ideal restaurant to get them started.

3   Students make notes of their answers to the
    questions. Encourage them to be as imaginative
    as possible – they can go anywhere in the world
    with whoever they like!

b   Students should now have answers to all of
    the questions in Exercise 14a. Divide the class
    into groups of four and tell them to ask each other
    the questions and answer individually. To maximise
    speaking practice, it is better if one student at a
    time is questioned by the other three. Circulate
    and help with questions as required.

c   Listen to feedback from each of the groups. Ask
    them to explain the best answers from their group
    and as a class decide on which is the best place to
    eat (and who with).

Check your progress

1 Grammar

a   2 have to   3 doesn't have to   4 have to
    5 don't have to   6 has to   7 don't have to

b   2 an   3 much   4 many   5 Many   6 a
    7 some; much   8 any; some   9 any

2 Vocabulary

a   2 eggs   3 sugar   4 orange   5 water   6 carrots
    7 bread   8 apple   9 meat   10 fish
    [Mystery word: vegetables]

b   2 dentist   3 doctor   4 nurse   5 pilot   6 lawyer
    7 firefighter   8 engineer

How did you do?

Check with students on their progress and
if necessary spend time with students helping
them in the areas they need more work on.

Memo from Mario

Eat for life

Hold them, smell them, pass them

▶ In preparation, bring these items to your lesson: *an apple, a carrot, rice, an egg, beans, bread, tomatoes, sugar, a small piece of meat, onions.*

▶ Also bring in these items (from the Vocabulary bank on Page 65) *knife, fork, spoon, plate, glass, bowl, napkin, cup, saucer, dish, straw, chopsticks, mug, menu.*

▶ Ask the students to stand in two concentric circles facing inwards.

▶ If you can clear a space for this, so much the better, but the two standing circles can also be among the desks.

▶ Take your place in the inner of the two circles and have the fruit, vegetables and kitchen items near you.

▶ Take the apple, hold it, look at it and smell it. Take your time. Then pass it to the student on your left while saying the word *apple* loud and clear.

▶ Ask the student on your left to do the same as you did and so on round the circle.

▶ If the pronunciation of the word gets wobbly, cross the circle, take back the object from the student who has it and give it to the student two to his/her right, saying the word again loudly and clearly. (In this way the 'wobbly' student has a chance to say the word correctly).

▶ When you have passed about five of the foods round the circle, ask the inner and outer circles to change places and do the rest of the food with the other group.

▶ Ask the inner and outer circles to swap places again.

▶ Repeat the above process with the first seven kitchen items, though in this case replace smelling them with tapping them to hear what sort of sound they make.

▶ Ask the inner and outer circles to swap again.

▶ Do the last seven kitchen items.

RATIONALE

It makes sense to teach highly sensory items in a multi-sensory way. In the case of the foods you are teaching through touch, sight, smell and hearing and the kitchen items, through touch, sight, and hearing. This kind of procedure makes remembering the words much easier for the students.

You may find that your more kinaesthetic students misbehave less when invited to stand and move than when nailed to their desks!

It is interesting that the outer circle people who do not take part in the action often learn the words as well or better than the inner circle 'actors'. The pressure is off them; people often seem to learn rather well by watching another's learning process. This is certainly what happens when, in the family, younger kids observe their older siblings learning something from one of the parents.

One good thing about this exercise is the way you can correct a student's pronunciation without focusing on them publicly … simply by making sure they hear the correct model a couple of times before having another go at saying the word.

Learning languages

Unit overview

TOPIC: Languages and language learning

TEXTS

Reading and listening: a text about a man who spoke many languages
Listening: a professor talking about language learning
Reading: a text about the different words teenagers use
Writing: a text about your language; a letter to a friend about an English course

SPEAKING AND FUNCTIONS

Comparing things
Talking about language learning

LANGUAGE

Grammar: Comparatives and superlatives
Vocabulary: Language learning
Pronunciation: Unstressed syllables: schwa sound /ə/ in *than*

1 Read and listen

Warm up

Write the title of the unit on the board. Ask students what they think the best way is to learn languages and make a list of their ideas. How long do they think it takes to learn a language well? Do they know any people who speak more than one language – how did these people learn?

[a] Ask students to look at the picture and read the title of the text. Students predict what the text is about, then read quickly to check their answers.

Answer
An Italian man who spoke many languages.

[b] ▶ **CD2 T1** Read through the sentences with students and check understanding. Go through the first item as an example if necessary. Play the recording for students to listen and read the text at the same time. Students complete the exercise and compare answers in pairs. Play the recording again, pausing as necessary for students to check or change their answers.

TAPESCRIPT
See the reading text on page 56 of the Student's Book.

Answers
1 T   2 F (He never left Italy.)   3 F (Chinese was the hardest language to learn.)   4 T   5 T

[c] In open class, ask students which languages are commonly spoken in their country. Do people who move to their country from abroad learn their language? Listen to some of their ideas.

[d] In pairs, students discuss which is the world's most commonly spoken language. Check answer.

Answer
Chinese

2 Listen

Warm up

To introduce comparatives, tell students about a (made-up) friend who speaks six languages. Write the languages on the board, grading his ability from 1 to 10, e.g. *English 10, French 7, Russian 6, Italian 5, Spanish 3, German 1*. Ask students to make a sentence comparing his abilities. Elicit the following sentence and write it on the board. *His French is better than his Russian.* Tell students that *better* is the comparative form of the adjective *good*. Elicit similar sentences comparing the other languages.

[a] ▶ **CD2 T2** Tell students they are going to listen to two students talking about the languages they are learning. Play the recording while students listen and read the texts.

[b] ▶ **CD2 T2** Play the recording again and ask students to fill in the names of the languages. Check answers.

TAPESCRIPT

Alessandro: My Spanish is good – it's better than my German. Of course, for me Spanish is easier than German. That's because it's got a lot of words that are almost the same as Italian. The grammar's very similar, too.

Paula: Portuguese pronunciation is difficult for me. But of course, English pronunciation is more difficult! I never know how to pronounce a new word, because the writing and the pronunciation are often very different.

Answers
1 Spanish   2 German   3 Spanish   4 German
5 Italian   6 Portuguese   7 English

Grammar

✱ Comparative adjectives

a Focus on the adjective *easy* in the grammar table and ask students to find a word similar to it in Alessandro's text in Exercise 2b (*easier*) and read the full sentence. Explain that he uses this word to compare Spanish and German and it is followed by *than*. Now ask students to find examples in the texts of other adjectives of comparison.

Students complete the table. They can compare their answers in pairs, before a whole class check.

> **Answers**
> easier, more difficult, better

Now ask students if they notice anything about the spellings in the comparative column of the table. Elicit the spelling rules:
Short adjectives: Add *-er*.

Adjectives ending in *-y*: Change the *-y* to *-i* and add *-er*.
Longer adjectives: Use the word *more* before them.
Irregular adjectives: Learn them!

> **Language notes**
> 1 The above is a simplified version of the rule: in actual fact, we only double the last consonant in short adjectives ending *t, d, g, m, n* where the last syllable ends consonant-vowel-consonant. Examples: *big – bigger, red – redder, hot – hotter*, BUT *long – longer, quiet – quieter, loud – louder*.
> 2 Students may produce comparatives like *more bigger than ...* or *It's hotter that ...* . Remind them that in English we compare two things using *more ... than*.

b Read through sentences 1–5 with students. Go through the example, if necessary. Students complete the sentences. Check answers.

> **Answers**
> 2 longer than   3 smaller than   4 more difficult than   5 farther from; than

> ### ✱ OPTIONAL ACTIVITY
>
> Ask students to change the adjectives in the sentences in Exercise 3b, and rewrite them so that the meaning is the same. Do the first one as an example.
>
> > **Answers**
> > 1 Latin is older than Italian.
> > 2 The Nile is shorter than the Amazon River.
> > 3 India is bigger than Iceland.
> > 4 For most Europeans, learning Italian is easier than learning Chinese.
> > 5 My country is closer to Paris than Sydney.

Grammar notebook

Students should copy the comparative table into their grammar notebooks.

 ## Pronunciation

See notes on page 65.

Speak

Read through the adjectives in the box with students, making sure they know them all. Do the first item as an example, giving your own opinion, e.g. *I think books are more interesting than CD-ROMs.* Students work in pairs or small groups and make comparisons. Find out how many have the same opinions. Ask: *How many of you think that dogs are more intelligent than cats?* etc.

> **Language note**
> We do not normally use *beautiful* (or *pretty*) to describe a man; we use *good-looking, handsome* or *attractive*.

 ## Listen

a ▶ **CD2 T4** Read through the sentences with students and check understanding. Go through the first item as an example if necessary. Play the recording for students to listen and read the questions at the same time. Students complete the exercise and compare answers in pairs.

> **Answers**
> 1 English   2 25,000   3 more than 1 million
> 4 *e*   5 10

b
> **Answers**
> 1 about 500,000–600,000   2 50,000
> 3 by saying nothing
> 4 by saying nothing and running away

TAPESCRIPT

Interviewer: Professor Crystal, you are one of the world's top experts on language. Thanks for coming in today.

David Crystal: It's a pleasure.

Interviewer: OK, so my first question is: what's the language with the most words?

David Crystal: That's a difficult one, as we don't know for sure how many words each language has. The correct answer is probably English, but again nobody knows how many words English really has. If you look at the two biggest dictionaries of the English language, they list about 500,000 – 600,000 words. But there are lots of words that are not in these dictionaries, and every year, about 25,000 new words come into the English language around the world. So, English now has well over one million words.

Interviewer: One million words! How many words does a normal person know?

David Crystal: Well, it depends on the person's education. People who read a lot know more words than people who don't. Most people have an active vocabulary of around 50,000 words and a passive vocabulary about a third larger.

Interviewer: And now on to a completely different question. When people are silent, does that mean different things in different languages?

David Crystal: Oh, absolutely. If in Japan a man says to a woman *Will you marry me?* and she is silent, this means *yes*. In English it probably doesn't mean *yes* – it could mean that the woman is not sure. In Igbo, a language they speak in West Africa, if a man says *Will you marry me?* and the woman doesn't say a word and stays there, it means *no*, but if she doesn't say anything and runs away, it means *yes*!

Interviewer: And another question, Professor Crystal. Which is the most frequent letter in English?

David Crystal: The letter E – but it's not the most interesting letter!

Interviewer: Really? So tell me – which is the most interesting letter, and why?

David Crystal: The letter X. It is not a very frequent letter in English, but no other letter has more meanings than the X when we use it alone.

Interviewer: Oh, really? Can you give me some examples?

David Crystal: Certainly. One of the first things that a child learns when he or she is learning to write is that when you write someone an email or send a text message and you add some Xes at the end it means …

Interviewer: … kisses!

David Crystal: That's right! And when a student does their homework and the teacher finds something that is wrong, the teacher writes …

Interviewer: An X!

David Crystal: … and there are many more examples in my book, *The Cambridge Encyclopedia of the English Language*. I give ten meanings for the letter X!

Interviewer: Ten meanings! Unbelievable! Now, my next question is about …

7 Vocabulary
✳ Language learning

a Go through the words in the box with the class. Students work in pairs and try to work out the meanings of each word or phrase.

b ▶ **CD2 T5** Ask students to read through the whole text, ignoring the spaces. Check any vocabulary problems. Go through the first item with them as an example.

Students work individually to complete the spaces, then compare their answers in pairs. Check answers.

TAPESCRIPT
Advice for language learners

It can sometimes be a little difficult to learn a foreign language fluently. But there are many things you can do to make your learning more successful.

When you speak a foreign language, it's normal to have an accent. That's OK – other people can usually understand. It's a good idea to listen to CDs and try to imitate other speakers, to make your pronunciation better.

If you see a new word and you don't know what it means, you can sometimes guess the meaning from words you know, or you can look up the word in a dictionary.

A lot of good language learners try not to translate things from their first language. Translation is sometimes a good idea, but try to think in the foreign language if you can!

It's also normal to make mistakes. When your teacher corrects a mistake in your writing or speaking, think about it and try to see why it's wrong. But it's more important to communicate so don't be afraid to speak!

> **Answers**
> 2 imitate 3 means 4 guess 5 look up
> 6 translate 7 make mistakes 8 corrects
> 9 communicate

Vocabulary notebook
Students may find it useful to copy down any new words or expressions from this section. If necessary, they could write translations beside each one.

8 Grammar
✳ Superlative adjectives

If you set the background information as a homework research task, ask students to tell the class what they have found out.

Norway is a country (population c. 4,805,437 in 2009) in Scandinavia. The capital of Norway is Oslo.

Sweden is a country (population c. 9,234,209 in 2007) in Scandinavia. The capital of Sweden is Stockholm.

Papua New Guinea is a country (population c. 6,300,000 in 2007) in the south western Pacific Ocean. The capital of Papua New Guinea is Port Moresby.

Indonesia is a country (population c. 237, 512, 352 in 2008) in south east Asia. It is made up of 17,508 islands. The capital of Indonesia is Jakarta.

Nigeria is a country (population c. 148,000,000 in 2008) in West Africa. It has one of the fastest growing economies in the world. The capital of Nigeria is Abuja.

Somalia is a country (population c. 9,558, 666 in 2008) in eastern Africa. The country gained independence from Italy and Great Britain in 1960.

To introduce this topic, ask students the following questions.

Do you know any towns with very short names?
Do you know any towns with very long names?
Do you know any long English words?
Do you know any short English words?

a Read the amazing facts with the class. Check that they understand any new words. Students guess which statements are not true.

Answer
The longest word in the English language is not *dispercombobulation* and the easiest language is not Portoni.

b Read through the four questions with students, then with books closed (or the text covered) students try to remember the answers. In pairs, students compare answers. Books open, students read the texts again quickly to check their answers.

Answers
1 South Africa 2 *e* 3 Somalia 4 D

c Students read through the adjectives in the box and the spelling rules in the table. Go through the examples in the table with students eliciting the rules for superlatives (short adjectives: add *-est*; longer adjectives: add *most* before the adjective).

Students now add the adjectives from the box to the table and complete the comparative and superlative forms. You may wish to do this on the board as a whole class activity, inviting students to come and fill in the chart for their classmates to check.

Answers
(short) – (shorter) – shortest
(small) – smaller – smallest
big – bigger – biggest
(easy) – (easier) – easiest
happy – happier –happiest
difficult – more difficult – most difficult
fantastic – more fantastic – most fantastic
important – more important – most important
(bad) – (worse) – worst
(good) – (better) – best
(many) – (more) – most

Language note
It is important for students to know when to use the comparative or superlative form of the adjective. Ask if anyone can guess the rule. (We use the comparative when we compare two things, and the superlative when we compare more than two things.)

d Read through sentences 1–6 with students and check any problems with understanding. Go through the example with students. Students complete the exercise. Check answers.

Answers
2 happiest 3 most important 4 smallest
5 worst 6 longest

Grammar notebook
Students should note down the comparatives and superlatives and the spelling rules from this unit and learn them.

Culture in mind

9 Read and listen

a Divide the class into pairs and read the instructions with students. In L1 students think of three words which they would say and their parents wouldn't. Make sure students make a note of the words.

b Students think of words used by their parents but not by them. Once again, make sure students make a note of their words.

c Divide the class into new pairs. Students compare the words chosen in Exercises 8a and 8b. As feedback, listen to some of their ideas in open class and write any interesting words on the board. If you know how English teenagers would say the words, you may like to give a translation.

d ▶ **CD2 T6** Tell students they are going to read and listen to a text about the way teenagers speak in the UK. Point out that they may not understand every word at this stage and that you will focus on particular vocabulary items later.

e Look at the words with students and tell them that they all appeared in the reading text on page 60.

Stronger classes: Students attempt the exercise before looking back at the text. Check answers.

Weaker classes: Let students look back at the text to help them match the words to their definitions. Check answers.

Answers
2 a 3 d 4 b 5 c 6 e

f Students use the words from Exercise 9e to complete the sentences. Tell them that some of the words change form because of the other words in the sentence. Check answers and ask students to explain why the answer to 2 is *inventing* (*-ing* after the verb *to love*) and 5 is *complained* (sentence is in past simple tense).

Answers
2 inventing 3 hang around 4 expression
5 complained 6 gates

10 Write

Students can do the preparation in class and complete the writing assignment as homework. Read through the tasks with the class and make sure they realise they only have to choose ONE of the activities.

a Students who choose this topic should use the listening texts in Exercise 2b as a guide. Students write about their own language ability.

b Students who choose this topic should look carefully at the questions first, and think about possible answers. Tell students to think about vocabulary they will need for their evaluation of their imaginary course.

11 Speak

a Read through the questions with students and check understanding. Encourage students to give their own opinions.

b Divide the class into small groups and ask them to discuss their answers. In open class listen to their ideas and write some of the best suggestions on the board. If students enjoy this topic, you may like to create a list of generic goals for the group. You could create a wall poster for reference.

Memo from Mario

Learning languages

1 A grammar letter to your class

▶ To introduce the grammar in this unit, write your students a grammar letter.

▶ To make clear what I mean, here is an example of a letter I have used to introduce comparatives to a low level class.

Dear Everybody,

I was 13 when I met Michael. He was 14. Michael was bigger than me, he was stronger than me, he had more hair on his body than me and he was a better fighter than me. I think I was a bit better at Spanish than Michael.

Today Michael is a GP (doctor). He understands people better then I do.

He is kinder to his wife than I am to mine.

Please write me a letter about a friend of yours. Please compare yourself to your friend.

Warmly yours,

Mario

▶ The above letter will be of no interest to your class, but a letter <u>you</u> write comparing yourself to a friend is likely to hold their interest.

▶ In the lesson give your letter to the students but before they write back to you do the work the authors suggest in Exercises 3 and 5.

▶ Ask the students to write their 'comparative' letter to you as homework.

▶ You may want to work on the mistakes they make in using the comparatives in their letters.

> **RATIONALE**
> There are umpteen ways of presenting new grammar but the teacher's personal grammar letter to the class is one of the more lively ones.

VARIATION FOR OTHER LEVELS

You can use this technique with almost any area of grammar. I remember needing to introduce the so-called 'second conditional' to a group of mid-teen students. My letter opened like this:

> *Dear All,*
> *What would things be like if I was a woman? I wouldn't wear high heeled shoes cos …*

At the core of this technique is the feeling that the students are learning the language from you, their linguistic parent, and that the coursebook, while a huge support, can only be as good as the way you mediate it.

2 Peer comparisons

▶ The technique that follows is useful for revising the grammar from this unit.

▶ Organise your class into seated circles of eight to ten students.

▶ Each student needs to have a pen and piece of paper.

▶ Ask each person to write their own name at the top of their piece of paper.

▶ Ask each person to pass the piece of paper to their right.

▶ Each person now writes a sentence comparing themselves to the person whose name is at the top of the sheet.

  e.g. *I am a bit taller than Ali.*

▶ Having written the comparative sentence, each person passes the paper on to the right.

▶ They add another sentence in which the writer compares themselves to the person named at the top of the page and so on.

▶ The activity continues until each student gets their own piece of paper back with the sentences each classmate has written about them.

▶ Ask the students, if they wish to, to put their pieces of paper up on the walls for all to read.

> **RATIONALE**
> Part of learning a language is saying real things about real people, however I would not risk doing this exercise if you have a class with a rough group dynamic, with a lot of 'outsiders' or students who have not yet integrated into the dominant culture of the class.

Pronunciation

Unit 2 Exercise 7

✱ /n/ (ma_n_) and /ŋ/ (so_ng_)

a ▶ **CD1 T9** Before listening, check students understand the difference between these two sounds. Ask students to repeat the word after you. Drill this several times. Now play the recording while students listen and repeat each word.

TAPESCRIPT

man, fun, town, Japan, Britain, Italian
thing, song, sing, morning, writing

b ▶ **CD1 T10** Follow the same procedure for this exercise as for Exercise 1a.

TAPESCRIPT

1 Jenny likes dancing and painting.
2 Dan enjoys running in the morning.
3 We sing songs for fun.

Unit 3 Exercise 3

✱ /ɜː/ (wo_r_ld)

a ▶ **CD1 T13** Play the recording for students to listen and repeat. You may want to focus on *birthday* and *university* and point out where the stress falls in them to make sure students pronounce them correctly. Drill any words students have problems with.

TAPESCRIPT

her, world, work, learn, birthday, university

b ▶ **CD1 T14** Before listening, ask students to underline the /ɜː/ sound in the sentences. Go through the first one with them as an example. Play the recording for students to repeat the sentences. If there are any problems, drill the sentences a few more times.

TAPESCRIPT

1 All over the wo_r_ld.
2 He always wo_r_ks hard.
3 Le_ar_n these wo_r_ds!
4 They we_r_en't at unive_r_sity.

Unit 4 Exercise 3

✱ *was* and *were*

a ▶ **CD1 T20** Put the following phonetic symbols on the board: /ɒ/, /ɜː/, /ə/. Read out the first sentence with the class and elicit which sound they heard in the word *was* (/ə/). Play the recording

for students to listen and write which sound they think they heard in *was* and *were*. Ask students for their answers and write them under the relevant heading on the board. Play the recording again, pausing for students to repeat the words. Drill any words further, if necessary.

TAPESCRIPT

1 Erin was an American woman.
2 There were a lot of papers.
3 Was the water clean?
4 Were the people sick?

> **Answers**
> 1 /ə/   2 /ɜː/   3 /ə/   4 /ɜː/

b ▶ **CD1 T21** Go through the example with students (on the board) and tick the appropriate column. In order to make sure students have heard the correct pronunciation you could pronounce it in all three ways for them to see why /ə/ is the correct pronunciation. Play the recording for students to listen and decide which sound they hear. Check answers, playing and pausing the recording again as necessary.

TAPESCRIPT

1 I was unhappy.
2 We were late yesterday.
3 Was it noisy?
4 Yes, it was.

> **Answers**
> 1 /ə/   2 /ə/   3 /ə/   4 /ɒ/

✱ *-ed* endings

c ▶ **CD1 T22** Put the column headings /d/ or /t/ and /ɪd/ on the board. Do the two examples with students and check they can hear the difference. Tell them they are going to hear the verbs in the box and they must decide which ending they hear. Play the recording. Students note down the verbs according to the pronunciation of the endings. Check answers. Play the recording again, pausing as necessary to drill and repeat each verb.

TAPESCRIPT

1 We walked a long way.
2 We visited an interesting museum.
3 I used a red pen to do the test.
4 We wanted another hamburger.
5 I watched a great programme last night.
6 My painting was awful, so I started again.

Grammar notebook

Students should note down the different pronunciations and write examples for each one.

Unit 5 Exercise 7
✳ Word stress

a ▶ **CD1 T28** Write the list on the board. Repeat the first word in isolation and ask students how many syllables it has. Write the number of syllables on the board. If necessary, remind students what a syllable is. In pairs, students now work out how many syllables the other words have. Play the recording for students to listen and check answers. Play the recording again, pausing for students to repeat.

TAPESCRIPT/ANSWERS

1	surfing (2)	4	cycling (2)
2	basketball (3)	5	skateboarding (3)
3	sport (1)	6	champion (3)

b Write the stress patterns on the board. Go through the first example with students, writing *surfing* under the two-syllable pattern. Students now use their answers from Exercise 4a and match the words with the stress patterns. Play the recording again for students to check answers. Play the recording once more, pausing as necessary for students to repeat each word.

Answers
1 surfing ●●
2 basketball ●●●
3 sport ●
4 cycling ●●
5 skateboarding ●●●
6 champion ●●●

Unit 6 Exercise 3
✳ have to / don't have to

▶ **CD1 T33** Read the instructions with the class. Play the recording and ask them to listen for the /f/ sound in *have* and the weak form of *to*. Students listen and repeat. Play the recording again, if necessary.

TAPESCRIPT

1 I have to go.
2 You don't have to shout.
3 He doesn't have to come.
4 We have to learn English.

Unit 7 Exercise 5
✳ The schwa /ə/ (*water*)

▶ **CD1 T40** Write the words in the box on the board and read them out. Ask students to listen carefully and explain that the schwa /ə/ is the most common vowel sound in English. Read the words again and ask students to identify the schwa sound in the words. Then play the recording for students to listen and check. Make sure they do not try to stress the schwa sound as it is always in a distressed syllable.

TAPESCRIPT

water, sugar, tomato, banana, exercise, vegetable

▶ **CD1 T41** Play the recording and ask students to listen out for the schwa sound. Play the recording again and ask students to underline the syllables with the schwa sound. Check answers playing the recording again.

TAPESCRIPT/ANSWERS

a carrot	some onions
an orange	a lot of fruit
some bread	a lot of calories
some apples	a lot of vegetables

Unit 8 Exercise 4
✳ *than*

a ▶ **CD2 T3** Write the first sentence on the board and read it out as an example. Ask students to tell you where the stressed syllables are and underline them on the board. Students read the other sentences while listening to the recording and mark the stressed syllables. Check answers, playing the recording again.

TAPESCRIPT/ANSWERS

1 Pronunciation is more difficult than grammar.
2 Spanish is easier than German.
3 My speaking is better than my writing.
4 Is French more interesting than English?

b Write *than* on the board and ask students to pronounce it: /ðən/. Explain that *than* is pronounced in its weak form when it is unstressed. Students repeat, paying particular attention to the schwa sound /ə/. Play the recording again, for students to repeat.

Project 1

A presentation about a well-known sports person

Divide the class into groups of about four to six. Read through the instructions with the class.

1 Brainstorm

a Students follow the instructions and look through the texts in Units 2 to 5 again.

b This part of the project can start off as a class project. Write up the three bullet points on the board. Then ask students to suggest events and people for each category.

c Read the instructions with students. Ask groups to appoint a note taker and give them a few minutes to come up with ideas and agree on who they are going to research. Monitor and help as necessary, making sure each student in the group is getting a chance to speak.

2 Research

Students decide which part of the project they will find out about. They should brainstorm ideas for resources: names of magazines, newspapers, books they have heard of, website addresses, etc. They should try to answer all the questions with as much additional interesting information as they can find. Give students a week or so to collect the information and bring it to class.

3 Presentation

Students work on this in class. They will need to go through all the information they have collected and decide what they are going to use and how. It is important to let them know how long the presentation should be. If you have a large class and you want all the presentations to be done in one lesson, for example, it would be advisable to keep the length of each presentation to a maximum of ten minutes.

A presentation can take the form of a large poster, with handwritten or printed text, pictures, photos, drawings, etc. Students can then use the poster as a background for the oral presentation. Alternatively, members of the group can talk about the person using visuals, music, etc.

Read through the examples with the class and let groups decide on a way to present the information. They will need to practise the presentation. They can do this in their groups in class.

Students should do their presentations in the next lesson.

Project 2

A class survey

1 Prepare the survey

You may find it useful to take in some magazine questionnaires and copy them for use in Exercise 1c.

a Read through the instructions with the class. In groups of three or four, students discuss the topics and choose one.

b Read through the instructions and the example with students, reminding them of different question forms.

c Look at the model questionnaire extract with students and show them some examples from magazines if you have any. Go through the example answers with students and explain that they must think of three answer options for each question they have written in Exercise 1b, or make it a *yes/no* question.

Students complete the exercise; make sure each student makes a copy of the questionnaire.

d Students ask the other students in their group the questions and note down their answers. Then students circulate round the class asking as many students as they can, noting down their answers.

2 Write up the results

a Students regroup in their original questionnaire group (from Exercise 1) and discuss their answers. Look at the model charts with students, explaining that they should draw up their results in this way. They can work out how many people they interviewed and what percentage answered.

b Using their own information from Exercise 1, each student now writes sentences to describe their results. Monitor and help as necessary.

c This can be set for homework. Students now transfer all their information on to a poster and add illustrations and more details if they want.

3 Present your information

Groups present their posters and their findings to the rest of the class. Each group appoints a spokesperson. If there are any interesting results, these can be discussed with the class.

Get it right! key

Unit 2: Present simple

2 wears 3 have 4 thinks

Unit 3: Present simple vs. present continuous

a is being (is)   studies (is studying)
visits (is visiting)   meets (is meeting)

b 2 studying 3 seeing 4 swimming
5 coming 6 enjoying 7 planning
8 travelling 9 selling 10 raining

Unit 5: Past time expressions

2 I passed my exam last Friday.
3 I bought a present for you yesterday.
4 I visited my cousins a week ago.

Unit 7: Countable and uncountable nouns

Countable: bottle, sausage, pen, cat, T-shirt

Uncountable: homework, music, advice, information, news, shorts

Unit 7: *a/an*, *some* and *any*

2 homework 3 shorts 4 news 5 sausages
6 eggs 7 water

Unit 7: *much* and *many*

2 many 3 much 4 many 5 many

Workbook key

1 Welcome

A People

1 2 Tomoko's from Japan. She's 16. She's a student. She's in room 107.
3 Devrim's from Turkey. He's 15. He's a student. He's in room 209.
4 Helena and Samantha are from Britain. They're 18. They aren't students. They're in room 112.
5 Patrick and Alan are from America. They're 16. They aren't students. They're in room 205.

2 **a** you – your   he – his   she – her   we – our
they – their

b 2 My; He; his 3 My; her 4 your
5 We; Our 6 Their; They

3 2 Helen has got a little brother.
3 Helen hasn't got a lot of DVDs.
4 Jordan has got a bicycle.
5 Jordan and Helen have got black hair.
6 Helen has got a big bedroom.
7 Jordan hasn't got a big family.
8 Jordan and Helen haven't got a dog.

B Rooms and homes

1 **a**

B	A	T	B	E	D	T	O
T	A	B	L	E	C	E	R
B	R	O	O	M	H	L	D
A	R	M	C	H	A	I	R
T	F	W	O	O	I	O	A
H	R	O	O	D	R	T	O
A	I	D	K	N	I	S	B
R	D	N	E	T	U	O	P
M	G	I	R	R	O	F	U
R	E	W	O	H	S	A	C

b 1 living room 2 kitchen 3 dining room
4 bathroom 5 bedroom

2 **a** 1 is 2 are 3 are 4 are 5 is 6 aren't

b 1 There is 2 There is 3 There are
4 There are 5 there is; there are

3 2 behind 3 on 4 between 5 next to 6 under

C Activities

1 **a** 2 close 3 run 4 swim 5 listen
6 read 7 jump 8 laugh 9 cry
10 write 11 shout 12 smile

b 2 read 3 listen 4 open 5 swim
6 run 7 laugh 8 close

2 2 Don't run!
3 Don't close the door!
4 Don't open the window!
5 Don't sing!
6 Don't come in!

3 2 Louisa never reads a book.
3 Sue sometimes listens to music.
4 Ben often reads a book.
5 Louisa hardly ever goes to the cinema.
6 Ben sometimes goes to the cinema.
7 Louisa usually gets up early.
8 Sue always gets up early.

4 2 can read 3 can't write 4 can't sing
5 can walk; can't run

D In town and shopping

1 **a** café; station; bookshop; disco; cinema; post office; shoe shop; clothes shop

b 2 café 3 shoe shop 4 clothes shop
5 cinema 6 disco 7 bookshop 8 station

2 2 past 3 half 4 to 5 past 6 twenty
7 past 8 quarter

3 1 shoes 2 shirt 3 trainers 4 → jumper
4 ↓ jacket 5 trousers 6 socks 7 skirt
8 scarf 9 dress 10 T-shirt

4 2 twelve euros
3 twenty-one dollars
4 seven pounds, forty-nine
5 twenty-four euros, ninety-nine
6 one hundred and twenty-five pounds
7 one hundred and twelve dollars fifty
8 one hundred and nineteen euros, ninety-nine

2 Free time

1 2 four 3 40,000 4 sugar 5 are 6 80,000
7 reads 8 honey

2 **a** 2 studies 3 get up 4 writes 5 sleeps
6 drive 7 like 8 gets

b 2 doesn't like cats 3 don't read books
4 don't watch TV 5 doesn't like aeroplanes

c 2 Do / listen 3 Does she like 4 Do they
study / they do 5 Does he speak
6 do / live 7 do / go 8 does she wear

d 1 meet 2 go 3 do / go 4 drink 5 don't
go 6 get up 7 play 8 doesn't get up
9 Does / work 10 works 11 doesn't like
12 come 13 don't go 14 do

3 **a** Students' own logos

b 2 reading 3 running 4 playing computer
games 5 dancing 6 painting 7 listening to
music 8 going to the cinema

c 2 doing A 3 looking after G 4 collecting F
5 making B 6 hanging out E 7 drawing D
8 keeping C

4 **a** 2 dancing 3 going 4 smiling 5 studying
6 flying 7 swimming 8 running

b 2 likes/enjoys/loves painting pictures
3 doesn't like / doesn't enjoy / hates playing
football
4 likes/enjoys/loves running
5 like/enjoy/love listening to music
6 likes/enjoys/loves dancing
7 don't like / don't enjoy / hate flying
8 doesn't like / doesn't enjoy / hates studying

c Students' own answers

5 **a** ▶ CD2 T7 TAPESCRIPT/ANSWERS
1 listen 2 open 3 wrong 4 wings 5 spin
6 go in 7 coming 8 driving

b ▶ CD2 T8 TAPESCRIPT/ANSWERS
1 Anne <u>rings</u> me every weekend.
2 I enjoy <u>speaking</u> another language.
3 We <u>run</u> every day.
4 Let's go <u>swimming</u>.
5 We usually <u>swim</u> in the summer.

6 1 Geography 2 Spanish 3 creative
4 Drama 5 lunch-time 6 orchestra
7 sailing 8 parents 9 free

7 Music activities: playing the piano
Places: cinema, beach
Other activities: reading, dancing, painting
Sports activities: playing football, swimming

8 Sally: 5, 6
James: 3, 7
Richard: 2, 8
Nadia: 1, 4

▶ CD2 T9 TAPESCRIPT

Sally: My favourite hobby is dancing. I also learn
the guitar – I go to guitar lessons on Wednesday
after school and I really enjoy that. And I often
play and sing with my friends on Saturday nights.

James: I spend a lot of time talking to my friends on the phone. Writing emails is fun too, but my computer isn't very good. It's a bit old.

Richard: I like swimming, but we don't live near the sea so I go to the swimming pool here in my town. My other hobby is going for long bike rides – my friends and I all like riding bicycles.

Nadia: I really enjoy going to the cinema – I love watching films. And at home I play computer games. I usually play with my cousin. It's great fun!

9 Matthew

Unit check

1 cinema 2 like 3 watches 4 talking
5 teaches 6 doesn't 7 games 8 different
9 person

2 b 3 a 4 a 5 b 6 c 7 c 8 b 9 c

2 running 3 playing 4 cinema 5 hobbies
6 writing 7 keeping 8 painting 9 dancing

3 Helping other people

1 2 a 3 b 4 c 5 b

2 **a** 1 are 2 is 3 aren't 4 isn't 5 am 6 are
7 are

b 2 What is she watching?
3 Are you getting dressed? I'm getting ready
4 Who are you talking to?
5 He is giving me the answers to the homework.
6 Why are you crying? I'm not crying! I'm laughing!

c Possible answers:
2 Irene is sitting under the tree. She is sleeping.
3 Danny is reading a book. He is sitting by the window.
4 Olga and Joanne are watching TV. Alex is washing up.
5 Tony is painting a picture. Sam is playing the guitar.
6 Frances is riding her bike. The dogs are running next to her.

d 2 e 3 f 4 a 5 c 6 b

e 2 am doing 3 don't / stay 4 goes
5 is not using 6 are watching
7 is doing 8 do / do 9 Are / playing
10 don't understand

3 **a** ▶ CD2 T10 do the cooking 2
do the shopping 1
do the washing-up 5
do the washing 4
clean the windows 6
tidy up 3

b 2 is doing the cooking
3 are tidying up
4 are doing the washing
5 is washing-up
6 are cleaning the windows

c 2 bucket 3 pillow 4 bin 5 cloth
6 hanger 7 drawers 8 wardrobe

Mystery word: CUPBOARD

4 **a** ▶ CD2 T11 TAPESCRIPT
1 bored bird; 2 born burn; 3 walk work;
4 short shirt

b ▶ CD2 T12 TAPESCRIPT
1 more 2 door 3 always 4 learning
5 girl 6 working 7 talking 8 birthday

c ▶ CD2 T13 1 All over the world 2 I was born in Turkey 3 Her parents are working in Portugal 4 The girls are organising their research. 5 Laura was early for work this morning.

5 2 See? 3 problem 4 on 5 though 6 So

6 **a** 2 Gemma plays in the orchestra.
3 Some students bring sandwiches and eat them at school.
4 We usually walk, but sometimes we catch the bus.

b Subjects: Geography, Art
Other nouns: exam, uniform
Verbs: write, teach

7 **a & b** 1 doing 2 volunteer 3 carry
4 having 5 eight 6 make
7 together 8 cooking 9 wash

▶ CD2 T14 TAPESCRIPT
(See page 25 of the Teacher's Resource Book.)

8 Students' own answers

Unit check

1 1 morning 2 up 3 moment 4 the 5 is
6 hate 7 right 8 works 9 shopping

2 2 c 3 c 4 b 5 c 6 b 7 a 8 c 9 b

3 2 do the washing 3 do the shopping 4 do the cooking 5 do the ironing 6 do the washing up
7 tidy up 8 clean the windows 9 have a rest

4 Who's your hero?

1 2 F 3 T 4 T 5 F 6 T

2 **a** 2 was 3 weren't 4 Were 5 was 6 was
7 Were 8 was

b ▶ CD2 T15 TAPESCRIPT
(See page 90 of the Workbook.)
1 was 2 Was 3 was 4 wasn't 5 was
6 was 7 were 8 was 9 were 10 weren't
11 was

c 2 hated 3 climbed 4 stayed 5 listened
6 cried 7 planned 8 decided 9 talked
10 stopped 11 studied 12 cleaned

d 2 cleaned 3 listened 4 cried 5 stopped
6 talked

e 2 didn't answer 3 didn't cook 4 didn't
speak 5 didn't study 6 didn't do

f 1 stayed 2 didn't like 3 visited 4 talked
5 didn't want 6 walked 7 didn't have
8 didn't play 9 started

3 **a** 1 B 2 D 3 A 4 C

b 2 Take it off! 3 Put it down! 4 Put them on!

c 2 grows up 3 Turn off 4 sit down 5 go out

d 2 up 3 on 4 down 5 off 6 down
7 on 8 off

4 **a** ▶ CD2 T16 TAPESCRIPT/ANSWERS
1 closed 1 2 watched 1 3 needed 2
4 started 2 5 discovered 3 6 decided 3
7 walked 1 8 studied 2 9 planned 1
10 worked 1

b ▶ CD2 T17 TAPESCRIPT
1 She wanted a drink.
2 They watched a good film.
3 He walked a long way.
4 We visited our friends.
5 I hated that book.
6 She climbed the hill.
7 We decided to go home.
8 He started to read.

5 **a** 2 e 3 a 4 d 5 b 6 f

b 1 forget 2 unforgettable 3 memorials
4 memory 5 memories

6 **a** up: come up, climb up, pick up
down: cut down, come down, put down

b goes off turns on gets up puts on
sets off goes on slow down gives up

c Students' own answers

d Students' own answers

Skills in mind

a Students' own answers

b 2 F 3 T 4 F 5 F 6 T

c 2 popular 3 thief 4 rich 5 beautiful

Unit check

1 1 travelled 2 born 3 was 4 planned 5 didn't
6 trees 7 discovered 8 weren't 9 wasn't

2 2 b 3 a 4 b 5 a 6 b 7 c 8 b 9 c

3 2 come up 3 switch on 4 get in 5 forget
6 sit down 7 put down 8 take off 9 go out

5 Making friends

1 2 a; 3 g; 4 f; 5 h; 6 c; 7 b; 8 e

2 **a** 2 wanted 3 said 4 enjoyed 5 wasn't
6 met 7 became 8 left

b 2 left 3 won 4 went 5 came/began
6 met/had

c 1 Liz 2 Pat 3 Sandra 4 Maria 5 Judy
6 Angela

d 1 Did you meet a famous athlete?
2 Did he speak to you?
3 Did the volunteers stay in the Olympic village?
4 Did you work hard?
5 Did people enjoy the Olympic Games?

e ▶ CD2 T18 TAPESCRIPT
(See page 97 of the Workbook.)
1 were 2 played 3 won 4 happened
5 started 6 scored 7 had 8 said 9 read
10 saw 11 found 12 wasn't

3 **a** Down: 1 March 2 weeks 3 February
4 yesterday 7 ten 9 last

Across: 3 Friday 5 hour 6 months
8 April 10 years 11 day

b B 7 C 6 D 9 E 5 F 10 G 1 H 3 I 2
J 8

c 2 I 3 F 4 J 5 D 6 A 7 E 8 B

4 **a** ▶ CD2 T19 TAPESCRIPT/ANSWERS
1 happened 2 listened 3 began 4 arrived
5 studied 6 became

b ▶ CD2 T20 TAPESCRIPT
morning friendship medal athlete
because July tonight today yesterday
teenager volleyball exercise November
important fantastic beginning

Oo	oO	Ooo	oOo
friendship	July	teenager	important
medal	tonight	volleyball	fantastic
athlete	today	exercise	beginning

5 2 I don't think so 3 to be honest 4 on the other hand 5 I didn't mean to 6 never mind

6 **a** 2 got 3 came 4 saw 5 took

b 2 forget 3 speak 4 drink 5 give

7 ▶ CD2 T21 TAPESCRIPT/ANSWERS

A 3 B 2 C 1 D 2 E 1 F 3

Narrator: 1

Girl: I met my friend Greg when we were five years old. We started school together on the same day and we became friends very quickly after that. We're at different schools now but I often see him at the weekend. We've both got bikes and we do a lot of cycling together.

Narrator: 2

Girl: Peter's another good friend of mine. I met him three years ago when his family came to live in the flat next to us. I see him almost every day. We usually walk to school together and we sometimes help each other with our homework.

Narrator: 3

Girl: Michael's 18 and he's my boyfriend. I met him a year ago – we met at my cousin's sixteenth birthday party. He asked me to dance and then we started talking and I really liked him. We're still going out together. I see him about three times a week and we go to the cinema together every Saturday, because we really enjoy watching films.

8 Students' own answers

Unit check

1 1 surfing 2 didn't 3 was 4 looked 5 began 6 said 7 became 8 ago 9 friendship

2 2 c 3 b 4 a 5 a 6 c 7 a 8 b 9 a

3 2 an hour ago 3 last 4 yesterday 5 basketball 6 skiing 7 skateboarding 8 helmet 9 court

6 Successful people

1 **a** 2 e 3 f 4 b 5 a 6 c
A 4 B 3 C 1 D 5 E 6 F 2

b 2 Doctors don't have to be good at painting.
3 A teacher doesn't have to know everything.
4 We have to do the washing-up after lunch.
5 You don't have to get up early tomorrow.
6 Roberto doesn't have to work during the holidays.

c 2 have to 3 has to 4 have to
5 doesn't have to 6 don't have to

d 2 Yes, they do 3 No, he doesn't
4 No, she doesn't 5 Yes, she does
6 No, they don't

e 2 Do Giovanna and Stefano have to do the ironing? No, they don't
3 Does Giovanna have to clean the windows? Yes, she does
4 Do Helena and Stefano have to wash up? Yes, they do.
5 and 6 Students' own answers

2 **a**

F	G	L	P	I	L	O	T	X	R	F	I	N
L	O	S	R	E	P	S	S	E	N	I	I	U
I	E	A	R	C	H	I	T	E	C	T	X	R
G	D	L	I	L	X	N	I	B	S	M	E	S
H	E	A	K	P	I	J	S	S	R	Y	F	E
T	N	W	Z	S	H	C	E	O	E	T	I	L
A	T	Y	Q	I	J	T	V	E	T	P	R	U
T	I	E	L	N	D	E	R	E	S	R	E	F
T	S	R	E	G	N	A	L	D	F	D	F	O
E	T	U	L	E	T	C	J	O	R	D	I	S
N	I	K	A	R	G	H	D	A	C	B	G	R
D	L	Y	T	I	O	E	Y	H	P	D	H	M
A	T	L	I	L	M	R	V	Q	S	X	T	A
N	I	O	P	I	D	O	C	T	O	R	E	E
T	J	E	N	G	I	N	E	E	R	H	R	B

b 2 pilot + flight attendant 3 doctor + nurse
4 firefighter 5 vet 6 engineer 7 architect
8 dentist

c 1 in a shop 2 in an office 3 salary
4 in a factory 5 night shift 6 wages
7 earns

3 **a** ▶ CD2 T22 TAPESCRIPT

1 We have to leave now.
2 They don't have to go out.
3 She has to do the washing.
4 He doesn't have to study tonight.
5 Do you have to cook this evening?
6 Does he have to drive to the shop?

b 2 had to 3 has to 4 have to 5 had to
6 have to

▶ CD2 T23 TAPESCRIPT

1 Sam has to help his parents at the weekend.
2 I had to go to the dentist yesterday.
3 Teresa has to work on Saturday mornings.
4 We have to buy a present for Dad's birthday.
5 My sister had to buy a new computer.
6 You have to get up early tomorrow.

4 **a** 2 dog walking   3 delivering newspapers
4 washing cars   5 helping elderly (people)

b 2 to earn   3 pocket money   4 to save
5 to spend   6 to waste

5 Students' own answers

6 2 c (photo A)   3 a (photo B)   4 b (photo D)
5 d (photo E)

7 **a** 1 pocket money   2 job   3 earn
4 newspapers   5 babysitting

b Students' own answers

Writing tip

1 b   2 c   3 a

Unit check

1 1 dentist   2 doctors   3 job   4 player   5 dream
6 have   7 hours   8 has   9 successful

2 2 a   3 b   4 a   5 c   6 a   7 c   8 a   9 a

3 2 part-time   3 pocket money   4 job   5 pilot
6 full-time   7 teacher   8 work   9 home

7 Eat for life

1 2 healthy   3 green   4 different   5 bad
6 stress-free

2 **a** Across: 1 cheese   2 oranges   3 tea
9 potatoes

Down: 1 carrots   2 eggs   3 butter   5 sugar
7 apples   8 water

b 2 Potatoes / carrots   3 Cheese / butter
4 water or tea   5 eggs   6 Sugar

c 2 coffee   3 milk   4 tomatoes   5 onions
6 grapes

3 **a** Countable: tomatoes, onions, oranges,
potatoes, carrots, eggs, apples

Uncountable: milk, bread, cheese, tea, butter,
sugar, water

b 2 is   3 are   4 is   5 is   6 are   7 is   8 are

c 2 an / some   3 a / an   4 an / some
5 some / some   6 some / some
7 a / an   8 a / some

d Students' own answers

e 1 many calories   2 much sugar
3 much weight   4 much exercise
5 many hours   6 many emails

f 1 much   2 many   3 much   4 many
5 much   6 much

4 **a** cup   spoon   fork   straw   knife   plate
glass   bowl   saucer

b 1 plate   2 knife   3 fork   4 spoon   5 glass
6 straw   7 cup   8 saucer   9 bowl

5 **a** ▶ CD2 T24   TAPESCRIPT/ANSWERS
1 min(e)ral wat(e)r
2 bacon (a)nd eggs
3 bread (a)nd butter
4 some fruit (a)nd veget(a)bles
5 (a) terr(i)ble breakfast

b ▶ CD2 T25   TAPESCRIPT/ANSWERS
Bacon and eggs for Jenny.
Bread and butter for Tim.
Bananas and apples for Harry,
Fruit's always the right food for him.

Breakfast is really important,
You have to eat lots of good stuff!
You can't just drink mineral water –
Why not? Well, it's just not enough!

6 1 as well   2 and stuff   3 know what you mean
4 no problem   5 couple of

7
Positive adjectives	Negative adjectives
delicious	unhealthy
successful	difficult
interesting	sick
healthy	boring
brilliant	crazy
beautiful	unhappy

8 **a** 2 Max   3 Maria   4 Diana

b

Meat and fish	Fruit and vegetables	Other food
fish	salad	tomato sauce
chicken	onions	pasta
	carrots	milk
	potatoes	rice
	oranges	cheese
		bread
		curry
		yoghurt
		lasagne
		carrot soup

9 Students' own answers

Unit check

1 1 some   2 breakfast   3 beef   4 fish   5 doesn't
6 vegetables   7 eats   8 apple   9 oranges

2 2 c   3 b   4 a   5 b   6 c   7 a   8 c   9 b

3 3 T 4 O 5 F 6 O 7 T 8 F 9 D 10 T
11 D 12 O 13 D 14 F 15 F 16 T 17 O 18 T

8 Learning languages

1 2 d 3 f 4 a 5 b 6 e

2 **a** small; local; old; excellent; Russian; different; strange; good; determined; big; exciting

b

-er	More ...	Irregular
quiet – quieter	difficult – more difficult	bad – worse
big – bigger		far – farther/further
easy – easier	expensive – more expensive	
cheap – cheaper	successful – more successful	
noisy – noisier		
old – older	relaxing – more relaxing	

c Possible answers:
2 Coffee is more expensive in Efes Café.
3 Sandwiches are cheaper in Café Paradiso.
4 The atmosphere is more relaxing in Café Paradiso.
5 Café Efes is bigger than Café Paradiso.
6 Efes Café is noisier than Café Paradiso.

3 **a** 2 c 3 d 4 a 5 b 6 h 7 f 8 g

b 1 guess 2 look up 3 have 4 imitate
5 make 6 translate

c 2 mother tongue 3 native speaker / foreign
4 fluent 5 bilingual 6 accurate 7 dialect

4 **a**

-est	Irregular	Most ...
big – the biggest	bad – the worst	beautiful – the most beautiful
easy – the easiest	good – the best	important – the most important
thin – the thinnest	short – the shortest	delicious – the most delicious
heavy – the heaviest		creative – the most creative
rich – the richest		intelligent – the most intelligent

b 2 biggest 3 worst 4 most beautiful
5 easiest 6 richest 7 heaviest

c 1 most expensive 2 bigger than 3 older
4 best 5 the friendliest 6 more difficult
7 most delicious 8 better than 9 most successful

d Students' own answers

5 **a** ► CD2 T26 TAPESCRIPT/ANSWERS
1 <u>Cars</u> are <u>fa</u>ster than <u>bi</u>cycles.
2 <u>Choc</u>olate is <u>swee</u>ter than <u>but</u>ter.
3 <u>Pau</u>la is <u>more</u> <u>cre</u>ative than her <u>brother</u>.
4 <u>Robert</u> is the <u>youngest</u> student in our <u>class</u>.
5 <u>Veg</u>etables are <u>heal</u>thy.
6 It was the <u>most</u> ex<u>pen</u>sive <u>jack</u>et in the <u>shop</u>.

b ► CD2 T26 TAPESCRIPT/ANSWERS
Cars are fast (er) than bic (y)cles.
Chocol (a)te is sweet (er) than butt (er).
Paul (a) is more creative than her broth (er).
Rob (e)rt is th (e) youngest student in ou (r) class.
Veg (e)tables are healthy.
It was th (e) most expensive jack (e)t in th (e) shop.

6 1 hang around 2 expressions 3 decades
4 groovy 5 ace 6 group 7 creative 8 rents

7 Students' own answers

8 **a** Mary 5B Juliette 1E Carla 4A Alice 3D

b 2 F 3 T 4 T 5 F 6 F

► CD2 T27 TAPESCRIPT

My name's Adrian. I'm 16 and I'm interested in art. I want to be a painter when I leave school.

I've got four sisters. Mary is the oldest, but she isn't the tallest – she's shorter than Carla and Alice. Mary's got very short hair – our parents don't like it but I think it looks cool. She's got a boyfriend called Terry and she talks about him all the time – it gets a bit boring, really.

Juliette is my favourite sister. She's the youngest – she's only ten but I think she's very intelligent and she's also the funniest person in our family – she can really make you laugh. She loves animals and she keeps a pet rabbit in the garden.

Carla and Alice are twins – they were born on the same day and now they're both twelve. They look similar, but Carla's got longer hair and bigger eyes than Alice. They have arguments about music all the time – Carla loves all the young girl bands but Alice hates them. Alice is a sporty kid – she's a good swimmer and she's in the girls' football team at school.

9 Students' own answers

Unit check

1 1 speak 2 than 3 difficult 4 easier 5 worst
6 guess 7 look 8 accent 9 imitate

2 2 b 3 b 4 a 5 b 6 a 7 b 8 b 9 c

3 2 accent 3 corrects 4 means 5 guess
6 foreign 7 accurate 8 decade 9 expression

People

Name ....

Class .... Date ....

1 Greetings and introductions

Complete the dialogue with the words in the box.

> hi ~~name's~~ OK Nice I'm How about friend fine

Simon: Hi. My 0 _name's_ Simon.

John: Hello, Simon. 1 .... John.

Simon: Oh, 2 .... , Mary. 3 .... are you?

Mary: I'm 4 .... , thanks. How 5 .... you?

Simon: 6 .... , thanks. John, this is my 7 .... , Mary.

John: 8 .... to meet you.

Mary: Hi, John.

`8`

2 have/has got

a Write short answers to the questions.

0 Have you got a dog? Yes, _I have_ .

1 Has Paul got a big family? No, ...

2 Have your parents got a car? Yes, ...

3 Has Julia got blue eyes? No, ...

4 Have you got an English dictionary? No, ...

5 Have they got a nice house? Yes, ...

`5`

b Write the questions.

0 you / a bicycle *Have you got a bicycle?*

1 Jack / brown hair ....

2 Mr and Mrs Smith / a daughter ....

3 Susan / green eyes ....

4 John's brothers / a cat ....

5 Jane / long hair ....

`5`

3 The verb be

Fill in the spaces with the correct form of the verb *be* (positive or negative).

0 Giulia and Paolo _are_ Italian.

1 Where .... you from?

2 What .... your name?

3 How .... you?

4 .... your name Jack?

5 They .... from America. They're from Canada.

6 We .... all students. Jack's a teacher!

7 My name .... Sarah, it's Sally.

8 .... your friends OK?

9 Is Simon from England? – No, he ....

10 I .... a teacher. I'm a student.

`10`

Rooms and homes

Name ....

Class .... Date ....

1 Colours

Write the colours.

0 uble _blue_

1 worbn ....

2 wolyel ....

3 energ ....

4 plerpu ....

5 agenor   5

2 Furniture and rooms

a Label the furniture.

0 _bath_

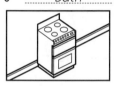

1 ....

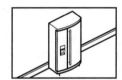

2 ....

3 ....

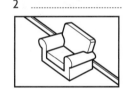

4 ....

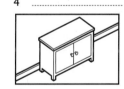

5 ....

6 ....

7 ....

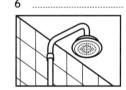

8 ....

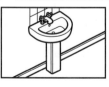

9 ....

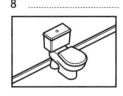

10   10

b Complete the sentences.

0 There's a sofa in the _living room_ .

1 There's a shower in the ....

2 There's a cooker in the ....

3 There's a bed in the ....

4 There are two sinks: there's a sink in the
   .... and in the   5

3 There is / There are

Correct the sentences.

0 There's five chairs in the living room.
   There are five chairs in the living room.

1 There are yellow sofa in the hall
   ....

2 There's old chair in the bedroom.
   ....

3 There's two computers behind the door.
   ....

4 There are new bed in the bedroom.
   ....

5 There's five people in the kitchen.
     5

4 Prepositions of place

Circle the correct words.

0 The milk is (in) / under the fridge.

1 My red coat is between / on the bed.

2 The table is between / on the two armchairs.

3 There's a bathroom next to / between
   my bedroom.

4 The garden chairs are in / behind the tree.

5 Your school bags are on / in the kitchen floor.   5

Activities

Name ....

Class .... Date ....

1 Verbs for activities

Write the verbs under the pictures.

0 ___shout___ 1 .... 2 .... 3 .... 4 .... 5 ....

| 5 |

2 Imperatives

Complete the sentences. Use the verbs in the box (positive or negative).

| write | ~~smile~~ | close | laugh | swim | look |

0 I want to take a photo. __Smile__ at me.

1 I've got a great new T-shirt. .... at it!

2 The pool is very dirty. .... in it!

3 It isn't funny! .... !

4 It's cold in here. .... the window!

5 I haven't got your address. .... it down for me.

| 5 |

3 can/can't for ability

a Write five things you can do.

0 _I can play the piano._

1 ....

2 ....

3 ....

4 ....

5 ....

| 5 |

b Now write five things you can't do.

0 _I can't swim._

1 ....

2 ....

3 ....

4 ....

5 ....

| 5 |

c Write the short answers.

0 Can Jim speak English?
   Yes, _he can_ .

1 Can you play the guitar?
   No, ...

2 Can your sister swim?
   Yes, ...

3 Can your father speak French?
   No, ...

4 Can your brothers play football?
   Yes, ...

5 Can Bill write poetry?
   No, ...

| 5 |

4 Object pronouns

Put the object pronouns in the sentences.

| you | her | them | us | me | ~~him~~ |

0 Nick is a good boy. The teachers like _him_ .

1 My father likes bananas but I hate ....

2 My brother and I like our aunt. She gives .... good holidays.

3 Can you help .... please? I've got a problem.

4 Are you there? We can't see ....

5 This is my cat and these are .... kittens.

| 5 |

In town and shopping

Name _____

Class _____ Date _____

1 Places

Complete the sentences.

0   You buy shoes at a _shoe shop_ .

1   You buy train tickets at a _____ .

2   You buy jeans at a _____ .

3   You buy books at a _____ .

4   You buy a coffee at a _____ .

5   You buy stamps at a _____ . [5]

2 *There is/are* negative and questions + *a/an* or *any*

a Complete the sentences.

0   _There aren't_ any cinemas in this town.

1   _____ library near here?

2   _____ disco in our town.

3   _____ clothes shops in this street?

4   _____ old cinema in your town?

5   _____ bookshops here. [5]

b Write the short answers.

0   Are there any books on Italy in this bookshop?
    No, there aren't.

1   Is there an airport in Birmingham?
    Yes, _____ .

2   Are there any good music shops here?
    No, _____ .

3   Is there a disco near your house?
    No, _____ .

4   Are there any supermarkets in this street?
    Yes, _____ .

5   Is there a good bookshop here?
    No, _____ . [5]

3 What's the time?

Look at the clocks and write the times.

0   _three o'clock_   1   _____

2   _____   3   _____

4   _____   5   _____ [5]

4 Clothes

Label the pictures.

0   _skirt_   1   _____

2   _____   3   _____

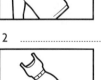 

4   _____   5   _____ [5]

5 Money and prices

Write the prices.

0   £3.60   _three pounds sixty_

1   $12   _____

2   £5.45   _____

3   m 11.30   _____

4   $162   _____

5   m 44.25   _____ [5]

Entry Test A

1 1 I'm   2 hi   3 How   4 fine   5 about
6 OK   7 friend   8 Nice

2 **a** 1 he hasn't
2 they have
3 she hasn't
4 I haven't
5 they have

b 1 Has Jack got brown hair?
2 Have Mr and Mrs Smith got a daughter?
3 Has Susan got green eyes?
4 Have John's brothers got a cat?
5 Has Jane got long hair?

3 1 are   2 is   3 are   4 Is   5 aren't   6 aren't
7 isn't   8 Are   9 isn't   10 'm not

Entry Test B

1 1 brown   2 yellow   3 green   4 purple
5 orange

2 **a** 1 oven   2 fridge   3 bed   4 armchair
5 sofa   6 cupboard   7 table
8 shower   9 sink   10 toilet

b 1 There's a shower in the bathroom.
2 There's a cooker in the kitchen.
3 There's a bed in the bedroom.
4 There are two sinks: there's a sink in
the kitchen and in the bathroom.

3 1 There's a yellow sofa in the hall.
2 There's an old chair in the bedroom.
3 There are two computers behind the door.
4 There's a new bed in the bedroom.
5 There are five people in the kitchen.

4 1 on   2 between   3 next to   4 behind
5 on

Entry Test C

1 1 read   2 listen   3 write   4 swim   5 run

2 1 Look   2 Don't swim   3 Don't laugh
4 Close   5 Write

3 **a** and **b** Students' own answers.

c 1 I can't
2 she can
3 he can't
4 they can
5 he can't

4 1 them   2 us   3 me   4 you   5 her

Entry Test D

1 1 station   2 clothes shop   3 bookshop
4 café   5 post office

2 **a** 1 Is there a
2 There isn't a
3 Are there any
4 Is there an
5 There aren't any

b 1 there is   2 there aren't   3 there isn't
4 there are   5 there isn't

3 1 five o'clock
2 twelve o'clock
3 ten o'clock
4 six o'clock
5 one o'clock

4 1 jeans   2 jumper   3 jacket   4 dress
5 trousers

5 1 twelve dollars   2 five pounds forty-five
3 eleven euros thirty   4 one/a hundred
and sixty two dollars   5 forty-four euros
twenty-five

Teaching notes for communication activities and grammar practice

Unit 2

Communication activity 2a

Areas practised

Present simple (positive and negative, questions and short answers); *like + -ing*
Hobbies and interests

Useful expressions

It's your turn / my turn; yes, that's right / no, wrong; move back a square; throw the dice; I'm the winner!

You will need: a dice for each group; some coloured counters or small objects, e.g. erasers, coins, etc.

- Divide the class into groups of four or five. Give a copy of the board game to each group.
- Each group member places their counter on the START square.
- The first person in the group rolls the dice and moves their counter accordingly.
- They must then look at the prompt on the square they land on and make a sentence using it. The sentence doesn't have to be true.
- The other group members decide if the sentence is grammatically correct. If it is correct the person stays on that square until it is their turn again. If the sentence is not correct they must move back one square.
- The game continues in this way until everyone has finished.
- Monitor and check students are using the positive and negative forms of the present simple correctly and make a note of any repeated errors to go through as a class after the activity.

Communication activity 2b

Areas practised

Present simple (questions and short answers)
School subjects

- Copy one questionnaire for each student in the class and give them out.
- Give students a few minutes to read the questionnaire. Make sure that they understand the phrases.
- Tell students they must ask and answer using the present simple. Remind them of the present simple questions and short answers by going through the first question on the questionnaire as a class. Elicit more questions.

- Explain that students must walk around and ask each other the questions on their questionnaire. They note down the name of each person beside the corresponding question.
- Give students a set time (e.g. three minutes) to go around asking and answering the questions.
- Monitor and check students are using the question and answer forms correctly, noting down any repeated errors to go through at the end of the activity.
- Ask students to feedback to the rest of the class on what they have found out about the other students in the class. If there are any interesting findings, encourage students to discuss them in more detail when they feedback.

Grammar practice key

1
2 They don't watch videos every day.
3 We don't play the piano after school.
4 Paula doesn't like football.
5 You don't study English.
6 My uncle doesn't teach Italian.
7 We don't like music.
8 Juan and José don't play football every day.
9 My classes don't start at 8.00 am.

2
2 I play computer games after school.
3 Susana writes emails every day.
4 My parents like winter.
5 We like football.
6 You like parties.
7 My sister drives a car.
8 Dario swims in the river every morning.
9 Clare and Lucy know the answer.

3
2 My sister loves speaking English.
3 My parents hate playing computer games.
4 You love watching TV.
5 We like swimming in the river.
6 Frank hates playing football.
7 Our dogs love running in the park.
8 I hate doing homework.
9 My grandparents love driving their car.

4

2 My parents like going to the cinema.

3 We love swimming in the river.

4 My dad doesn't like playing computer games.

5 She studies English.

6 My brother loves reading books.

7 They don't like talking in English.

8 My friend listens to pop music every day.

9 Julie loves flying.

5

2 Does she live in London?

3 Do they go swimming in the summer?

4 Do you and your friends play football in the park?

5 Does he speak English and Spanish?

6 Does Anne have lunch at two o'clock every day?

7 Do you go to guitar classes on Thursdays?

8 Do they fly to New York every winter?

9 Does she work in a school?

6

2 No, I don't.   3 Yes, I do.   4 Yes, they do.

5 No, it doesn't.   6 Yes, she/he does.

7 Yes, we do.   8 No, I don't.   9 No, we don't.

Unit 3

Communication activity

Areas practised

Present simple and present continuous
Housework vocabulary

Useful expression

catch a thief

- Divide the class into student A and B pairs. Copy and cut up one sheet for each pair.

- Give students a few minutes to look at the pictures.

- Explain that students must ask and answer questions, using the present simple or the present continuous, to find all the information about what police officer Bill usually does (his daily routine) and what he is doing today in the Hotel De Luxe. Go through the example with a stronger pair. Explain that they must write the information in their notebooks. At the end of the activity, students should have eight facts about Bill's routine and eight facts about what he is doing today.

- Monitor and check students are using the tenses correctly and are forming questions and answers correctly. Note down any repeated errors to go through as a class after the activity.

- Stronger classes can then retell the story, using the present simple and present continuous tenses.

Grammar practice key

1

2 Helen 's/is washing the car.

3 Dad 's/is doing the ironing.

4 Are you going shopping?

5 Paul and Mark aren't / are not cleaning the bathroom.

6 I 'm/am doing my homework.

7 Is Ruth working in Belize?

8 They aren't / are not tidying up.

9 I 'm/am making my bed.

2

2 Juan and Fred are doing the shopping.

3 I 'm/am cooking a chicken for our friends.

4 Peter and Bill are not tidying the living room.

5 Lisa 's/is listening to music.

6 David 's/is playing the guitar.

7 Catherine is not having a shower.

8 Are Mike and Sarah doing the washing-up?

9 Is Daniel making the beds?

3

2 ✓

3 ✓

4 ✗ Do you read the newspaper every day?

5 ✗ Do you like your English classes?

6 ✓

7 ✓

8 ✓

9 ✗ Are you doing the washing-up now?

4

2 f   3 b   4 h   5 g   6 i   7 a   8 c   9 e

Unit 4

Communication activity

Areas practised

Past simple: the verb *be*; *was born / were born*
Past simple: regular verbs

- Divide the class into A and B pairs. Copy and cut up one sheet for each pair.

- Students read through their texts silently. Go through the first item of each text as an example with the class, making sure they understand which verb form to use. Students then write the correct form of the verbs in their notebooks.

- Student A must now check their text with student B. Student A should read out their text to student B. If a verb is wrong, student B must not tell A the correct answer right away. Student A should try to work it out.
- Students then swap roles.
- Monitor and check students are using the correct verb forms. Note down any repeated errors to go through as a class after the activity.

Answers student A
1 was born 2 was 3 lived 4 moved
5 was 6 stayed 7 worked 8 started
9 appeared 10 directed 11 starred
12 worked 13 married 14 was
15 appeared

Answers student B
1 was born 2 moved 3 was 4 started
5 was 6 was 7 trained 8 was 9 was
10 worked 11 married 12 separated
13 continued 14 starred 15 accepted

Grammar practice key

1 2 Was 3 was 4 were 5 wasn't 6 was
7 A Was B wasn't 8 A Were B were
9 A Were B wasn't, was

2 2 were born 3 was born 4 wasn't born
5 were (you) born 6 wasn't born
7 was (your brother) born

3 2 started, didn't finish 3 Did (she) use
4 studied 5 didn't clean 6 lived 7 walked
8 Did (you) watch 9 rained, didn't play

4 2 Pick up 3 climb up 4 Get out
5 Put down 6 Get in 7 Take them off
8 Come down

Unit 5
Communication activity

Areas practised
Past simple: regular and irregular verbs
Past time expressions; Sports

- Divide the class into small groups of four or five. Copy and cut up one sheet for each group.
- Explain to students that they must make three different card piles: one pile with the verb cards, one pile with the sports pictures and one with the time expressions. Check students have sorted the cards correctly.

The cards should then be piled face down so that students can't see them.
- Demonstrate the activity by asking a stronger student to turn over one card from each pile. Make sure they have a verb, a sport picture and a time expression. The student must now make up a sentence using all three parts (the sentence does not have to be true!). The other members of the group decide if the sentence is grammatically correct. If the sentence is correct, the next student can have a turn. If the sentence is wrong, then the student tries again with the same cards.
- Continue in this way until students have used all the cards. Cards can then be shuffled for students to play the game again if they need more practice.
- Monitor and check students are forming the past tenses correctly and that the time expressions are being put in the right place. Make a note of any repeated errors to go through as a class after the activity.

Grammar practice key

1 2 began 3 didn't want 4 talked
5 didn't study 6 went 7 left 8 didn't beat 9 thought, were

2
2 Did they have breakfast before they went to school?
3 Did your brother play football last weekend?
4 Did you do your homework last night?
5 Did the team win the competition yesterday?
6 Did your parents go on holiday last summer?
7 Did we buy food for the party at the weekend?
8 Did you see that science programme on television last night?
9 Did they tell you about their holiday?

3 2 g 3 d 4 c 5 f 6 e 7 a

4

yesterday	last	ago
morning	week	ten years
afternoon	February	an hour
evening	Sunday	a month
		thirteen days

Unit 6
Communication activity
Areas practised
have to / don't have to
Jobs

- Divide the class into pairs. Copy and cut up one sheet for each pair.
- Students spread the cards face up over their table.
- Ask one pair of students to choose a person in the picture and two sentence prompts. Students then use the three items to make a sentence about the person they have chosen. Explain that one part of the sentence must use *has to* and the other part must use *doesn't have to*.
- Encourage students to choose sensible options for the *has to* part, but they can use their imaginations for the *doesn't have to* part.
- Monitor and check that students are using the sentence parts correctly.
- Ask pairs to feedback to the rest of the class.

Alternatively, this can be played with two piles of cards (one of pictures and one of sentence prompts). Students choose one person card and two sentence prompts unseen and make up a sentence in the same way as the procedure above.

Grammar practice key

1
2 Does she have to do the ironing every day?
3 Do they have to study tonight?
4 Do you have to wear a uniform?
5 Do vets have to learn English?
6 Do we have to go to the party tonight?
7 Does he have to get good results?

2
2 Yes, you do.   3 No, you don't.
4 Yes, he does.   5 No, I don't.
6 Yes, they do.   7 Yes, we do.
8 No, they don't.   9 No, you don't.

3
2 ✓
3 ✗ Does my mother have to go to work?
4 ✗ Do your parents have to drive to work?
5 ✓
6 ✓
7 ✗ Does my brother have to come?
8 ✓
9 ✗ Do they have to learn Spanish?

2 don't have to   3 have to   4 had to /
didn't have to 5 didn't have to   6 don't have
to   7 didn't have to   8 have to / don't have
to   9 had to / didn't have to

Unit 7
Communication activity
Areas practised
some and *any*; Possessive pronouns; Sleeping and waking.
Revision of *There is/are* questions and short answers; *How much/many* questions and short answers; Present continuous

- Divide the class into student A and B pairs. Copy and cut up one sheet for each pair.
- Tell the students that they must not show their pictures to their partners. Give students a few minutes to look at their pictures.
- Explain that they must ask and answer questions using the language in the box to find ten differences between the pictures. Ask a stronger pair to read out the example and make sure students understand which question and answer forms to use.
- Monitor and check students are taking turns to ask and answer questions and that they are using question and answer forms correctly. Note down any repeated errors to go through as a class after the activity.
- Ask pairs to feedback to the class. Did they find all ten differences?

Answers picture A
1 There are 10 students in the class.
2 One student is wearing glasses.
3 One student is asleep.
4 One student is daydreaming about football.
5 There is half a litre of water.
6 Two students are playing a game of football.
7 One girl is talking on her mobile phone.
8 One boy is eating a sandwich.
9 One girl is reading a book.
10 The teacher is female and is writing on the blackboard.

Answers picture B
1 There are 12 students in the class.
2 Two students are wearing glasses.
3 Two students are asleep.
4 One student is daydreaming about being a star.
5 There is one litre of water.
6 Four students are playing a game of tennis.

7 Two girls are talking on their mobile phones.

8 One boy is eating an apple.

9 One boy is playing a computer game.

10 The teacher is male and is talking to someone at the door of the classroom.

Grammar practice key

1

2 ✗ Have you got any oranges?

3 ✓

4 ✓

5 ✗ There aren't any onions in this recipe.

6 ✗ There isn't any milk in this glass.

7 ✗ We've got some homework tonight. / We haven't got any homework tonight.

8 ✓

9 ✗ I haven't got any good ideas for the band. / I've got some good ideas for the band.

2

2 many   3 much   4 many   5 much   6 many
7 much   8 many   9 much

3

2 Is there a tomato in the fridge?

3 Have some birthday cake!

4 He has got a big bedroom.

5 I have got an umbrella.

6 Is there an onion in the pan?

7 There are some dogs in the park.

8 I've got an idea!

9 They go on an expensive holiday every year.

4

2 mine   3 his   4 theirs   5 ours   6 hers
7 mine   8 ours   9 yours

Unit 8

Communication activity

Areas practised

Comparative adjectives; Superlative adjectives

- Divide the class into groups of four. Copy one game for each group.

- Each student chooses a coin or other small object (an eraser, sharpener, etc.). Use a coin as a dice: show students which side of the coin is heads (they move forward one square) and which side is tails (they move forward two squares).

- Each player should choose one column and start at the square marked START.

- Students take turns to toss the coin to see how many spaces they can move their counters.

- Players move their counters and read the prompts on the square they land on.

- They should talk for 30 seconds on the corresponding subject using the superlative of the adjective in brackets. The rest of the group must time the speaker.

- If a player can talk about the subject for 30 seconds, he/she stays on that square. If the player can't, he/she misses a turn. The first player to finish is the winner.

- Monitor groups to see that they are using the correct superlatives. Make a note of any repeated errors to go through as a class after the activity.

Grammar practice key

1

2 more intelligent than

3 shorter than

4 tidier than

5 more friendly than

6 more boring than

7 smaller than

8 more exciting than

9 more interesting than

2

2 ✓

3 ✗ Books are more interesting than computer games.

4 ✗ I think English is easier than French.

5 ✗ My English spelling is better than my English grammar.

6 ✓

7 ✗ Dogs can run faster than cats.

3

2 worst   3 smallest   4 best   5 longest
6 most important   7 happiest   8 shortest
9 easiest

4

2 the oldest   3 the most beautiful
4 the smallest   5 easier than   6 worse than
7 better than

- Give students a few minutes to read through

Communication activity 2a

(16) my father / hates	**(17)** write emails	**(18)** ice cream	**(19)** I / like	**(20) FINISH**
(15) my team / football	**(14)** my sister / not like	**(13)** my brother / get up	**(12)** my grandmother / paint	**(11)** listen to music
(6) my mother / not like	**(7)** my friends / swimming	**(8)** my aunt / play computer games	**(9)** I / not study	**(10)** my grandfather / not read
(5) my uncle / enjoy	**(4)** I / cinema	**(3)** my piano teacher / piano	**(2)** my friend's sister / dance	**(1) START**

 # Communication activity 2b

Find someone who ...	Name
... likes listening to the radio in the morning.	
... hates dancing.	
... goes to the swimming pool every Saturday.	
... loves football.	
... writes email messages every day.	
... gets up at six o'clock in the morning.	
... plays the guitar.	
... doesn't have a pet at home.	
... walks to school every day.	
... speaks English every day.	
... doesn't like Art.	
... travels to school by bus every day.	

Grammar practice 2

1 **Make the positive sentences negative.**

1   I like bananas.
   I don't like bananas.

2   They watch videos every day.

3   We play the piano after school.

4   Paula likes football.

5   You study English.

6   My uncle teaches Italian.

7   We like music.

8   Juan and José play football every day.

9   My classes start at 8.00 am.

2 **Make the negative sentences positive.**

1   We don't like English.
   We like English.

2   I don't play computer games after school.

3   Susana doesn't write emails every day.

4   My parents don't like winter.

5   We don't like football.

6   You don't like parties.

7   My sister doesn't drive a car.

8   Dario doesn't swim in the river
   every morning.

9   Clare and Lucy don't know the answer.

3 **Complete the sentences. Use the –ing form of the verbs in the box.**

play	play	watch	do	drive	speak
run	~~dance~~	swim			

1   I hate _dancing_ at parties.

2   My sister loves _____ English.

3   My parents hate _____ computer games.

4   You love _____ TV.

5   We like _____ in the river.

6   Frank hates _____ football.

7   Our dogs love _____ in the park.

8   I hate _____ homework.

9   My grandparents love _____ their car.

4 **Put the words in order to make sentences.**

1   piano / don't / I / the / play
   I don't play the piano.

2   going / cinema / my / like / to /
   parents / the

3   river / love / the / swimming / we / in

4   games / playing / my / like / doesn't /
   computer / dad

5   English / studies / she

6   my / reading / loves / brother / books

7   in / don't / English / like / they / talking

8   pop / friend / to / day / my / music /
   every / listens

9   flying / loves / Julie

RESOURCES   UNIT 2

5 Write the questions. Use the clues to help you.

1 I don't like school. (he)

   Does he like school ?

2 I live in London. (she)

   .... ?

3 I go swimming in the summer. (they)

   .... ?

4 I don't play football in the park. (you and your friends)

   .... ?

5 I speak English and Spanish. (he)

   .... ?

6 I have lunch at two o'clock every day. (Anne)

   .... ?

7 I go to guitar classes on Thursdays. (you)

   .... ?

8 I fly to New York every winter. (they)

   .... ?

9 I don't work in a school. (she)

   .... ?

6 Write the answers. Use the clues to help you.

1 Do you always speak in class? (✓)

   Yes, I do.

2 Do you like school? (✗)

   ....

3 Do you always have lots of homework? (✓)

   ....

4 Do your friends walk to school? (✓)

   ....

5 Does your school have a cafeteria? (✗)

   ....

6 Does your French teacher speak Chinese? (✓)

   ....

7 Do you and your friends eat at school? (✓)

   ....

8 Do you watch television in the evening? (✗)

   ....

9 Do you and Lucy go on holiday? (✗)

   ....

Communication activity 3

Student A

Police officer Bill usually works at a police station. Today he is working undercover in the Hotel De Luxe. He is looking for a thief. Look at the pictures and ask your partner for information.

A: What does he usually do at 7.30 am?

B: He has breakfast at 7.30 am.

B: What is he doing at 7.30 am today?

A: He is cooking breakfast in the Hotel De Luxe today.

Student B

Police officer Bill usually works at a police station. Today he is working undercover in the Hotel De Luxe. He is looking for a thief. Look at the pictures and ask your partner for information.

B: What is he doing at 7.30 am today?

A: He is cooking breakfast in the Hotel De Luxe today.

A: What does he usually do at 7.30 am?

B: He has breakfast at 7.30 am.

© Cambridge University Press 2010   Resources Unit 3

RESOURCES   UNIT 3

Grammar practice 3

1 Write sentences or questions. Use the present continuous form of the verbs.

1 She / take / a photo
   She's taking a photo.

2 Helen / wash / the car
   ....

3 Dad / do / the ironing
   ....

4 You / go / shopping
   .... ?

5 Paul and Mark / not clean / the bathroom
   ....

6 I / do / my homework
   ....

7 Ruth / work / in Belize
   .... ?

8 They / not tidy up
   ....

9 I / make / my bed
   ....

2 Complete the sentences. Use the present continuous form of the verbs in the box.

tidy ~~have~~ listen do play
make do cook have

1 We __*are having*__ a party.

2 Juan and Fred .... the shopping.

3 I .... a chicken for our friends.

4 Peter and Bill .... not .... the living room.

5 Lisa .... to music.

6 David .... the guitar.

7 Catherine .... not .... a shower.

8 .... Mike and Sarah .... the washing-up?

9 .... Daniel .... the beds?

3 Right (✓) or wrong (✗)? Correct the wrong sentences.

1 What are you usually doing on Saturdays? [✗]
   What do you usually do on Saturdays?

2 I am listening to my new CD now. [ ]
   ....

3 Don't turn the TV off! I'm watching it! [ ]
   ....

4 Are you reading the newspaper every day? [ ]
   ....

5 Are you liking your English classes? [ ]
   ....

6 I make my bed every morning. [ ]
   ....

7 Patricia washes her hair every Thursday. [ ]
   ....

8 Is Dad cooking dinner now? [ ]
   ....

9 Do you do the washing-up now? [ ]
   ....

4 Match the two parts of each sentence.

1 Does she [d]
2 Is she [ ]
3 Today, Sarah [ ]
4 Kevin [ ]
5 Are they [ ]
6 Do they [ ]
7 At the moment, Jane and George [ ]
8 We never [ ]
9 My mum always [ ]

a are tidying their bedrooms.
b is going on holiday with her friends.
c do the ironing.
d ~~cook at weekends?~~
e does the ironing on Tuesdays.
f cooking an apple pie for her family?
g drinking lemonade with their friends now?
h goes on holiday every summer with his family.
i go to Spain every year

Communication activity 4

Student A

Read text A and write the correct form of the verbs in your notebook. Who is it? Read your text to student B. He/She will help you correct it and tell you who it is. You start.

Then look at text B. Listen to student B and correct him/her. See if they guessed the person!

Text A

He [1] (be born) on 27 October 1952 in the Italian town of Misericordia in Arezzo. His family [2] (be) poor and they [3] (live) without electricity for a long time when he was young.

He [4] (move) to Florence when he [5] (be) 12 years old and [6] (stay) there until 1962. He [7] (work) in various jobs until 1972 when he [8] (start) acting.

He [9] (appear) in various films and [10] (direct) his first film in 1983. The actress Nicoletta Braschi [11] (star) in his first film and they [12] (work) together. The couple [13] (marry) in 1991. He directed and produced the film *La Vita è Bella* (*Life is Beautiful*). It [14] (be) a success in lots of countries.

In 1999 he [15] (appear) in a French film, *Astérix et Obélix Contre César*. He continues to make films and he lives in Rome with his wife.

Text B

She **was born** on 20 June 1967 in Hawaii. She **moved** to Australia when she **was** four years old.

She **started** acting when she **was** six years old. When she **was** a teenager she **trained** in dance and drama.

Her first American film **was** *Dead Calm* in 1989. It had a lot of good reviews. Her next film **was** *Days of Thunder*. She **worked** with her future husband on this film. She **married** her husband in 1990.

She **separated** from her husband in 2001 and she **continued** to make lots of films. In 2002 she **starred** in the film *The Hours*. She **accepted** an award for her part in that film at the Golden Globe ceremony.

(Nicole Kidman)

Student B

Read text B and write the correct form of the verbs in your notebook. Who is it? Then look at text A. Listen to student A and correct him/her. See if they guessed the person!

Read your completed text B to student A. He/She will help you correct it and tell you who it is.

Text B

She [1] (be born) on 20 June 1967 in Hawaii. She [2] (move) to Australia when she [3] (be) four years old.

She [4] (start) acting when she [5] (be) six years old. When she [6] (be) a teenager she [7] (train) in dance and drama.

Her first American film [8] (be) *Dead Calm* in 1989. It had a lot of good reviews. Her next film [9] (be) *Days of Thunder*. She [10] (work) with her future husband on this film. She [11] (marry) her husband in 1990.

She [12] (separate) from her husband in 2001 and she [13] (continue) to make lots of films. In 2002 she [14] (star) in the film *The Hours*. She [15] (accept) an award for her part in that film at the Golden Globe ceremony.

Text A

He **was born** on 27 October 1952 in the Italian town of Misericordia in Arezzo. His family **was** poor and they **lived** without electricity for a long time when he was young.

He **moved** to Florence when he **was** 12 years old and **stayed** there until 1962. He **worked** in various jobs until 1972 when he **started** acting.

He **appeared** in various films and **directed** his first film in 1983. The actress Nicoletta Braschi **starred** in his first film and they **worked** together. The couple **married** in 1991. He directed and produced the film *La Vita è Bella* (*Life is Beautiful*). It **was** a success in lots of countries.

In 1999 he **appeared** in a French film, *Astérix et Obélix Contre César*. He continues to make films and he lives in Rome with his wife.

(Roberto Benigni)

RESOURCES   UNIT 4

Grammar practice 4

1 Complete the sentences. Use the correct past simple form of the verb *be*.

1 How many people __were__ (be) there at the party?

2 _____ (be) there a football match on television last night?

3 My sister _____ (be) very happy yesterday because she passed her exams.

4 There _____ (be) lots of trees in the rainforest.

5 My teacher _____ (not be) very good last year. This year my teacher is great!

6 The bus _____ (be) late yesterday.

7 A: _____ (be) it noisy at the party?

   B: No, it _____ (be not).

8 A: _____ (be) there lots of questions in the exam?

   B: Yes, there _____ (be).

9 A: _____ (be) you at school last week?

   B: No, I _____ (not be). I _____ (be) ill.

2 Complete the sentences with *was/were born* (✓) or *wasn't/weren't born* (✗).

1 I _was born_ in Spain. ✓

2 My grandparents _____ in 1930. ✓

3 My sister _____ at home. ✓

4 My best friend _____ in this country. ✗

5 Where _____ you _____ ? ✓

6 I _____ in a hospital. ✗

7 When _____ your brother _____ ? ✓

3 Complete the sentences. Use the past simple form of the verbs.

1 I _cooked_ (cook) a meal for my family last night.

2 I _____ (start) my homework last night but I _____ (not finish) it.

3 _____ she _____ (use) my mobile phone yesterday?

4 My brother _____ (study) Italian last year.

5 They _____ (not clean) their bedrooms.

6 When you were born, your family _____ (live) in Madrid.

7 We _____ (walk) to school last week.

8 _____ you _____ (watch) that James Bond film on television last night?

9 It _____ (rain) yesterday so the children _____ (not play) in the garden.

4 Circle the correct phrasal verb.

1 Here are your shoes. Please *put them on* / *climb them up.*

2 Look at the mess! *Pick up* / *Get in* all your clothes and tidy your room.

3 Look at that tree! Let's *come down* / *climb up* to the top!

4 '*Get out* / *Put down* of my room or ... !!' he shouted.

5 '*Climb up* / *Put down* your pencils now,' the teacher told the students.

6 '*Pick up* / *Get in* the car immediately,' the police officer said.

7 'They're my trainers. *Take them off* / *Get them in* right now!'

8 '*Come down* / *Put down* now before you fall,' the mother shouted to her child.

UNIT 4

RESOURCES

Communication activity 5

go	play	watch	want	listen	win
beat	begin	think	yesterday morning	yesterday evening	last night
last week	last month	last year	last Saturday	four days ago	ten years ago

© Cambridge University Press 2010   **Resources Unit 5**

Grammar practice 5

1 Complete the sentences. Use the correct past simple form of the verbs.

1 When _did_ you _leave_ (leave) school?

2 The summer holidays .... (begin) three weeks ago.

3 My parents .... (not want) to go on holiday last year.

4 I .... (talk) to my teacher after my bad exam results.

5 My sister .... (not study) for her exams.

6 My grandparents .... (go) swimming in the sea last weekend.

7 The train .... (leave) an hour ago.

8 Milan .... (not beat) Juve in the final last weekend.

9 We .... (think) you .... (be) on holiday!

2 Put the words in order to make past simple questions.

1 Saturday / go / night / you / on / did / out / ?

Did you go out on Saturday night?

2 breakfast / school / they / before / did / went / they / to / have / ?

....

3 football / did / your / play / weekend / brother / last / ?

....

4 homework / you / did / night / do / last / your / ?

....

5 team / did / the / yesterday / win / competition / the / ?

....

6 holiday / go / last / parents / on / summer / your / did / ?

....

7 food / weekend / the / for / did / at / we / the / buy / party / ?

....

8 programme / last / television / night / that / did / see / you / science / on / ?

....

9 holiday / you / about / their / tell / did / they / ?

....

3 Match the questions with the answers.

1 When did you start school? | b |

2 What did you do last night? | |

3 Where did you go on holiday last summer? | |

4 Did you have toast for breakfast this morning? | |

5 Where were you last Saturday night? | |

6 What time did you get home yesterday? | |

7 Did Jesse Owens win the gold medal in the 1936 Olympic Games long jump? | |

a Yes, he did.

b ~~12 years ago.~~

c No, I didn't.

d We went to Paris.

e At 4.30 pm.

f I was at a party.

g I watched television.

4 Write the words from the box in the correct lists.

| ~~ten years~~ week morning February an hour a month afternoon Sunday evening thirteen days |

yesterday	last	ago
		ten years

Communication activity 6

be determined	be hard-working	remember things well	have a good voice	know how to drive
like looking after people	have a good imagination	be good at medicine	know how to type	like animals
like aeroplanes	like children	have a good memory	like computers	practise every day
sing well	have good school results	like teeth	like people	speak English

Grammar practice 6

1 **Put the words in order to make questions.**

1 have / school / I / to / to / now / do / go / ?

   Do I have to go to school now?

2 ironing / day / she / every / have / does / to / do / the / ?

   ----

3 tonight / have / do / study / they / to / ?

   ----

4 uniform / to / do / wear / you / have / a / ?

   ----

5 English / vets / do / to / learn / have / ?

   ----

6 party / we / tonight / to / have / go / do / the / to / ?

   ----

7 results / get / to / he / does / have / good / ?

   ----

2 **Write the answers to the questions. Use the clues to help you.**

1 Does she have to wear school uniform? (✗)

   No, she doesn't.

2 Do I have to go to visit Aunt Matilda? (✓)

   ----

3 Do we have to do the washing-up now? (✗)

   ----

4 Does he have to speak English in his job? (✓)

   ----

5 Do you have to go out tonight? (✗)

   ----

6 Do nurses have to wear a uniform? (✓)

   ----

7 Do you and Dad have to go away? (✓)

   ----

8 Do dentists have to like animals? (✗)

   ----

9 Do I have to tidy my bedroom today? (✗)

   ----

3 **Right (✓) or wrong (✗)? Correct the wrong sentences.**

1 Does they walk to school every day? ☒

   Do they walk to school every day?

2 Do writers have to have good ideas? ☐

   ----

3 Do my mother have to go to work? ☐

   ----

4 Does your parents have to drive to work? ☐

   ----

5 Do you have to study during the holidays? ☐

   ----

6 Do we have to go to England this year? ☐

   ----

7 Do my brother have to come? ☐

   ----

8 Do secretaries have to be good at Physics? ☐

   ----

9 Does they have to learn Spanish? ☐

   ----

4 **Complete the sentences. Use the correct form of *have to* (present or past, positive or negative).**

1 I *had to* stay at home last night.

2 It's a holiday, so we .... go to school.

3 It's a very expensive restaurant. You .... pay a lot of money to eat there.

4 I .... walk to school yesterday.

5 Ruth went to a basketball match last weekend. It was free, so she .... pay to go in.

6 We've got a dishwasher now, so we .... do the washing-up.

7 We .... wear school uniform today so I wore my jeans and a T-shirt.

8 I .... do the cooking today.

9 My parents .... go to work yesterday.

© Cambridge University Press 2010 **Resources Unit 6**

UNIT 6

RESOURCES

Communication activity 7

Student A

Ask and answer questions to find ten differences between your picture and your partner's picture. Use the phrases and words in the box to help you. You start.

> How much/many ... ?   Is/Are there ... ?   There is/are ...   some   any

A: *How many students are there in your picture?*

B: *There are ... students in my picture.*

Student B

Ask and answer questions to find ten differences between your picture and your partner's picture. Use the phrases and words in the box to help you. Student A starts.

> How much/many ... ?   Is/Are there ... ?   There is/are ...   some   any

A: *How many students are there in your picture?*

B: *There are ... students in my picture.*

UNIT 7

Grammar practice 7

1 Right (✓) or wrong (✗)? Correct the wrong sentences.

1 I haven't got some paper. ☒

I haven't got any paper.

2 Have you got some oranges? ☐
....

3 There aren't any apples in the kitchen. ☐
....

4 Is there any food in the fridge? ☐
....

5 There aren't some onions in this recipe. ☐
....

6 There isn't some milk in this glass. ☐
....

7 We've got any homework tonight. ☐
....

8 Have the band got any new songs? ☐
....

9 I've got any good ideas for the band. ☐
....

2 Complete the sentences with *much* or *many*.

1 How __*many*__ brothers have you got?

2 How .... teachers are there?

3 How .... money have you got?

4 How .... rooms are there in your house?

5 How .... homework have you got today?

6 How .... apples do you eat?

7 How .... milk do you drink?

8 How .... months are there in a year?

9 How .... sugar have you got?

3 Put the words in order to make sentences.

1 are / computers / the / in / there / some / classroom

There are some computers in the classroom.

2 a / there / in / fridge / is / tomato / the / ?
....

3 have / birthday / some / cake / !
....

4 got / has / big / bedroom / he / a
....

5 got / umbrella / an / I / have
....

6 onion / the / an / is / in / there / pan / ?
....

7 there / dogs / some / park / in / are / the
....

8 idea / an / got / I've / !
....

9 an / every / they / expensive / go / holiday / on / year
....

4 Complete the sentences. Use the correct possessive pronoun.

1 They're your jeans. They're ___*yours*___ .

2 It's my book. It's ....

3 It's his mobile phone. It's ....

4 It's their car. It's ....

5 They're our friends. They're ....

6 It's her dog. It's ....

7 They're my CDs. They're ....

8 It's our computer. It's ....

9 It's your glass. It's ....

Communication activity 8

Talk for 30 seconds about …

START	START	START	START
the (young) person in your family	your (bad) day at school	the (good) film you know	your (boring) subject
your (good) subject	the (old) person you know	the (horrible) place to go on holiday	the (good) place to go out in your town or area
the (sad) film you know	the (easy) subject to learn	the (dangerous) sport you can think of	the (boring) film you know
your (new) CD or recording	your (good) band	the (happy) day of your life	the (good) pet to have
the (interesting) thing to do at the weekend	the (nice) person in your class	the (delicious) food to eat	the (beautiful) place to visit
the (bad) food to eat	the (popular) band in your country now	the (bad) song on the radio these days	the (great) pop band in the world
the (famous) person in your country at the moment	the (interesting) TV programme at the moment	the (friendly) person in your class	your (expensive) item of clothing
your (bad) night out	the (old) person in your family	the (good) place for shopping in town	the (small) object in your schoolbag
FINISH	FINISH	FINISH	FINISH

RESOURCES   UNIT 8

Grammar practice 8

1

Complete the sentences. Use the comparative form of the adjectives in the box.

> long   small   tidy   friendly   exciting
> intelligent   boring   ~~beautiful~~   interesting

1   I think Claudia Schiffer is *more beautiful than* Julia Roberts.

2   People say humans are
    .... monkeys.

3   The River Nile is ....
    the River Amazon.

4   I tidied my bedroom today. My room is
    .... yours now.

5   Some people say that Scottish people are
    .... English people.

6   I don't like French. I think it is
    .... German.

7   Spain is .... Australia.

8   I love the *Lord of the Rings* books. I think
    they're .... the *Harry
    Potter* books.

9   I think History is ....
    Geography.

2

Right (✓) or wrong (✗)? Correct the wrong sentences.

1   My homework is more difficult that yours.   ☒

    My homework is more difficult than yours.

2   London is busier than Birmingham.   ☐

    ....

3   Books are interesting than computer games.   ☐

    ....

4   I think English is easyer than French.   ☐

    ....

5   My English spelling is gooder than my
    English grammar.   ☐

    ....

6   Italian is more modern than Latin.   ☐

    ....

7   Dogs can run fast than cats.   ☐

    ....

3

Complete the sentences. Choose the correct adjective and use the superlative form.

> bad   important   long   ~~difficult~~   easy
> small   good   short   happy

1   The *most difficult* exam I had this year
    was History. I couldn't remember anything!

2   The .... day of my life was when I
    got my exam results. I failed them all.

3   I think the mouse is the ....
    mammal.

4   I went to Corsica on holiday last year. It was
    great! The .... holiday of my life!

5   Some people think the Nile is the
    .... river in the world but it's
    actually the Amazon.

6   My parents think the .... thing
    in life is to be happy.

7   My .... memory is my 13th birthday
    party when all my friends and family came
    to my house.

8   The .... word in English is *a.*

9   The .... way to get to Italy is to fly.

4

Complete the text with the comparative or superlative form of the adjectives.

The (1) *best* (good) holiday I had was when
I went to Rome for two weeks last summer.
It has some of (2) .... (old) buildings in
the world and some of (3) .... (beautiful)
architecture. I visited (4) .... (small)
country in the world – The Vatican City – and I
saw some amazing sights. I spoke some Italian –
it was (5) .... (easy) I imagined! My Italian
pronunciation was (6) .... (bad) my English
pronunciation! The waiters were very nice and
they helped me a lot. However, after two weeks
and lots of practice, my Italian was (7) ....
(good) my English! Maybe I'll go to England
next summer!

UNIT 8

RESOURCES

English in Mind

Second edition

Brian Hart
with Mario Rinvolucri, Herbert Puchta & Jeff Stranks

Teacher's Resource
Book 1B

Pronunciation • Vocabulary bank • Projects • Get it right! • Irregular verbs and phonetics

Speaking & Functions	Listening	Reading	Writing
Talking about arrangements Discussing holiday plans Last but not least: information gap: talking about holidays	Radio show about family holidays Dialogue about holiday plans	Magazine article: Family holidays can be fun! Travel brochure: Welcome to Cape Town – the city that has everything! Photostory: Having fun?	Email about a trip
Making predictions Talking about your future life Talking about fortune telling	Future predictions Song: *When I'm Sixty-four*	Article: Getting the future wrong! Culture in mind: Fortune telling	Text predicting the future
Describing actions Relating Hermann Maier's life story Describing the weather Last but not least: information gap about famous sportspeople	A weather forecast Dialogue about the life of Hermann Maier	Article: Jungle survival Photostory: Keep on running	Email giving advice to a friend
Talking about intentions Talking about a song	Dialogue about a New Year's Eve party Song: *Wonderful World, Beautiful People*	Article: In New York for New Year's Eve Culture in mind: Reggae Music	Email about New Year's Eve
Expressing future possibilities Discussing bravery Last but not least: talking about situations where you were brave / not brave	Dialogues about bravery	Article: Subway hero Photostory: Chicken	Description of a film, book or TV programme
Giving advice and recommendations Talking about what somebody is like	Dialogue about different customs around the world A quiz about UK culture	Quiz: What do you know about UK culture? Culture in mind: Heroic Ulises on a journey of hope	Email giving tips to a tourist
Talking about life experiences Last but not least: talking about things you've never done	Conversation about strange world records	Article: You've never seen anything like this! Article: He holds the record – for records! Photostory: What's the next thing?	Email about a visit to Los Angeles

1 Welcome

This unit is designed to serve as a review giving students the opportunity to revise and practise language they already know and have studied in the previous level of *English in Mind*. It is also a tool for teachers to find out how much students know already and which areas students may need to do more work on before continuing with the course.

A | AT SCHOOL

1 Read and listen

a ▶ **CD2 T28** Students read the question and then read through the text. Play the recording for students to listen and read. Check any problems. Students complete the exercise and compare answers in pairs. Play the recording again, pausing as necessary for students to check or change their answer.

TAPESCRIPT
See the reading text on page 6 of the Student's Book.

> **Answers**
> Mrs Terrell is busy because she does more than just teach. She has to prepare lessons, correct students' homework and tests, check the internet for new ideas and look after her two children.

b Read through the sentences with students and check understanding. Explain that students must decide if the sentences are true or false. Read through the text again. Students compare answers with a partner before feedback in open class.

> **Answers**
> 1 False
> 2 True
> 3 True
> 4 False

2 School subjects

a Ask students to write the name of each school subject. Monitor and check spelling.

> **Answers**
> 2 History
> 3 Geography
> 4 Science
> 5 PE
> 6 ICT

✱ **OPTIONAL ACTIVITY**

Write these school subjects on the board and put students in small groups.

English
Maths
History
Geography
ICT
French
Biology
Chemistry
Spanish
Music
Technology
Physics
Drama

Then write these two categories in columns for the students to copy in their notebooks. Ask them to put the school subjects into the correct category.

Arts   **Sciences**

> **Answers**
> Arts: English, History, Geography, French, Spanish, Music, Drama
> Sciences: Maths, ICT, Biology, Chemistry, Technology, Physics

b Check that all students know the school subjects, then divide the class into pairs and play the game. It might be a good idea to set a time limit of two minutes.

Present simple

Write the following sentences on the board:

A: Do you like French?

B: Yes I do. My mum's French and she speaks to me in French but my dad is English and he doesn't speak French.

Read the sentences with students. Ask them to identify the verbs in the affirmative, negative, interrogative and the short answer. Make sure students understand how to form the affirmative, negative, interrogative and the short answer.

Students read through sentences 1 – 6. Go through the first item with them as an example. Students complete the exercise. Check answers.

> ### Answers
> 1 do; makes
> 2 does; speak
> 3 Does; want; doesn't
> 4 Do; play; don't; does; plays
> 5 Do; go; don't
> 6 does; live; lives

 ## have to / don't have to

a Students read the question and then read through the blog. Check any problems. Students complete the exercise and compare answers in pairs.

> ### Answers
> The writer thinks that school rules are a good idea.

b Students read through the blog again. Go through the first item with them as an example. Students complete the blog with *have / has to* or *don't / doesn't have to*. Check answers.

> ### Answers
> 2 has to
> 3 have to
> 4 have to
> 5 don't have to
> 6 has to
> 7 have to
> 8 have to
> 9 doesn't have to

B | WORK AND FREE TIME

 ## Read and listen

a Read through the words in the box with students. Check understanding. Then read through the phone messages. Ask students to complete them with the words from the box.

b ▶ **CD2 T29** Play the recording for students to check their answers. Play the recording again, pausing as necessary for students to clarify any problem answers.

TAPESCRIPT

1 Hi Dad, it's Ava. Listen, I'm helping Sarah with her homework so I can't prepare lunch. Can you do the cooking, please? Thanks, bye.

2 Hi Ava, Mum speaking. When you come home, please can you tidy the living room? We've got guests tonight, and there's a real mess. Thanks darling, and see you later.

3 Hi Ava, Tom speaking. Be a good sister, please. Mum wants me to do the shopping. But I can't, I'm meeting some friends now. The shopping list's in my room, on the keyboard of my computer. OK? And, by the way, you're my favourite sister ... not! Hehehehehe

4 Hi Ava, Mum again. Please don't forget to do the washing up too. The dishwasher's broken - sorry.

5 Hi Tom, it's Mum speaking. Could you do me a favour, please. You know we've got guests tonight, and I was just thinking. Please could you clean the windows in the living room. I know you don't like doing it, but please help. Thanks!

6 Hi Tom, it's Dad. Can you help me? I want to look good for the guests tonight. There's a clean shirt and trousers in my room. Please, can you iron them for me? Thanks! Bye!

> ### Answers
> 1 do the cooking
> 2 tidy
> 3 do the shopping
> 4 do the washing-up
> 5 clean the windows
> 6 do the ironing

2 Jobs

Ask students to write the names of each job. Monitor and check spelling.

Answers
2 vet
3 architect
4 firefighter
5 dentist
6 lawyer
7 flight attendant
8 shop assistant

✳ OPTIONAL ACTIVITY

Call out a profession and the students have to describe what that person does, e.g.

T: Nurse

S: Someone who looks after sick people.

3 Work and money

Read the sentences with students. Go through the first sentence as an example. Students complete the exercise. Check answers.

Answers
2 pocket money
3 spends
4 full-time
5 waste
6 earn; save

4 Sports

Ask students to write the names of the sports.

Answers
1 surfing
2 swimming
3 snowboarding
4 skiing
5 volleyball
6 ice hockey
7 basketball
8 cycling

✳ OPTIONAL ACTIVITY

Put students into small groups and ask them if they can think of a sport for each letter of the alphabet. Where they can't think of one, tell them not to worry, but to continue with the rest of the alphabet. Set a time limit of three minutes.

Eg: *athletics, boxing, cricket, dancing ...*

5 Present continuous

Write the following sentences on the board:

A: *Are you learning French?*

B: *Yes I am.*

C: *No, I'm not learning French, I'm learning German.*

Read the sentences with students and ask them to identify the tense the verbs are in. Make sure students understand how to form the affirmative, negative, interrogative and the short answer.

Students read through sentences 1 – 8. Go through the first item with them as an example. Students complete the exercise. Check answers.

Answers
2 's/is playing; 'm/am doing
3 is; doing; 's/is painting
4 is; watching; 's/is sleeping
5 are having
6 aren't listening
7 Are; working; 're/are visiting
8 aren't; helping

C AT THE SCHOOL CANTEEN

1 Read and listen

a ▶ CD2 T30 Students read the question and then read through the dialogue. Play the recording for students to listen and read. Check any problems. Students complete the exercise and compare answers in pairs. Play the recording again, pausing as necessary for students to check or change their answer.

TAPESCRIPT
See the dialogue on page 10 of the Student's Book.

Answers
No, Mia isn't a vegetarian.

b Go through questions with the students. Check understanding. Read through the dialogue again. Do the first question as an example. Students complete the exercise. Check answers.

Answers
1 The dinner lady thinks that Mia is too slim to be on a diet.
2 Mia learnt about healthy eating in Biology.
3 Mia thinks that eating a little meat is OK, but it's not good to eat the fat from the meat.
4 Mia has to stop their conversation because she has got a project team meeting.
5 She doesn't want mashed potato because she doesn't like it.

2 some/any

Students read through sentences 1 – 5. Go through the first item with them as an example. Students complete the exercise. Check answers.

Answers
1 any; some
2 some
3 some; any
4 some
5 some

3 a/an; some/any; much/many

Students read through sentences 1 – 5. Go through the first item with them as an example. Students complete the exercise by circling the correct words. Check answers.

Answers
1 some
2 some; a
3 some
4 much; some; any
5 an; any

4 Food

Ask students to write the names of the food.

Answers
2 rice
3 beans
4 bread
5 eggs
6 vegetables
7 chicken
8 mushrooms
9 cheese

5 Comparative and superlative adjectives

Write these sentences on the board:

It was the hottest day of the year last Saturday.

Your book is longer than mine, so my book is shorter than yours!

Remind students of comparative and superlative structures and ask them to identify the comparatives and superlatives in the sentences and to say when we use these structures.

Students read through sentences 1 – 6. Go through the first item with them as an example. Students complete the exercise. Check answers.

Answers
1 better
2 worse
3 healthiest; healthier
4 more important; most important
5 hungriest
6 more stressful; healthier; most relaxed

> **Language note**
> Remind students of the irregular comparative and superlative forms.
> *good – better - best*
> *bad – worse – worst*
> *far – further – furthest*

D WHAT A STORY!

1 Read and listen

a ▶ CD2 T31 Students read the question and then read through the article. Play the recording for students to listen and read. Check any problems. Students complete the exercise and compare answers in pairs. Play the recording again, pausing as necessary for students to check or change their answer.

TAPESCRIPT
See the dialogue on page 12 of the Student's Book.

Answers
Jessica Watson was the youngest person to sail around the world on her own.

b Read through the sentences with students and check understanding. Explain that students must cover up the article and try to remember how the sentences end. Then, read through the article again. Students compare answers with a partner before feedback in open class.

Answers
1 210 days
2 Sydney, Australia
3 she is too young
4 followed Jessica's blog on
5 welcomed her
6 Jessica's parents

2 Past simple: questions

Warm up
Write these sentences on the board:
How old were you on your last birthday?
Did you have a birthday cake?
How many cakes did your brother eat?
Go through the structure of past simple questions with your students.

a Students read through the exercise. Go through the first item with them as an example. Students complete the exercise. Check answers.

Answers
1 How old was Jessica on her trip?
2 How high were the highest waves she saw?
3 How many times did her boat nearly turn over?
4 What direction did she sail in first?
5 How many people followed her blog?

b In pairs, students ask and answer the questions from Exercise 2a. Monitor and make sure pairs are taking turns to answer.

3 Past time expressions

Students read through the exercise. Go through the first item with them as an example. Students complete the exercise. Check answers.

Answers
2 four days ago
3 six months ago
4 two hours ago
5 seven months ago
6 twelve minutes ago
7 two months ago
8 six days ago

> **Language note**
> Remind students of the past time expressions used with the past simple.
> *yesterday*
> *yesterday morning*
> *last night*
> *last week*
> *a month ago*
> *three years ago*
> *on Sunday*

4 Past simple: regular and irregular verbs

a Read through the verbs with the students and check meaning. Go through the first item with them as an example. Students complete the exercise. Check answers.

Answers
1 changed
2 called
3 bought
4 missed
5 listened
6 arrived
7 saw
8 went

b Read through the exercise with the students.
Remind them that they will be using the past simple
forms they have written in Exercise 4a. Go through
the first item as an example. Students complete the
exercise. Check answers.

> **Answers**
> 1 listened
> 2 bought
> 3 went
> 4 called
> 5 changed
> 6 missed; arrived
> 7 saw

5 Past simple: negative

Write these sentences on the board:

I don't like potatoes or spinach.

He isn't sixteen, he's fourteen.

Go through the structure of a past simple negative
sentence with the students. Read through the
sentences with the students and check meaning.
Go through the first item with them as an example.
Students complete the exercise. Check answers.

> **Answers**
> 2 We didn't start our trip from Venice in Italy.
> 3 He wasn't very angry about the result of the
>   match.
> 4 She wasn't very sad about the news.
> 5 We didn't play football all evening.
> 6 Our friends didn't spend their holidays in
>   Greece.
> 7 We didn't have a good time at the weekend.
> 8 I didn't do very well in the test yesterday.

2 We're going on holiday

Unit overview

TOPIC: Future plans and holiday arrangements

TEXTS
Reading and listening: magazine holiday adverts; teenagers discussing holiday plans
Listening: a radio show about holidays
Reading: a text about South Africa
Writing: an email describing a trip you are going on

SPEAKING AND FUNCTIONS
Talking about future plans
Talking about holidays and holiday activities

LANGUAGE
Grammar: Present continuous for future arrangements
Vocabulary: future time expressions; holiday activities
Pronunciation: /θ/ (_think_) and /ð/ (_that_)
Everyday English: _Hang on; at all; don't worry; either; it's (our) fault; then_

1 Read and listen

If you set the background information as a homework research task ask the students to tell the class what they have found out.

BACKGROUND INFORMATION
The Red Sea is a salt water inlet of the Indian Ocean between Africa and Asia. It is the habitat of over 1,000 invertebrate species and 200 soft and hard corals and is the world's northern-most tropical sea.

Egypt is a country (population c. 75.5 million in 2008) mainly in North Africa covering an area of about 1,010,000 square km. Egypt is famous for its ancient civilisation and some of the world's most famous monuments, including the Giza pyramid complex and its Great Sphinx. Egypt is widely regarded as an important political and cultural nation of the Middle East.

Thailand The Kingdom of Thailand (population c. 63 million in 2007) lies in the heart of south east Asia. The capital and largest city of Thailand is Bangkok. It is also the country's centre of political, commercial, industrial and cultural activities.

Slovenia is a country (population c. 2 million in 2008) in southern Central Europe. The capital of Slovenia is Ljubljana.

Warm up
Ask students where they normally go on holiday and what they do when they are there. Find out if anyone has been on an adventure holiday. Help students with vocabulary and write any interesting words on the board.

a Ask students to look at the text and photos and, in pairs, discuss which holidays they would like to go on. Listen to some of their ideas in open class.

b ▶ **CD2 T32** Tell students they are going to hear a radio show in which people talk about their holidays. Read the instructions with the class.

Play the recording while students listen and complete the exercise. Let students compare answers with a partner before playing the recording again, pausing for clarification and to check answers.

TAPESCRIPT
Radio host: Hello, and welcome to _Holiday Dreams_ – our programme with tips for holidays for you and your family. Today's topic is adventure holidays for families with teenage children. And with me in the studio is tour operator, Ken Taylor. Ken, it's becoming a big thing to offer adventure holidays for families and their teenage children. Why is that?

Ken: Well, to be honest, I think it's the parents. Many of them are saying 'I want to enjoy a great holiday with my teenage children before they leave home and don't want to come with us any more!'

Radio host: I see. And we're asking YOU to phone us and tell us about holidays you're taking. And here's the first caller, Debbie from Brighton. Debbie, you're going on a great holiday. Tell us about it.

Debbie: Hi! That's right. We're going camping – in Kenya. We're staying there for two weeks. We're starting off with a safari camp, then we're going walking in the desert.

Radio host: Walking in the desert. That sounds exciting. But maybe a bit tiring and dangerous, too.

Debbie: Well, we aren't going on our own: we're taking a guide with us. And there are people to carry our rucksacks and help us with cooking and putting up our tents.

Radio host: Sounds fantastic. Hope you have a great holiday.

Debbie: Thank you.

Radio host: And this is Mark from Saundersfoot in Wales. Tell us about the holiday you're going on.

Mark: Right. Well, my parents and I are going on a volunteer holiday.

Radio host: A volunteer holiday? What's that all about?

Mark: Well, we're going to Thailand, and we're helping in an elephant conservation project. We have to wash and feed the elephants. I'm really looking forward to it.

Radio host: It sounds like a lot of work.

Mark: Well, yes but we're going to have lots of fun too.

Radio host: Wow. Thank you, and here's Monica. Where are you going?

Monica: To Slovenia.

Radio host: Slovenia? Is it possible to have an adventure holiday there?

Monica: Yes, of course! We're visiting the Soča valley. It's one of the world's most beautiful places for water sports. The Soča is the number one place for river sports.

Radio host: Oh, really. That sounds great.

Monica: Yes, Dad and I are going on a canoeing tour, and Mum is doing a course in salsa dancing.

Radio host: OK, thanks. Now, Ken, from what these teenagers are saying ...

> **Answers**
> Debbie 1
> Mark 4
> Monica 3

c ▶ **CD2 T33** Ask students to read through the dialogue and check understanding.

Stronger classes: They can complete the sentences by reading the text alone and then listening to check.

Weaker classes: Play the recording while they read, pausing as necessary to give them time to find their answers.

Check answers.

TAPESCRIPT

Sara: Hey, Anna! How's your day going?

Anna: Good! My mum and I are planning the family holiday.

Sara: Excellent! Where are you going?

Anna: Well, listen to this! We're going to Thailand!

Sara: Wow! Really? When?

Anna: In two months' time. We're leaving on 8 May.

Sara: How are you getting there?

Anna: First we're flying to Bangkok.

Sara: Oh. And are you staying in Bangkok?

Anna: Oh no! We're travelling on to Chang Mai. And ... this is the best bit! We're doing some work at the elephant conservation centre!

Sara: Amazing! What are you doing there?

Anna: We're looking after the elephants. We're doing things like washing them and cleaning their feet.

Sara: It sounds brilliant! Are all your family going with you?

Anna: Yes! But it's a bit expensive. Dad almost fainted when he heard how much we're paying.

> **Answers**
> 1 going 2 leaving 3 flying 4 staying
> 5 travelling 6 doing 7 doing 8 looking
> 9 doing 10 going

2 Grammar

✱ Present continuous for future arrangements

a Students should already be familiar with the present continuous for activities happening now. Ask students *Where is Anna going on holiday? (Thailand). What tense is this? (present continuous).* To check understanding, ask them, in L1 if necessary: *Is this happening now or in the future? (future). Is this a plan or an arrangement? (arrangement).* Now read through the examples from the dialogue and remind students of the negative and question forms, giving a few examples of these if necessary. Students go through Exercise 1c and underline any more examples of the present continuous. Check answers.

> **Answers**
> How's your day going?
> My mum and I are planning the family holiday.
> Where are you going?
> How are you getting there?
> ... how much we're paying.

Now read through the Rule box with students. You may want to remind them of the spelling rules for the -ing form of verbs.

b Students read through sentences 1–6. Check any problems. Go through the first item with them as an example, if necessary. Remind them to use short forms where possible. Students complete the exercise. Check answers.

> **Answers**
> 2 're having / are having
> 3 's taking / is taking; 're leaving / are leaving
> 4 A: Are you going; B: 'm staying / am staying
> 5 isn't coming / is not coming; 's working / is working
> 6 'm seeing / am seeing

Grammar notebook

Remind students to note down the rules and some examples of the present continuous for future use.

3 Vocabulary

✱ Future time expressions

a Students read through the time expressions and in pairs decide how they say them in their own language. Discuss any similarities and differences in these expressions. Ask students a few questions using the future time expressions and the present continuous, e.g. *Nicola, what are you doing tomorrow after school? Anna, what are you doing on Saturday?*

> **Language note**
>
> It may be useful to point out to students that there is no article before *next week/month* etc. in English. We don't say ~~The next week~~ ...

b Students read through questions 1–4. Check any problems and do the first one as an example, if necessary. Students complete the exercise. Students can compare answers in pairs. Then ask a few students to read out their answers to the class.

Vocabulary notebook

Students could start a section called *Future time expressions* in their notebooks and note down any new words from this unit.

4 Speak

a In pairs, students tell each other what they are doing and when. Make sure students swap roles to allow both to ask and answer. Listen to some of their sentences in open class.

b Go through the example sentences with students highlighting the use of the present continuous. Students work with another partner and tell him/her what they and their previous partner are doing and when. Make sure students swap roles to allow both to speak. Ask a few students to give feedback on what their partner's plans and arrangements were.

✱ **OPTIONAL ACTIVITY** ─────────────

For further practice of this structure, a fun activity is for students to take on the personality of a famous person and repeat Exercise 4 imagining what their character is doing in the future. Encourage stronger classes to ask questions using all of the future time expressions in Exercise 3a. Listen to some of the best dialogues in open class. You may like to ask students to keep the identity of the famous people secret and ask other students to guess who is talking.

Grammar notebook

Students can note down the future time expressions and their translations from Exercise 3a.

5 Read

If you set the background information as a homework research task, ask students to tell the rest of the class what they found out.

> **BACKGROUND INFORMATION**
>
> **South Africa** is a country (population c. 47,900,000 in 2008) located at the southern tip of Africa. Cape Town is a large town which became a British colony in 1806. The discovery of diamonds and later gold triggered the Anglo-Boer War as the Boers and the British fought for control of the South African mineral wealth. Under British rule, blacks and whites were segregated in a system called apartheid. This was continued after South Africa was declared a republic in 1961, despite opposition both in and outside of the country. In 1990 the then president F.W. de Klerk began to dismantle this legislation, and in 1994 the first democratic election was held in South Africa. This election brought Nelson Mandela and the current ruling party, the African National Congress, to power, and the country rejoined the Commonwealth of Nations.

a Read through the questions with students and check understanding. Students answer the questions. Encourage them to guess if they are not sure. Do not give them the answers at this stage.

b Ask students to read the text to check their answers to Exercise 5a. Tell them that they do not need to understand every word and to focus on the task. If you have a weak class, you may prefer to read the text aloud with the class first.

Answers
1 b 2 a 3 c 4 b

c In open class ask students to try to remember which adjectives were used to describe the words. Listen to their ideas before letting them look back at the text to check. Check answers in open class, paying attention to pronunciation.

Answers
the beaches: sunny; ideal
the shopping: great
the setting: fantastic
the climate: pleasant

6 Vocabulary

✱ Holiday activities

a ▶ **CD2 T34** Books closed. Elicit as many holiday activities as you can. Remind students of the activities Sara and Anna talked about in Exercise 1c. Put students' suggestions on the board. Students now open their books at page 17 and read through the activities in Exercise 6a. Go through the first one as an example. Students complete the exercise. Play the recording for students to listen and check answers. Play the recording again, for students to repeat.

TAPESCRIPT/ANSWERS

A: sailing
B: sunbathing
C: hiking
D: canoeing
E: windsurfing
F: camping
G: horse riding
H: kayaking
I: climbing
J: scuba diving
K: surfing
L: snorkelling
M: sightseeing
N: parachuting
O: golf

b In pairs, students discuss which of the activities in Exercise 6a they like doing on holiday. Elicit the following expressions, *like / don't like / love / hate + -ing*. Go through the example with students, if necessary. Set a time limit for this and ask for some students to give feedback to the class about themselves and their partner.

c **Stronger classes:** With books closed, write the following verbs on the board: *hire, travel, stay, buy, spend*. Ask them to check the meaning of the verbs in a dictionary. Remind them that there may be several uses of one verb.

Weaker classes: Read through the verbs in the box with them and sentences 1–5. Check they know the meaning of each verb and the words in the sentences 1–5.

Give them some examples with the verbs in context to help them understand the meaning (e.g. *I always hire a car when I go on holiday. I like to travel by plane when I go to Spain.*). Students complete the exercise. Check answers.

Answers
2 stay 3 travel 4 spend 5 hire

Language notes

1 Point out to students that we use *by* with means of transport: *by ferry/car/plane/train/coach* but we say *on foot*.

2 The verb *spend* can also be used in the expression *to spend money*.

Vocabulary bank

Refer students to the vocabulary bank on page 65. Read through the words and phrases in open class and check understanding.

Vocabulary notebook

Students could start a section called *Holiday activities* in their notebooks and note down any new words from this unit.

7 Speak

a Divide the class into pairs and give them a time limit of two minutes in which to make a list of all the different kinds of holidays and holiday places in the unit. Stronger classes can do this exercise with books closed before looking back at the unit to check their answers. Weaker classes can look back at the text to find answers. Go through answers in open class, paying attention to pronunciation.

b Working individually, students have two minutes to think of a holiday destination they think their family would like. Give them an example of your own to get them started. Circulate and help with vocabulary as required.

c Read through the questions with students and encourage them to make detailed notes about their holiday plans.

d In pairs, students act out dialogues using the questions from Exercise 7c. Encourage them to answer in detail and to practise the dialogue more than once until it feels more natural. Listen to some of the dialogues in open class.

8 Pronunciation

See notes on page 155.

Photostory: Having fun?

9 Read and listen

Warm up

Tell students that, despite the weather, camping holidays are quite popular in the United Kingdom.

Ask students if they have ever been camping. Did they enjoy it? What things did they do while they were camping? If they haven't been camping, would they like to go? Ask students to name the characters in the photostory.

a ▶ **CD2 T37** Read the questions through with students and ask students to guess the answers. Play the recording while students listen and read to find the answers. Play the recording again, pausing as necessary for students to check their predictions.

Answers
They are in a tent. In the first photograph, they are bored and not enjoying themselves. They are enjoying themselves in the last photograph and they feel a lot happier. Debbie talks to her Dad on the phone.

TAPESCRIPT
See the text on page 18 of the Student's Book.

b Read through sentences 1–6 with students and check understanding. Students match the beginnings and endings of the sentences to make a summary of the story. Check answers in open class.

Answers
2 a 3 e 4 f 5 b 6 c

10 Everyday English

a Read the expressions aloud with the class. In pairs, students find them in the photostory and decide who said them. Check answers. Students can then translate them into their own language.

Answers
1 Joel 2 Debbie 3 Debbie 4 Debbie
5 Debbie 6 Pete

b Students complete the sentences with the expressions from Exercise 10a. Do the first item as an example, if necessary. Remind students to read through the whole dialogue before deciding which expressions to use. Check answers.

Answers
2 then 3 it's/fault 4 Hang on 5 either
6 don't worry

✱ OPTIONAL ACTIVITY

Divide the class into pairs and ask them to practise the dialogue. You may like to read through the dialogue yourself first to give them an example. When students have practised the dialogue, they take it in turns to close their books and try to remember their part. Their partner can give them prompts to help them remember. Can any students remember the whole dialogue without looking at their books?

Vocabulary notebook

Encourage students to add these expressions to the *Everyday English* section in their vocabulary notebooks.

Discussion box

Weaker classes: Students can choose one question to discuss.

Stronger classes: In pairs or small groups, students go through the questions in the box and discuss them.

Monitor and help as necessary, encouraging students to express themselves in English and to use any vocabulary they have learned from the text. Ask pairs or groups to feedback to the class and discuss any interesting points further.

11 Improvisation

Divide the class into pairs. Tell students they are going to create a role play between Pete and Joel. Read through the instructions with students. Give students two minutes to plan their dialogue. Circulate and help with vocabulary as necessary. Encourage students to use expressions from Exercise 10. Students practise their conversation in pairs. Listen to some of the best conversations in open class.

12 Team Spirit ⊙ DVD 1 Episode 4

Warm up

Books closed. In open class, ask students to tell you as many words as they can connected to camping and write the words on the board. If students don't know a word in English, encourage them to describe it (*What size is it? What is it used for?*), before telling them the word.

a Read through the instructions with students and check they understand all of the words in the box. Did they think of all the words in the warm up exercise? Students work in small groups and rank the objects in order of importance. Circulate and monitor, making sure everybody has the chance to give their opinion and that students are giving reasons for their choices. When students have ranked the objects, have an open class discussion to decide on the most important objects.

b Watch Episode 4 of the DVD for students to find out more about the camping trip.

13 Write

If you set the background information as a homework research task ask the students to tell the class what they have found out.

BACKGROUND INFORMATION

The Tate Modern in London is Britain's national museum of international modern art.

The Design Museum is a museum by the River Thames near Tower Bridge in central London.

The London Eye (also known as the **Millennium Wheel**) at a height of 135 m (443 ft) is the biggest Ferris wheel in Europe. It is located on the South Bank of the River Thames between Westminster Bridge and Hungerford Bridge.

The Palace of Westminster, also known as the **Houses of Parliament**, is where the two Houses of the Parliament of the United Kingdom (the House of Lords and the House of Commons) meet. The palace lies on the north bank of the River Thames in the City of Westminster, close to the government buildings of Whitehall. It contains around 1,100 rooms, 100 staircases and 4.8 kilometres of corridors.

Portobello Road is a road in the Notting Hill district of west London. On Saturdays it is home to Portobello Road Market, a street market known for its second-hand clothes and antiques.

Harrods is a department store in Knightsbridge, London. The store was established in 1834 and is one of the largest department stores in the world. Its food hall is world famous.

Hyde Park is one of the largest parks in central London and famous for its Speakers' Corner. The park is divided in two by the Serpentine River and is 1.4 km². The park has become a traditional location for mass political demonstrations and is also used for large open-air concerts.

Warm up

Ask students what they know about London. Try to elicit famous buildings, attractions, people and historical events. If any of the students have visited London, ask them to describe what they saw there. Encourage students to compare London to their own capital city.

a Tell students they are going to read an email from a girl called Cynthia which describes her plans for a visit to London. Students read the email and find out how Cynthia feels. Check answers and point out the use of the present continuous in the email.

> **Answer**
> Excited, because she is going to do a lot of wonderful things in London.

b Read through the instructions with students and check understanding. Encourage them to use the email from Cynthia as a guide. Give them as much time as possible to plan and organise their

ideas in class. Monitor and check their progress. In a subsequent lesson, ask students to read each other's emails and give each other feedback.

14 Last but not least: more speaking

Read through the instructions with students. Divide the class into pairs and give each student a letter A or B. B students turn to page 73 for information about their holiday. Students ask each other questions to find out about their holidays. With weaker classes, you may like to ask some questions yourself as examples. Encourage students to use the present continuous tense in their dialogues. Circulate and help with pronunciation and intonation. Listen to some of the dialogues in open class as feedback.

Check your progress

1 Grammar

a 2 more difficult 3 easiest 4 worst 5 bigger
6 better 7 worse 8 most important

b 2 's meeting Gerard in a café
3 are going to the cinema
4 are having lunch
5 she's doing her homework
6 her cousins are arriving from Canada

2 Vocabulary

a 1 communicate 2 mean 3 imitate 4 translate
5 accent 6 guess; look up

b in/on water: windsurfing, snorkelling, canoeing, surfing

not in/on water: climbing, camping, horse riding, sightseeing, sunbathing.

How did you do?

Check that students are marking their scores. Collect these in and check them as necessary and discuss any further work needed with specific students.

Memo from Mario

We're going on holiday

Vocabulary ranking – speaking activity

▶ Ask a student to come to the front and act as class secretary. Tell the class to shout out all the names of holiday activities in Exercise 6 to the 'secretary'.

▶ Ask if there are other sports or holiday activities people in the group have tried or know of.

▶ Add these to the list on the board or the IWB.

Phase 1

▶ Ask the students to work in groups of three and write the activities down in order of the courage you need to engage in them.

e.g. Does *camping* require more guts than *parachuting*?

▶ Make sure the students understand the idea of a courage ranking activity properly.

▶ Ask the groups of three to compare their lists and justify their rankings.

Phase 2

▶ Ask the students to change seats and form new groups of three. Then get them to rank the activities in order of the amount of physical strength needed for each.

e.g. Does *horse-riding* require more strength than *kayaking*?

▶ Ask the groups to compare and explain their rankings.

Phase 3

▶ Ask the students to make new groups of three again. Ask the students to rank the activities in terms of how much intelligence they require.

e.g. Does *scuba-diving* demand more intelligence than *golf*?

▶ The groups compare and explain their rankings.

RATIONALE

In this activity students are invited to think in some depth about these sporting activities and to think about them from different angles. Psychologically this unit is mainly about 'heroic' activities and follows on from their work on heroes and successful people in Combo 1A, a vital theme to teenagers who are trying to define who they are and where they want to go. The exercise focuses on three aspects of heroism: courage, strength and intelligence.

From a language point of view, the use and re-use of these words helps them to sink in without the students having to try and artificially memorise them.

It'll never happen

Unit overview

TOPIC: Making predictions about the future

TEXTS

Reading and listening: a text about predictions which went wrong
Listening: two teenagers talking about the future
Listening: a song
Reading: a text about fortune telling
Writing: a text predicting the future

SPEAKING AND FUNCTIONS

Asking and answering about future personal predictions
A discussion about fortune telling

LANGUAGE

Grammar: *will/won't*
Vocabulary: Expressions to talk about the future; expressions to talk about fortune telling
Pronunciation: *'ll*

1 Read and listen

If you set the background information as a homework research task, ask students to tell the class what they have found out.

BACKGROUND INFORMATION

Edwin Laurentine Drake (1819–1880), also known as Colonel Drake, was an American oil driller, popularly credited with being the first to drill for oil in the United States.

Rutherford Birchard Hayes was born in Delaware, Ohio, on 4 October 1822 and became the 19th President of the United States (1877–1881). Hayes was elected President by one electoral vote after the highly disputed election of 1876.

Warner Bros. Entertainment, Inc. (also known as **Warner Bros. Pictures**, or simply **Warner Bros.**) is one of the world's largest producers of film and television entertainment. Founded in 1918 by Jewish immigrants from Poland, Warner Bros. is the third-oldest American movie studio in continuous operation, after Paramount Pictures, founded in 1912 as Famous Players, and Universal Studios, also founded in 1912.

International Business Machines Corporation, abbreviated **IBM** and nicknamed **"Big Blue"** (for its official corporate colour), is a multinational computer technology and consulting corporation with headquarters in New York, United States. With over 388,000 employees worldwide, IBM is the largest and most profitable information technology employer in the world. Known for its highly talented workforce, IBM employees have earned three Nobel Prizes. In 2007 IBM ranked second in the list of largest software companies in the world.

Decca Records is a British record label established in 1929 by Edward Lewis. The name "Decca" dates back to a portable gramophone called the "Decca Dulcephone" patented in 1914 by musical instrument makers Barnett Samuel and Sons.

The Beatles were a rock and pop band from Liverpool, England that formed in 1960. During their career, the group primarily consisted of John Lennon (rhythm guitar, vocals), Paul McCartney (bass guitar, vocals), George Harrison (lead guitar, vocals) and Ringo Starr (drums, vocals). Their clothes, style and statements made them trendsetters, while their growing social awareness saw their influence extend into the social and cultural revolutions of the 1960s. After the band broke up in 1970, all four members embarked upon successful solo careers. The Beatles are one of the most commercially successful and critically acclaimed bands in the history of popular music, selling over one billion records internationally. In the United Kingdom, the Beatles earned more number one albums (15) than any other group in UK chart history.

Warm up

Books closed. Ask students to think of any films or television programmes which are set in the future. When are they set? What predictions do they make about life in the future? Listen to their ideas and encourage students to discuss whether they think the future seen in the films will come true.

a ▶ **CD2 T38** Books open. Tell students they are going to listen to five people making predictions. Pre-teach difficult vocabulary: *break down; storms; hurricanes; afford; stuff.* Students read the predictions and match them to the people in the pictures. Play the recording for students to check answers, pausing if necessary for clarification.

TAPESCRIPT

Presenter: We talked to some ordinary people to find out their predictions for the future. This is what they told us. First, Amy Hunter, a 40-year-old teacher from Balham.

Speaker 1: One day, there won't be any real toys any more. Kids will play with virtual toys. I think that'll be very sad.

Presenter: Now, student, Phil Elliot.

Speaker 2: In the future, there will be some great inventions. I bet very rich people will have their own personal space rockets so they can fly off into space whenever they feel like it!

Presenter: And next, let's hear what car mechanic, Mike Edge has to say.

Speaker 3: I think they'll have special machines that do X-rays of cars so that when they break down, we can find out immediately what's wrong with them.

Presenter: Now for housewife and mother, Melissa Frank.

Speaker 4: I'm sure one day scientists will invent little robots that are so cheap we can all afford to buy one and keep it at home to help in the house and stuff.

Presenter: And finally, fisherman Dan Morgan's view of the future.

Speaker 5: I reckon that one day we'll be able to totally control the weather. We won't have any more bad storms and hurricanes any more.

Answers
A 4   B 5   C 1   D 3   E 2

b Read through the instructions in open class. Students read the predictions again and mark them before comparing their views with other students. With weaker classes, read through the first prediction in open class and ask for individual views. As feedback, go through the predictions and have a class vote on each.

c To introduce the text, ask students if they know of any famous predictions that have gone wrong. Listen to any examples before asking students to read the text and see if they had heard any of the predictions. Tell students that they should read the text quickly and not worry about any difficult vocabulary at this stage.

d ▶ **CD2 T39** If students have found the text difficult, explain the following vocabulary: *drill for oil; hole; ground; X-rays; toys; tape.* Students read the text again and listen before they complete the sentences. Check answers.

Example answers
1 talking in films
2 won't be popular
3 will buy a computer
4 will want to use it

e Read through the instructions in open class. Make sure students have enough time to write three predictions before reading them to their partner. Circulate and monitor, helping with vocabulary as required. Listen to some of the best predictions in open class and encourage further discussion.

2 Grammar

will/won't

a Read the example sentences with the class. Ask them to find the word (positive or negative) that is next to each verb in each sentence (*will ('ll)/won't*). Students look for and underline other examples of *will ('ll)* or *won't* in the text. Check answers.

Answers
1a: ... I reckon that one day we'll be able to control the weather.
We won't have any more bad storms ...
There won't be any real toys any more.
Kids will play with virtual toys.
I think that'll be very sad.
... scientists will invent little robots ...
... there will be some great inventions
... very rich people will have their own personal space rockets

1b: They want to know what will or won't happen ...
... who will want to use it?
... X-rays won't work
... they'll never be important for war
Nobody will want that.
... computers will only weigh about 1.5 tons.
People won't buy this music.
Tonight it will be a little windy.

b Read the instructions and do the first item with students as an example, if necessary. Students complete the table and the rule. Check answers.

Answers
Positive: 'll
Negative: won't
Question: Will
Short answers: will; won't
Rule: 'll; won't

c Ask students to read through the verbs in the box and the dialogue. Go through the example with students. Students then complete the exercise. Check answers.

> **Answers**
> 2 'll be 3 won't go 4 'll stay 5 won't help
> 6 will give 7 'll find

d Students practise the dialogue in pairs. Ask two stronger students to act the dialogue out for the class.

Grammar notebook

Students may find it useful to note down the grammar table and the rules in their notebooks for future reference.

3 Pronunciation

See notes on page 155.

4 Listen

▶ **CD2 T41** Read the instructions aloud with the class and make sure they understand what they have to do while listening. (Tell them to ignore the last two columns at the moment.)

Play the recording. If necessary, pause after the example item and go through it with students to check they understand what to do. Continue with the recording for students to mark their charts, before comparing in pairs. Check answers.

TAPESCRIPT

Interviewer: Today on *Teen Talk*, we're going to talk about how teenagers see their future! You first, Sally – what do you think will happen in your future?

Sally: Well, it's hard to say. Maybe I'll get married but I'm sure I won't have children. I'm not sure I'd be a good parent, to be honest.

Interviewer: Do you think you'll go to university?

Sally: Well yes, I think I'll probably go to university.

Interviewer: And what about a job, after university?

Sally: Well, I don't know what kind of job I want. But I hope to get a good job, you know, and make good money!

Interviewer: How about living abroad? Do you think you'll do that?

Sally: Well, the thing is, I really, really like living here in England. So I don't think I'll live abroad, no.

Interviewer: Right. OK. Will you learn to drive?

Sally: I doubt it. There are too many cars already – so I doubt I'll learn to drive.

Interviewer: Last question. Do you think you'll be famous one day?

Sally: Famous? No, I'm sure I won't be famous!

Interviewer: OK. Now, here's Patrick. Hi, Patrick.

Patrick: Hi.

Interviewer: What about your future, Patrick? Do you think you'll get married and have children?

Patrick: Well, yes, I think I'll get married. I hope so, anyway! And I'm pretty sure I want children. I like kids.

Interviewer: OK. Now, do you think you'll get a good job?

Patrick: Yes, I'm sure I'll go to university and get a good job. I want to be a lawyer. I hope to go to one of the top universities, and then I hope to be one of the best lawyers in the country.

Interviewer: Well, good luck! And what about driving?

Patrick: Oh yes, I'm sure I'll learn to drive.

Interviewer: Do you think you'll be famous one day?

Patrick: Well, I don't think so – but you never know! I doubt I'll be famous, though.

Interviewer: Right. Thank you very much, Patrick ...

> **Answers**
> Sally: get married ✓; have children ✗; go to university ✓; get a good job ✓; learn to drive ✗; become famous ✗
> Patrick: get married ✓; have children ✓; go to university ✓; get a good job ✓; learn to drive ✓; become famous ✗

5 Vocabulary

✴ Expressions to talk about the future

a Read the instructions with students. Students answer the question and then think about how they say *I hope to* in their own language.

Answer
She wants to get a good job but she's not sure if she will.

b Read through sentences 1–8 with students and write the column headings on the board. Give an example of your own for each column before students start, e.g. *I think I'll teach in this school next year. I don't think I will go to England this summer. I'll probably go to England for Christmas.* Ask them which of these things you believe will happen (sentence A), which won't happen (sentence B), and which is possible that it will happen (sentence C). Students now classify the sentences under each heading. Check answers.

Answers
1 A 2 C 3 B 4 B 5 C 6 B 7 C 8 A

Vocabulary notebook

Students should note down these expressions and some translations or example sentences in their notebooks.

6 Speak

a Ask students to go back to the chart at the top of page 24 and to make predictions about their own future and complete the *Me* column.

b Read the example dialogue with students before they begin. Students then work in pairs to ask the questions and note down their partner's answers in the column marked *My partner*. Ask several pairs to demonstrate their dialogues to the class. Ask other students to say whether their partners think they will be married / live abroad, etc. Are there any interesting answers? If so, discuss these in more detail as a class.

c Students use the information in the table in Exercise 4 and go around the class asking other students their opinions. Students pool the information and draw up a chart showing the general opinions in the class.

7 Listen: a song

a ▶ CD2 T42

TAPESCRIPT
See the song on page 25 of the Student's Book.

b **Answers**
2 e 3 g 4 b 5 c 6 d 7 a 8 f 9 j 10 h

c **Answers**
1 c 2 b 3 a

d Students listen and sing along while you play the song again.

Culture in mind

8 Read and listen

Warm up
Books closed. Ask students if they think that the day they are born will affect their future life and personality. Ask if they know what their star sign is and what that says about their personality.

a Books open. Ask students to think of ways of predicting the future. Make a note of their ideas on the board and ask students to explain any methods which are not shown in the pictures.

b ▶ CD2 T43 Read the questions with students and check understanding. Students read the text, listen to the recording and find answers. Encourage them to focus on the task and not to worry about difficult vocabulary. With weaker classes, you may like to read the text aloud, pausing for clarification of difficult vocabulary. Check answers.

Answers
1 Palmistry 2 Astrology 3 Fortune cookies
4 Reading tea leaves 5 Palmistry
6 Fortune cookies 7 Astrology 8 Palmistry

✱ OPTIONAL ACTIVITY

Divide the class into pairs and tell students they are going to create dialogues based on palmistry. Students take it in turns to look at the lines on their partner's hands and invent predictions. It is not necessary for students to know the traditional meaning of the lines on the hand, but you may like to give them sample sentences to get them started, e.g. *This line is very thick/thin/short/long/broken, that means …* Encourage students to use their imaginations and if they enjoy the activity, let them change partners and repeat the procedure.

9 Vocabulary

✱ **Expressions to talk about fortune telling**

a Ask students to choose the correct definitions of the words in the text. Read the words aloud for them to hear the pronunciation. Check answers.

Answers
2 b 3 b 4 b 5 a 6 b 7 a 8 a

b Students complete the sentences using the words from Exercise 9a. Check answers.

Answers

1 fortune telling; nonsense	4 palm
2 influence	5 leaves; predict
3 centuries	6 reliable

Vocabulary notebook

Encourage students to add these words and any other interesting vocabulary from this section to their vocabulary notebooks.

10 Write

a As an introduction to this exercise, write the date one hundred years from now on the board and ask students to make predictions of what life will be like. Ask them to make predictions about computers, TV, music, pollution, animals, schools, etc.

Tell students they are going to read some predictions. Students read the text and complete with words from the box. Allow them to check their answers with a partner before open class feedback. Draw students' attention to the use of *will* to make predictions.

Answers

2 will happen 3 will be 4 won't be 5 will find 6 we'll recycle 7 will learn 8 They'll do

b Students can do the preparation in class and complete the writing assignment as homework. Read the title with the class and give them time to think about vocabulary they will need and to plan their composition. Encourage them to use the text in Exercise 10a as a guide. In the next class, let students read each other's work and decide who made the best predictions.

11 Speak

a Divide the class into pairs. Ask students to discuss the two questions and give their views on the fortune-telling methods. Circulate and monitor, helping with vocabulary as required. For feedback, expand into a whole class discussion. If they have personal experience of any of the techniques, ask them to tell their story. You could end with a class vote to decide which is the best method of fortune telling.

b In pairs, students invent a new fortune telling technique. To get them started, you could give the following example: Ask a student to open any book and, with eyes closed, point to a place on the page. He then opens his eyes and finds the noun nearest to his finger. He repeats this at random, finding ten different words on ten different pages. These words then form the basis of a prediction.

When students have invented a method, divide the class into small groups and let them practise on each other.

Memo from Mario

It'll never happen

1 Students control a dictation

▶ Explain to the students that you are going to give them a dictation and that you are going to 'become' a machine, a kind of text-playing machine.

▶ To work with you they need to use three commands:

Start!

Stop!

Go back to ... (and the word they want you to go back to)

▶ Tell them you understand these three commands and no others. Explain that if they do not use the *Stop* command you will simply go on reading.

▶ This is what a student controlled dictation can sound like:

Student:	*Start!*
You:	*Astrology is centuries old. The idea is ...*
Another student:	*Stop!*
Another student:	*Go back to OLD ...*
You:	*Old. The idea is that the position of the stars ...*
Another student:	*Stop!*

▶ Tell the students to close their books and you become a text playing machine and dictate the first two sections of 'Fortune telling' (page 26) to them.

▶ The students open their books and check that what they have written down is correct.

▶ Give them time to tell you how they felt during the dictation.

> **RATIONALE**
> Students spend a lot of time at school being told what to do. In this activity they have the chance, in a light-hearted way, to be the bosses and the teacher has to obey. Wow! What a relief. It is a bit like the suspension of normal rules you have at carnival time!

2 The present seen from the past

▶ Choose a time deep in the past that is well known in the students' own culture. This might be the start of the Han Dynasty for Chinese people or the time of Hegira for people of the Muslim faith. With Europeans it could be Roman times.

▶ Ask the students to tell you about the weapons, the transport, the houses and the communications systems of that time.

▶ Put this text up on the board or the IWB.

> This is the year .... (the time chosen) and I am a .... (Roman, Han Dynasty Chinese etc.)
>
> In the year 2015 I predict that people will drive cars ... they won't ride horses ... etc.

▶ Ask the students to copy what you have put up on the board or the IWB and write a dozen more predictions. Tell them it is fine if they mix in some false predictions.

▶ Put the students in pairs so they can listen to each other's forecasts.

> **RATIONALE**
> It is educationally valuable to think forward from the past. It inculcates a sense of history and gives us a frame for thinking about the unpredictability of the future.

4 Don't give up

Unit overview

TOPIC: Overcoming difficult situations; the weather

TEXTS

Reading and listening: a text about a girl surviving in the jungle
Listening: a text about a successful skier
Writing: an email about learning English

SPEAKING AND FUNCTIONS

Describing a famous sportsperson
A discussion about how you do things

LANGUAGE

Grammar: *too* + adjective; adverbs
Vocabulary: the weather
Pronunciation: /əʊ/ (*go*)
Everyday English: *In fact; Not really; in a way; Are you sure?; in a minute; the best thing to do*

1 Read and listen

If you set the background information as a homework research task ask students to tell the class what they have found out.

BACKGROUND INFORMATION

Lima is the capital and largest city of Peru. It is located on the coast overlooking the Pacific Ocean. Lima was founded by Spanish conquistador Francisco Pizarro on 18 January 1535, as La Ciudad de los Reyes, or "The City of Kings". After the Peruvian War of Independence, it was made the capital of the Republic of Peru. Today around one-third of the Peruvian population lives in this metropolitan area.

The Amazon rainforest also known as **Amazonia**, or the **Amazon jungle**, is a moist broadleaf forest of around 5.5 million km² that covers most of the Amazon Basin of South America. This region includes territory belonging to nine nations. The majority of the forest (60%) is contained within Brazil, followed by Peru with 13% of the rainforest, and with minor amounts in Colombia, Venezuela, Ecuador, Bolivia, Guyana, Suriname, and French Guiana. The Amazon represents over half of the planet's remaining rainforests, and it comprises the largest and most species-rich area of tropical rainforest in the world.

Werner Herzog (born in Munich on 5 September 1942) is an Academy Award-nominated German film director, screenwriter, actor and opera director. His films often feature heroes with impossible dreams or people with unique talents in obscure fields.

Warm up

Books closed. Ask students to close their eyes and relax. Read the following text to them: *Imagine that you are in the middle of the Amazon jungle. Look around you. What can you see? What can you hear? What can you smell? How do you feel? Are you hot? Are you thirsty? Imagine that you start to walk into the jungle. What do you see? Is there anything dangerous? Are you afraid?*

Tell students to open their eyes and describe what they imagined to a partner. Listen to some of their ideas in open class.

a Books open. Students look at the pictures and decide what the connection between them is. Check answers.

b Tell students they are going to read a text about a young girl who is stranded in the jungle after a plane crash. Students read the text quickly to answer the question. If necessary pre-teach the following vocabulary: *unconscious; survive; woodcutters*. Encourage students not to look up every new word but just to read and focus on finding the answer. Check answer.

> **Answer**
> She walked along it in order to reach civilisation. It also gave her clean water to drink and kept her cool.

c Write the title of the text *Jungle survival* on the board. In pairs, students discuss the difficulties and dangers of surviving in the jungle.

Weaker classes: brainstorm difficulties and write them on the board. In pairs, students discuss how they would overcome the problems. Circulate and monitor. In open class, listen to some of the students' ideas as feedback.

d ▶ **CD3 T1** Students read the text again in more detail and complete the sentences. Play the recording while they read. Let students check answers with a partner before playing the recording again, pausing to check answers and for clarification as necessary. Ask students what types of words are used to complete the gaps (*adverbs*) and what their purpose is (*to describe how an action takes place*).

Tell students they will do further work on adverbs in Exercise 4.

TAPESCRIPT
See the reading text on page 28 of the Student's Book.

Answers
1 heavily 2 quickly 3 slowly 4 safely

e Read through the questions with students and discuss in open class. Have they seen any other films about jungles? Do they think it would be difficult to make a film in a jungle?

2 Grammar
✷ too + adjective

a Read the sentences aloud and match the first one as an example with students. Students match the other items. Check answers. Then ask students to translate the underlined expressions into their own language. Do they notice any similarities or differences?

Now ask students to look at the adjectives in the second part of each sentence and ask them what they think the word *too* does to the adjective (*it intensifies it*). Elicit a few more adjectives and put them on the board, then elicit a few sentences from students using *too* + one of the adjectives on the board.

Answers
1 b 2 c 3 a

Language note
It may be useful to tell students that when we put *too* in front of an adjective it usually implies a negative meaning. Compare this with the use of *very* + adjective, which can have a positive meaning. Give examples to show the difference. *He's very friendly. / He's too friendly. His house is very clean. / His house is too clean (i.e. I don't like clean houses).*

b Students work in pairs or individually to complete the sentences. Check answers.

Answers
2 too cold 3 too old 4 too expensive
5 too long 6 too hard

c Read through the words in the box with students and do the first item as an example. Remind students of the differences between using *very* and too with adjectives (see Language note above). In pairs, students complete the exercise. Check answers.

Answers
1 very big 2 too big 3 too heavy
4 very heavy 5 very old 6 too old

✷ **OPTIONAL ACTIVITIES**

Ask students to find the opposites of the words in Exercise 2b. Check the answers by calling out one of the words in Exercise 2b and asking students to give you the opposite.

Answers
hard – easy; long – short; expensive – cheap;
cold – hot; young – old

Stronger classes: Give students some more adjectives, such as in the list 1–8 below. Ask them to find the opposites. Students can use a dictionary if necessary.
1 wide 2 new 3 beautiful 4 early
5 dark 6 dry 7 full 8 quiet

Answers
1 narrow 2 old 3 ugly 4 late 5 light 6 wet
7 empty 8 noisy

Grammar notebook
Students may find it useful at this point to note down the key points from this grammar section and any useful translations.

3 Vocabulary
✷ The weather

a Ask students to describe what the weather is like at different times of year and try to elicit the words in the box. Write any words connected to weather on the board and check pronunciation.

Read through the weather words and sentences with students and check understanding. You may like to pre-teach *burn*. Students complete the exercise before checking in open class.

Answers
2 Lightning 3 sun 4 thunder 5 hot
6 shower

Language note
It may be useful to point out to students that English uses the verb *be* for weather expressions, e.g. *It's hot. NOT It makes/does hot.* Ask them to translate the expressions into their own language and compare them with English.

b ▶ CD3 T2 To introduce the concept of weather forecasts ask students to tell you how they find out what the weather is going to be like the following day. Ask them to describe a weather forecast in L1.

Tell students they are going to listen to a weather forecast and fill the gaps with words from Exercise 3a. Play the recording while students complete the text. Give students time to compare answers before listening to the recording again, pausing for clarification where necessary. Check answers.

TAPESCRIPT

Weather man: And now for today's forecast. In the London area, the weather will be warm with temperatures of around 18 degrees. Although the sun will shine for a while, we can expect some strong winds this afternoon. And that will make it feel quite cool. Further north in the Birmingham area, things won't be too good, I'm afraid. After last night's thunderstorms, Birmingham is going to be very cool with an expected high of about 14 degrees. But no more thunder and lightning today, at least. And finally, in Scotland, it will be foggy for part of the morning then cloudy later on. But not snowing like it was yesterday, fortunately, so the roads should be safer once the fog clears.

Answers
1 warm 2 winds 3 thunderstorms 4 cool
5 thunder 6 lightning 7 foggy 8 cloudy

[c] Ask students to predict what the weather will be like tomorrow and write their sentences. Encourage them to use some of the vocabulary from Exercise 3a and 3b. Circulate and help with vocabulary as required. In pairs, students compare their predictions with a partner. In your next class, refer back to their predictions and see who was closest to the truth.

Vocabulary bank

Refer students to the vocabulary bank on page 65. Read through the words and phrases in open class and check understanding. For further practice of the vocabulary, ask students to describe typical weather at different times of year or in different countries, e.g. *What's the weather like in March? What's the weather like in Iceland?*

Vocabulary notebook

Encourage students to start a new section *Weather* in their notebook and add any weather-related vocabulary from this exercise.

4 Grammar

✱ Adverbs

[a] Read through the examples from the text with students. If necessary, refer them back to the text where they can see each sentence in context. Write the headings *Adjectives* and *Adverbs* on the board.

Look at the example sentences again and ask students the following questions: *How did the rain fall?* Elicit *heavily*. Do the same for the other sentences: *How hot was it? (extremely), How did the plane take her? (safely).*

Explain to students that adverbs describe adjectives and verbs. Ask them to look at each adverb and try to work out which adjective they come from (*heavy, extreme, safe*). Read through the rule with students and then they complete it. While they are doing this, put the adverbs and the elicited adjectives they come from on the board. Check answers. To check understanding at this point, call out a few adjectives and ask students for the adverb, e.g. *quick – quickly, soft – softly.*

Answers
verbs; –ly; i; –ly

[b] Refer students back to the text on page 28 and tell them to go through it and find examples of adverbs. Students can compare answers in pairs. Ask some pairs to read out their answers to the class.

Answers
Juliane fell quickly …
hit the trees hard …
her shoulder hurt badly …
and walked slowly along it.
they cleaned her cuts carefully …

✱ OPTIONAL ACTIVITY

At this point you can ask students to work out which adjectives these adverbs come from.

Answers
quick; hard; bad; slow; careful

[c] Read through the tables with students and go through the regular and irregular examples with them. Using the information from Exercises 4a and b, students now complete the tables. Check answers.

Answers
Regular adverbs: badly, loudly, quietly, luckily, easily
Irregular adverbs: well, hard

[d] Students read through sentences 1–4. Check for any problems. Go through the example with them, eliciting the second adverb (*well*). Remind students to read the whole sentence and to look carefully at the second sentence since they will find the information there to help them choose their adverb. Check answers.

Answers
1 well 2 quietly 3 late 4 hard

In small groups or in front of the class, students can act out some mini-scenes with adverbs. The other students have to guess the whole sentence or the adverb. Set a time limit of one minute for students to guess the answers. Students get one point for guessing the correct adverb and two points for guessing the whole situation correctly. The group/student with most points is the winner.

Example sentences/situations (or students can provide their own):
- *eating a banana slowly*
- *arriving late for your class*
- *speaking English quickly*
- *singing loudly in the shower/bath*
- *walking quietly out of the house*

5 Speak

a Read through the four questions with students. If necessary, do the first question and answer as an example. For example:
T: Silvia, do you study better early or late in the day?
Silvia: I study better late in the day.

Then, in pairs, students ask and answer. Do not ask for feedback at this stage.

b Read through the adverbs in the box and go through the example dialogue first. Students then continue from Exercise 5a asking and answering about other things they can do. Remind them to use present simple tenses when asking and answering. Set a time limit for this. After a few minutes, swap pairs and students can give information about their partner to a new partner, e.g. *Silvia can speak English well. She can play the piano badly!*

Grammar notebook

Students should copy down the tables from Exercise 4c and learn the adverbs. They can ask a partner to test them on the adverbs.

6 Pronunciation

See notes on page 155.

7 Listen and speak

If you set the background information as a homework research task ask students to tell the class what they have found out.

BACKGROUND INFORMATION

Hermann Maier (born 7 December 1972, in Altenmarkt im Pongau, Austria) is a champion alpine ski racer. Maier has won four overall World Cup titles (1998, 2000, 2001, 2004), two Olympic gold medals (both in 1998), three World Championship titles (1999: two, and 2005) and 54 races on the World Cup circuit. Maier ranks among the finest alpine ski racers in history.

a Read the instructions with the class and ask students to look at the photos. Ask them who they think Hermann Maier is. (*He is a champion alpine ski racer from Austria.*) They work in pairs to predict the correct order of the pictures. Do not check answers at this stage.

b ▶ **CD3 T5** Now play the recording. Students check or change their order, if necessary.

Weaker classes: It may help to pause the recording after each answer.

TAPESCRIPT

Boy: ... and so the teacher wants me to give a presentation about a sportsperson, and I don't know who to talk about.

Male: Well, I've got an idea. Do you want to hear it?

Boy: Absolutely!

Male: OK – talk about Hermann Maier.

Boy: The skier?

Male: Yes.

Boy: Tell me about him.

Male: OK. Well, he's Austrian, and like most Austrian boys he liked skiing, and he wasn't bad at it. He went to a special skiing school when he was 15, but the teachers at the school said he was too small and told him to go home.

Boy: Oh.

Male: So he went back home and for a time he worked as a bricklayer, you know, helping to build walls and houses and things.

Boy: So he stopped skiing?

Male: No, he didn't. He still wanted to be a good skier so he kept practising and then he won a couple of small races and in 1996 he got into the Austrian team.

Boy: Right.

Male: He won several World Cup races, but in 1998 he fell really badly – at more than a hundred kilometres per hour, at the Olympic Games in Japan.

Boy: Ouch.

Male: Yeah, but three days later he was back and he won the Olympic Gold medal in the Super Giant Slalom. Only three days later!

Boy: Wow! Brilliant! OK, Dad, thanks, that's a really good ...

Male: Whoa, wait – there's more!!

Boy: Oh – sorry.

Male: Here's the best bit. Three years later – 2001, I think it was – Maier was on his motorbike when a car hit him. It was a really bad accident. And the doctors operated on him for hours. He nearly lost one of his legs.

Boy: Wow.

Male: ... and they had to put metal in his legs and everything. And the doctors said 'No more skiing – you'll never ski again, you'll be lucky if you walk properly.'

Boy: But ...

Male: But he went back to skiing, and in 2004 he won the World Cup!! Isn't that amazing?

Boy: It is. I can use this. Thanks Dad, I think I've got my presentation now.

> **Answers**
> A 7 B 5 C 1 D 6 E 3 F 4 G 2

c ▶ **CD3 T5** Play the recording again, pausing it at the point where the first age/date is mentioned. Students write the date or age. Continue playing the recording. Check answers, replaying the recording as necessary.

> **Answers**
> 1 c 2 e 3 a 4 f 5 b 6 d

d In open class, discuss Hermann Maier's life story and ask students how they think he felt at various times in his life. Help students with vocabulary as necessary. Divide the class into pairs and ask them to take it in turns to tell Hermann Maier's life story. Circulate and check progress. Listen to some of their stories in open class as feedback.

Photostory: Keep on running

8 Read and listen

Warm up

Ask students what they do to keep fit. Do they ever go running? If so, how long do they run for? Students then look at the photostory. Ask them who features in this story (Jess and Joel) and ask them to predict what they might be discussing.

a ▶ **CD3 T6** Students read the photostory and answer the questions. Play the recording for students to check their answers and their predictions from the Warm up. Were any of their predictions correct?

TAPESCRIPT
See the text on page 32 of the Student's Book.

> **Answers**
> Jess and Joel are running. Jess isn't very happy because her stomach hurts. Joel tells her to keep running.

b Read through the sentences with students. In pairs, students complete the exercise. As feedback, ask individual students to read the sentences aloud, emphasising the correct information, e.g. Jess thinks running is good fun.

> **Answers**
> 2 ~~neck~~ stomach 3 ~~cry~~ stop 4 ~~stop~~ keep on
> 5 ~~wrong~~ right 6 ~~doesn't go~~ goes
> 7 ~~now~~ in a minute

9 Everyday English

a Read the expressions aloud with the class. Ask students to try to remember who said them without looking back at the text. In pairs, students find them in the text of the photostory and discover who said them. Check answers. Students can then translate the expressions into their own language.

> **Answers**
> 1 Joel 2 Jess 3 Jess 4 Joel 5 Joel 6 Joel

b Students read the dialogues and then complete them with the expressions from Exercise 9a. Go through the first item as an example, if necessary. Check answers.

> **Answers**
> 2 the best thing to do 3 Are you sure
> 4 not really 5 In fact 6 in a way

Vocabulary notebook

Encourage students to add the expressions to the *Everyday English* section in their vocabulary notebooks and, if necessary, to add translations to help them remember the meanings.

Discussion box

Weaker classes: Students can choose one question to discuss.

Stronger classes: In pairs or small groups, students go through the questions in the box and discuss them.

Monitor and help as necessary, encouraging students to express themselves in English and to use any vocabulary they have learned from the text. Ask pairs or groups to feedback to the class and discuss any interesting points further.

10 Improvisation

Divide the class into pairs. Tell students they are going to create a role play between Jess and Joel. Read through the instructions with students. Give students two minutes to plan their dialogue. Circulate and help with vocabulary as necessary. Encourage students to use expressions from Exercise 9. Students practise their conversation in pairs. Listen to some of the best conversations in open class.

11 Team Spirit ⊙ DVD 1 Episode 5

a Look at the photo with students and ask them to describe what is happening and to guess what Debbie is going to do. Listen to some of their ideas in open class. Read through the words in the box and the sentences with students. Check understanding of difficult vocabulary: *celebrate; bet; compulsory*. Students complete the sentences. Allow them to use a dictionary if necessary. Ask students what they think the next episode will be about and listen to some of their ideas in open class.

b Play Episode 5 of the DVD for students to check their answers.

> **Answers**
> 2 into 3 bet 4 after 5 hold 6 down
> 7 celebrate

12 Write

a Students read the question and then Spiros's email. Check any vocabulary problems.

> **Answer**
> Because he's finding English very difficult and he's getting terrible test results.

b This can be set for homework. Read through the phrases given and check students understand how and when to use them. Then look at the start of the email reply with students and explain that they must continue the reply using those phrases. Students plan their reply and complete the exercise in class or at home.

13 Last but not least: more speaking

Weaker classes: Look at the 'Famous sportswoman' card on page 34 and elicit the following questions from students:

What is her name?
When was she born?
Where was she born?
What sport does she play?

When did she begin playing?
What did she do in 2004/2006/2007?

Say the questions for students to repeat. Follow the procedure for stronger classes.

Stronger classes: Divide the class into pairs and ask students to follow the instructions. Circulate and check students are using the correct intonation patterns.

When students have completed their cards, give them two minutes to memorise the information. In pairs, students take it in turns to look at their cards and ask their partners questions to see how much he/she can remember. Encourage them to use full sentences.

> ✱ OPTIONAL ACTIVITY
>
> If students are interested in sport, ask them to complete a similar card with information on a sportsperson of their choice. When they have prepared the information (you may like to set this stage for homework) students can present their information to other students in the class.

Check your progress

1 Grammar

a 2 will 3 will 4 won't 5 Will 6 won't 7 will
8 won't 9 Will; will; will 10 won't; will

b 2 badly 3 easy 4 well 5 slowly 6 loud
7 slow; late 8 slow 9 hard; hardly

2 Vocabulary

a 2 hopes 3 Maybe 4 thinks 5 sure
6 probably 7 doubt

b 2 lightning 3 rain 4 shower 5 sun; hot
6 thunder 7 foggy

How did you do?

Check that students are marking their scores. Collect these in and check them as necessary and discuss any further work needed with specific students.

Memo from Mario

Don't give up
Adverbs the TPR* way

Prepare a sheet of commands including the adverbs introduced in this unit or use the one provided below. Photocopy it so you can give out one sheet per two students.

Adverbs in Unit 4: *slowly, badly, loudly, quietly, luckily, easily, fast, well, early, late, hard, quickly, heavily, safely, lazily, impatiently, carefully*

Walk slowly

Walk slowly and quietly

Walk loudly

Walk fast and loudly

Walk quickly

Walk fast and quietly

Walk quietly

Walk loudly and slowly

Walk carefully

Walk badly

Walk fast

Walk carefully and quietly

Speak slowly

Speak fast

Speak loudly

Speak quietly

Speak quickly

Speak carefully

Speak English badly

Shake hands carefully (with another person)

Shake hands slowly

Shake hands badly

Shake hands quickly

Shake hands slowly and carefully

Shake hands happily

Shake hands sadly

Hand on hand slowly

Hand on head fast

Hand on knee carefully

Hand on leg loudly (slap)

Hand on nose laughingly

Finger on eye gently

Elbow on leg slowly

Do what you can to clear enough space at the front of the classroom for the students to walk about in. This may mean pushing some of the tables and chairs back.

It would be even better to take the students to a clear space somewhere outside the classroom.

Bring the students into the space.

Give them the commands on your sheet, making sure that they show their understanding through their actions. If they don't understand, say the phrase again and demonstrate. Then give the command again.

Put the students in pairs and give one person in each pair a copy of the command sheet.

One student reads a command and the other carries it out. Half way through the activity, get the partners to swap roles.

Round off the activity by asking the students to call out commands which you execute!

* TPR = total physical response

> ### RATIONALE
> This activity gives the kinaesthetic students in your class a chance to come into their element. They love moving and DOING. In this exercise they have 15 minutes of unfettered learning time. They are learning language in their natural way.

5 Promises, promises

Unit overview

TOPIC: New Year's resolutions; reggae

TEXTS

Reading and listening: a text about New Year in New York
Listening: a dialogue about New Year's resolutions
Reading and listening: a text about two teenagers going out for the evening
Reading: a text about reggae music
Listening: a song – *Wonderful World, Beautiful People*
Writing: an email about New Year and plans

SPEAKING AND FUNCTIONS

Talking about future plans
Discussing the meaning of a song

LANGUAGE

Grammar: *be going to* (intentions and predictions); *must/mustn't*
Vocabulary: multi-word verbs; prepositions
Pronunciation: Stress on *must* and *mustn't*

1 Read and Listen

If you set the background information as a homework research task ask the students to tell the class what they have found out.

BACKGROUND INFORMATION

The City of New York (most often called **New York City**), located on the Atlantic coast of the north eastern United States, is the most densely populated major city in the United States, with an estimated 8,274,527 people occupying just under 790 km². In 2005, nearly 170 languages were spoken in the city and 36% of its population was born outside the United States. The city is sometimes referred to as 'The City that Never Sleeps'. The city has been home to several of the tallest buildings in the world, including the Empire State Building and the twin towers of the former World Trade Centre. It also has many world famous sights: The Statue of Liberty, Wall Street, Times Square and Broadway. New York City is a leading global city, exerting a powerful influence over commerce, finance, culture and entertainment worldwide. The city is also an important centre for international affairs, hosting the United Nations headquarters.

Times Square is a major intersection in Manhattan, New York City at the junction of Broadway and Seventh Avenue. Times Square, sometimes known as the 'Crossroads of the World', has achieved the status of an iconic world landmark and has become a symbol of its city.

A New Year's resolution is a commitment that an individual makes to a project or the reforming of a habit, often a lifestyle change that is generally interpreted as advantageous. The name comes from the fact that these commitments normally go into effect on New Year's Day and remain until fulfilled or abandoned.

Warm up

Books closed. In open class, brainstorm festivals and special days in the students' home countries. Ask them to explain what the days celebrate and what people do on those days. Write any interesting vocabulary on the board.

a Tell students that in many countries, New Year is the time of great celebrations. Ask students what they do on New Year in their country. With weaker classes, allow students to do this in L1.

b Students look at the text quickly and find answers. Encourage students not to look up every difficult word, but just to read and get the general idea of the text.

Answers
1 New Year's Eve 2 midnight 3 resolutions

c Students read the text and make sure their answers for Exercise 1b are correct.

d ▶ CD3 T7 Read through the sentences with students and check understanding. Play the recording while students listen and answer the questions. Allow them to compare answers with a partner before playing the recording again, pausing for clarification and to check answers.

TAPESCRIPT

See the reading text on page 36 of the Student's Book.

Answers
1 In New York.
2 A sparkling crystal ball
3 A clock striking 12 and everybody cheering.
4 People break them before the New Year is very old.

2 Listen

Warm up

Ask students if they have ever made a resolution at New Year or at any other time. Did they keep their promise or break it? How difficult was it to keep? What made them break their promise? You may like to give a couple of examples of your own to get them started.

▶ **CD3 T8** Tell students they are going to hear a conversation between a girl and her father in which they discuss their New Year's resolutions. Before listening, read through the sentences with students and ask them to predict who will say what. Play the recording. Students check answers with a partner before listening to the recording again, pausing to check answers.

TAPESCRIPT

Amy: Happy New Year, Dad!

Male: Happy New Year! Let's hope it brings us lots of luck, eh?

Amy: Yes, Dad. What are your resolutions this year?

Male: Resolutions? Well, I'm not going to eat unhealthy food any more. I'm going to give up eating chips, for one thing. And I'm going to make an effort to get fitter. Mum and I are going to check out that new gym.

Amy: Hmm ... both those resolutions sound familiar, Dad! They're the same as the ones you made last year!

Male: Yes, well, this year I really mean it! You can tell me off if I don't keep them this time. Anyway – what about your resolutions?

Amy: Well, first of all, I'm going to take up running and – listen to this – I'm going to tidy my room every weekend!

Male: That's not going to be easy!

Amy: And Jodie and I are going to set up a business!

Male: A business? Amy, you're only 16!

Amy: I know, Dad. But we can earn some money by walking people's dogs for them. We looked it up on the internet. It's going to be a great success.

Male: Ah, so are you going to take our dog for a walk now so that I don't have to do it every day?

Amy: Well, Dad, it'll cost you! But you don't have to pay the full price because you're family!! I'm sure we can work something out!

Answers
1 Dad 2 Dad 3 Dad 4 Amy 5 Amy 6 Amy

3 Vocabulary

✱ **Multi-word verbs**

▶ **CD3 T9** Ask students if they can remember what multi-word verbs are. Elicit a few examples from the ones they have seen in previous units. Students read through verbs 1–6 and the definitions. Do the first item with them as an example, if necessary. Students complete the exercise. Check answers. Then play the recording for students to listen and repeat the multi-word verbs. To check understanding at this point, give an example of your own and ask a few students to give you examples for the other verbs.

Ask students which verb is usually associated with New Year's resolutions (*give up*).

TAPESCRIPT/ANSWERS
1 take up – b start doing something
2 give up – d stop doing something
3 look up – f find out information about something from a book or computer
4 tell off – c speak angrily to someone for doing something wrong
5 work out – e find the answer to something
6 check out – a go to a place to see what it is like

> **Language note**
> Explain to students that some multi-word verbs can be split and a pronoun can be inserted between the first and second part. Highlight this using item 6 from Exercise 2. This is not possible with all multi-word verbs and has to be learned.

✱ OPTIONAL ACTIVITY

Stronger classes: Call out a list of verbs and ask students to give you the relevant preposition to go with them to make them into multi-word verbs.

Weaker classes: They can work in pairs. Students write these verbs down and look them up in a dictionary to find the various prepositions.
Climb (up/down)
Turn (up/down/around)
Work (out)
Take (up/down/in/out)
Keep (up/in/out)

Vocabulary bank

Refer students to the vocabulary bank on page 66. Read through the words and phrases in open class and check understanding. For further practice, divide the class into pairs and ask them to test each other, e.g. *A: Which verb means 'to ring'? B: go off.*

Vocabulary notebook

Students should start a new section in their notebook called *Multi-word verbs*. They should note down the new verbs from this unit.

4 Grammar

✱ *be going to*: intentions

a Books closed. Ask students if they can remember the dialogue between Amy and her Dad in Exercise 2. Ask them: *Who is going to be more healthy? (Dad). Who is going to be more organised? (Amy).* Then ask: *Were Amy and her Dad talking about the past or the future? (future).* Explain that they were talking about future intentions and elicit the form of *be going to* which was used. It may be useful to write this on the board at this stage. Students now open their books at page 37. Read through the Rule box in Exercise 4a with them and check they understand. You can do this by asking them a few questions, e.g. *Alicia, are you going to do your homework tonight?* and elicit the short answer *Yes, I am. / No, I'm not.* Students now complete the grammar table. Check answers.

> **Answers**
> Negative: aren't; isn't
> Questions: Are; Is
> Short answers: am; are; isn't

b Read through the words in the box with students and check understanding. They should remember most of these from the dialogue in Exercise 2.

Students read through items 1–6. Go through the example with students, asking why *are going to* is used (because it is a plural subject) to check students have remembered all the forms of *be*. Students complete the exercise. Remind them to change any pronouns as necessary to match the subject. Check answers.

Weaker classes: They may find it useful to listen to the Exercise 2 dialogue again before starting this exercise.

> **Answers**
> 2 is going to give up eating chips
> 3 is going to take up running
> 4 are going to check out the gym
> 5 is going to tidy her room every weekend
> 6 Dad: Are; going to start a business
>   Amy: are

✱ *be going to*: predictions

c Read through the rule with students and give them another example of your own, e.g. *Look at those black clouds. It's going to rain soon.* Check students understand that this is prediction because there is present evidence. Students read through items 1–6, then go through the example with them. Students complete the exercise. Remind them to use short forms where possible. Check answers.

> **Answers**
> 2 isn't going to be / is not going to be
> 3 're going to love / are going to love
> 4 're going to be / are going to be
> 5 isn't going to get / is not going to get
> 6 Are; going to win

d Students look at the pictures and read through sentences 1–6. Explain that they must match one sentence with each picture. Do the first one as an example, if necessary. In pairs, students complete the exercise. Check answers.

> **Answers**
> B 6 C 5 D 2 E 1 F 3

e This can be done for homework. Read through the instructions with students. Do the first item with them as an example. In pairs, students complete the exercise. Check answers.

> **Answers**
> 1 P 2 I 3 P 4 P 5 P 6 I

5 Speak

a Divide the class into pairs and ask students to think of three changes they would like to make in their town/city. Make sure students make a note of their ideas.

b Students compare their ideas with a student from a different pair. Encourage them to use sentences with *going to* as much as possible. Circulate and check they are using the language correctly. Ask some students to give examples of their plans using *going to* to the rest of the class.

6 Read and listen

Warm up

Books closed. Ask students if they have ever been out with friends to celebrate New Year or another festival. Ask them what their parents said to them before they went out. Allow students to use L1 for this activity to encourage discussion. If students go out with their friends, what time do they have to return home in the evening?

a Tell students that they are going to listen to a conversation between two teenagers and their parents. Look at the first picture with students and ask them to guess what the parents are saying. Elicit some ideas and write any good sentences on the board.

b ▶ **CD3 T10** Ask students to read through the dialogue and to try to think of the missing words. Play the recording while students listen and complete the dialogue. Tell them not to worry about understanding every word, but just to focus on the task. Students check answers with a partner before feedback. Play the recording again, pausing if necessary.

TAPESCRIPT

Kate: Mum? Dad? We're going now, OK?

Mum: OK, you two. Have a good time. But remember …

Ashley: Yes, Mum, we know.

Dad: You must be home at 12.30.

Mum: You can stay at the party for the midnight celebration, but you mustn't stay longer than that.

Kate: OK – no problem.

Ashley: It isn't far, so we're going to leave at 12.15 and walk back. We'll be home at 12.30.

Dad: Fine. Have you got your mobile phones?

Mum: Yes, you mustn't forget those.

Kate: We've got mine. Ashley lost his last week, remember?

Mum: OK. Call us if there's any problem, OK?

Ashley: We will – promise.

Dad: OK – off you go. Have a good time.

Kate: Thanks. See you later – I mean, at 12.30.

Answers
1 remember 2 must 3 mustn't 4 going
5 walk 6 forget 7 promise 8 mean

c Look at the second picture and ask students to guess what the parents are going to say. Write any interesting ideas on the board.

d ▶ **CD3 T11** Tell students they are going to hear a dialogue between Kate and Ashley and their parents when they arrive home late. Students guess why Kate and Ashley are late. Play the recording while students listen to check their ideas.

TAPESCRIPT

Dad: Look at the time! It's 2.15 in the morning. And the police are bringing you home!

Ashley: Mum, Dad – we can explain.

Mum: What on earth happened?

Ashley: Well, we left the party at 12.15, like we said …

Kate: And on the way home we saw an accident.

Ashley: There was a woman on a bicycle, and a car hit her.

Kate: But the car didn't stop, and the woman was hurt …

Ashley: So we called an ambulance and we waited until it came …

Kate: We couldn't leave her. We had to wait with her.

Ashley: And the police came too, and they asked us some questions, and then they brought us home.

Mum: But isn't your phone working? Why didn't you answer the phone? Why didn't you phone us? You promised!

Kate: I tried to, Mum, but my battery was flat.

Dad: Well, why didn't you ask the police to call us?

Kate: Oh, I never thought of that, Dad. Actually, we were very upset, you know?

Dad: Yes, of course … Sorry. Is the woman OK?

Ashley: Yes, she is … and she thanked us for our help. She says she's going to take us all out for a meal when she's better!

Answers
Kate and Ashley saw an accident and waited with an injured woman until her ambulance came. Then they helped the police with their inquiries.

e ▶ **CD3 T11** Divide the class into pairs and ask students to order the sentences. Play the recording again while students check their answers.

Answers
1 They left the party.
2 They saw an accident.
3 They phoned for an ambulance.
4 They waited with the woman.
5 The ambulance came.
6 The police came and asked them questions.

7 Grammar

✳ *must/mustn't*

a Read through the example sentences with students. Ask students why Kate and Ashley's mum and dad asked them to do these things (*because they were important*). Now students read through the Rule box and the grammar table and complete the table. Check answers. To check understanding at this point give an example of your own and elicit a few more from students, e.g. *I must remember to go to the supermarket after school today. Maria, is there anything you must remember to do today?* etc.

Answers
Positive: must
Negative: mustn't

b Students read through the verbs in the box and look at the pictures. Go through the example with them. Students complete the exercise. Check answers.

LOOK!

Read through the examples in the Look! box with students. Offer some more examples of your own to clarify the rule.

Language note

Students may be confused by the different uses of *have to* and *must*. Explain that we use *must* when we are setting the obligation, e.g. *Mother: You must come home at 10 o'clock (because I say so)*. We use *have to* when we are referring to an obligation set by another person, e.g. *Child: I have to go home at 10 o'clock (because my mother says so)*. To clarify this further, set out some rules for students: *You must do your homework; You must arrive on time.* Elicit what they should say when they explain these rules to another person: *At school, we have to do homework; we have to arrive on time*, etc.

8 Pronunciation

See notes on page 155-6.

Culture in mind

9 Read and listen

If you set the background information as a homework research task ask students to tell the class what they have found out.

BACKGROUND INFORMATION

Reggae is a music genre first developed in Jamaica in the late 1960s. The term *reggae* describes a particular music style that originated following on the development of ska and rocksteady. Reggae is based on a rhythmic style characterised by regular beats on the off-beat, known as the *skank*. Reggae is normally slower than ska, and usually has accents on the first and third beat in each bar. Reggae song lyrics deal with many subjects, including religion, love, sexuality, peace, relationships, poverty, injustice and other social and political issues.

Jamaica is an island nation situated in the Caribbean Sea. It is about 145 km south of Cuba. Its indigenous Taíno inhabitants named the island *Xaymaca*, meaning the 'Land of Wood and Water'. It is part of the British Commonwealth.

Rhythm and blues (also known as **R&B**) is the name given to a genre of popular music, originally created by African Americans in the late 1940s and early 1950s. By the 1970s, the term 'rhythm and blues' was being used as a blanket term to describe soul and funk.

New Orleans is a major United States port city, the largest city in Louisiana and located on the Mississippi River. It is well known for being the birthplace of jazz and its annual Mardi Gras and other celebrations and festivals. The city is often referred to as the 'most unique' city in America.

Jimmy Cliff was born **James Chambers** on 1 April 1948 and is a Jamaican ska and reggae musician. He is best known among mainstream audiences for songs such as *Sittin' in Limbo*, *You Can Get It If You Really Want*, and for his cover of Cat Stevens' *Wild World* plus his cover of *I Can See Clearly Now*.

The Wailers was a reggae group from Kingston, Jamaica. They formed in 1963 and consisted of Junior Braithwaite, Beverley Kelso, Bunny Livingston (aka Bunny Wailer), Robert Nesta Marley (aka Bob Marley), Peter McIntosh and Cherry Smith. They were previously called The Teenagers, The Wailing Rudeboys, The Wailing Wailers, and finally The Wailers. The Wailers recorded groundbreaking reggae songs such as, *Simmer Down, Trenchtown Rock, Nice Time, Stir It Up, Get Up, Stand Up,* and many others. They broke up in 1974 and Bob Marley went on to international fame with Bob Marley & The Wailers.

Warm up

Books closed. To introduce the topic of music, tell students about the type of music you listen to and when you usually listen to music. Ask students what types of music they like to listen to and why. Make a list of the different types on the board. How do they find out about new music? Through the radio, internet, friends, family?

a Books open. Read through the instructions with students and ask them to answer the questions. Students compare their answers with a partner before feedback in open class. Have a vote to find out which is the most popular time to listen to music.

b ▶ **CD3 T14** Ask students if they have ever heard of reggae music. Read through the questions with students and check understanding of difficult vocabulary in the text: *heartbeat, equal rights; hippies*. Students compare their answers with a partner before feedback in open class. Read the text and listen to the recording.

> **Answers**
> 1 More than 50 years ago.
> 2 Rhythm and blues.
> 3 It is easier to sing and dance to.
> 4 He combined reggae music and the 'peace and love' ideas that the hippies of the 1960s believed in.
> 5 He played with Peter Tosh and Bunny Wailer in The Wailers.

10 Vocabulary

✱ Prepositions

a Students complete the sentences with the correct prepositions. All of the items appear in the text, but see if students can complete the exercise without looking back at the text. With weaker classes, you may like to write the prepositions randomly on the board for students to choose from. Allow them to compare answers with a partner before allowing them to look back at the text to check answers.

> **Answers**
> 2 of 3 to 4 in 5 from 6 into

b Read through the sentences with students and check understanding. Students circle the correct word. Students check answers in pairs before feedback in open class.

> **Answers**
> 2 hit 3 charts 4 lyrics 5 combination
> 6 equal

Vocabulary notebook

Encourage students to start a new section *Music* in their notebook and add any music-related vocabulary from this exercise. They should also add the prepositional phrases from Exercise 10a to a section called *Prepositions*.

11 Listen: a song

If you set the background information as a homework research task ask students to tell the class what they have found out.

> **BACKGROUND INFORMATION**
> **Jimmy Cliff:** see background information Unit 5 Exercise 9.

 **CD3 T15** Tell students they are going to listen to a song called *Wonderful World, Beautiful People*. Read through the words in the box with students,

paying attention to pronunciation. Ask students to guess how the words might be connected to the title. Play the recording while students listen and complete the lyrics with the words in the box. Let students compare their answers with a partner before checking in open class. Play the song again and encourage students to sing along.

TAPESCRIPT

See the song on page 41 of the Student's Book.

> **Answers**
> 1 pretty 2 secret 3 world 4 love 5 helping
> 6 free

12 Speak

Read through the questions and check understanding. Divide the class into pairs and give students a short time to discuss their answers to the questions. Circulate and help with difficult vocabulary as required. After discussion in pairs hold a class discussion and note any interesting ideas on the board.

13 Write

The planning for this exercise can be done in class and the writing can be set as homework.

Remind students how people in New York celebrate New Year (see Exercise 1). Explain that Jessie is from Scotland and has written this email. Students read through Jessie's email; check any problems. To remind students how to structure their reply, ask them to match each item to a paragraph in Jessie's email. Students then complete the exercise. Collect these in to mark or students can swap with a partner and the partner can correct their email.

Memo from Mario

Promises promises

1 Visualising a dialogue

▶ This activity relates to Exercise 2 on page 36. Write these questions up on the board or the IWB.

What does Amy look like?
How old is she?
What is she wearing?

What does Dad look like?
How old is he?
What is he wearing?
Where are they both?

▶ Play the dialogue once through. Ask the students if they want to hear it a second time. Explain to the students that they will be asked to answer the questions above and therefore will have to use their imagination to visualise the scene in the dialogue. It might be a good idea to get them to close their eyes while listening.

▶ Ask the students, working on their own, to write down their answers to the questions on the board or the IWB.

▶ Ask them to share their answers with a partner. Write the first three lines of the dialogue up on the board, as far as, *this year …*

▶ Ask each student to imagine being a film director deciding how to shoot this first part of the scene. Get the students to draw a simple sketch of what the eye of the camera should see during these opening exchanges.

▶ Ask the students to get up, move around and compare the first frame of their story-board with other students.

▶ Ask them to sit down again.

▶ Write the father's long speech, *Resolutions … to … new gym*.

▶ Ask the students to draw one or two of the next frames in the film.

▶ Ask for volunteers to come and re-draw their visualisations on the board.

▶ Now play the whole text twice through and ask the students to visualise what is happening as the words are said. This is best done with eyes closed.

> **RATIONALE**
> The idea of turning the students into cinéastes is to divert their conscious attention from the language and thus allow it to settle elegantly into their unconscious minds.
>
> It is also a way of making the dialogue more multi-sensory by drawing on the students' spatial intelligence.

2 Parent-child two way written role-play

▶ Once the students have worked on the dialogue in Exercise 6 ask them to re-organise themselves into closed seated groups of six.

▶ Each student needs a clean piece of paper.

▶ Ask them to listen to this text which you read slowly, with plenty of pauses:

You are a parent. Your 15 year-old child promised to be back from the party at midnight, 12.00am.

You look at your watch. It is half-past midnight. No teenager.

You make yourself a cup of tea.

You hear the church clock. DONG!. It strikes 1.00 am. Still no sign of your child.

You feel worried. You try to read a book.

The church clock … half past one … this is really too much …

What has happened to your teenager?

An accident? Are they all right?

DONG! DONG! … three minutes pass and you hear the door of the house open quietly …

▶ Tell the students that they are in role as the parent. Ask them to **write** what the parent says to the returning teenager on the piece of paper in front of them.

▶ Tell them to pass their piece of paper to the left.

▶ Each student now has the parental reaction. Now, in role as the teenager, they reply to 'their parent'.

▶ Each student passes the piece of paper back to the parent, who then responds in writing to what they say.

▶ Each student is in role first as parent and then as child, then as parent, then as child. If I am a student the person to my right is my parent and the person to my left is my child.

▶ Stop this writing activity just as the energy level peaks … don't let it drag on to a slow death.

▶ With the students sitting in the same groups of six, simultaneously ask people to read out their dialogues, each person reading their own part.

▶ Allow time for brief open class feedback on the activity.

> **RATIONALE**
> The teenager parent dialogue in Exercise 6 may well stir quite a lot of memories of isomorphic situations in teenagers. The activity above allows safe channeling of the emotions that may surround these memories. The nature of the activity forces the writers to see the teenager-parent situation from both sides.

6 What a brave person!

Unit overview

TOPIC: Bravery and heroes

TEXTS

Reading and listening: a text about a man saving another man's life
Listening and speaking: two people discussing levels of bravery in different jobs
Writing: a text about a book, film or TV programme where somebody was in a dangerous situation

SPEAKING AND FUNCTIONS

Discussing possible future activities
Describing a situation when you were brave

LANGUAGE

Grammar: first conditional; *when* and *if*
Vocabulary: adjectives of feeling
Pronunciation: Stress in conditional sentences
Everyday English: *Well done; not a big deal; and that's that; Go on!; I beg your pardon?; after all*

1 Read and listen

If you set the background information as a homework research task ask the students to tell the class what they have found out.

> **BACKGROUND INFORMATION**
> **New York:** see background information
> Unit 5 Exercise 1.

Warm up

Books closed. Write the word *hero* on the board. Divide the class into pairs and ask them to discuss what a hero is. Can they think of any heroes or heroic deeds, perhaps from the news, films or books? Circulate and help with vocabulary. When students have some ideas, carry on the discussion in open class.

a Books open. Ask students to describe the pictures and guess what the text is about. Students read the text quickly to find the answer. Tell students not to worry about the meaning of every word, but to concentrate on the task.

> **Answer**
> A man who saved another man in the New York subway.

b ▶ **CD3 T16** Read questions 1–5 with students. Explain the meaning of: *platform, track, on top of, carriages.* Play the recording while students read and listen to the text in order to answer the questions. Pause where appropriate to check comprehension and help with difficult vocabulary. Let students check answers with a partner before feedback in open class.

TAPESCRIPT

See the reading text on page 42 of the Student's Book.

> **Answers**
> 1 He was sick and he collapsed.
> 2 It was about half a metre deep.
> 3 Because the driver couldn't stop in time.
> 4 His daughters.
> 5 His blue hat got dirty.

c In pairs, students discuss the question. Encourage them to use some of the language from the text to help them express their opinions.

d Read through descriptions with students and check understanding. Students find words in the text. With weaker classes, you may like to write the answers on the board in random order for them to choose from. Check answers.

> **Answers**
> 1 collapsed   2 make a decision   3 clapped
> 4 injuries

e If you have ever been brave tell the class about it. If you haven't, you could invent a story or tell the story of a famous hero in cinema or literature. Encourage the class to tell stories of heroic things they have done or heard about.

2 Grammar

✶ First conditional

a Read the instructions with the class and ask them to try to match the sentence halves without referring to the text. Students then check the text on page 42 and change their answers if necessary. Check answers as a class.

> **Answers**
> 1 b If he tries to get up, the train will kill him.
> 2 a If he doesn't move, he'll be OK.

Ask students to look at the first half of each sentence and find one word which is in the present tense (positive or negative form) and one word which refers to the future in the second half of each sentence (*will*).

b Read the Rule box with the class. To check understanding at this point, give a few examples of your own, gapping one word in each half to elicit the tenses from students, e.g. *If you ... hard, you'll pass your English exam.* Students complete the grammar table. This will remind them of the full and short forms of *will / will not* which they should remember from Unit 3. Check answers.

> **Answers**
> 'll; won't

c Students read through the sentences. Go through the first item with them as an example and show them how the *If* clause doesn't always have to come at the start of a sentence (see Language note below). Students complete the exercise. Check answers.

> **Language note**
> Draw students' attention to the fact that the *If* clause doesn't always come first in the sentence. It can also come at the beginning of the second clause. When this happens the comma is omitted from the sentence.

> **Answers**
> 1 If I see Jane, I'll tell her. / I'll tell Jane if I see her.
> 2 If I'm late, my parents will be angry. / My parents will be angry if I'm late.
> 3 If I remember, I'll bring it to school tomorrow. / I'll bring it to school tomorrow if I remember.
> 4 If you come to the party, you'll meet my new friend, Jake. / You'll meet my new friend, Jake if you come to the party.
> 5 If it doesn't rain tomorrow, we'll go to the beach. / We'll go to the beach tomorrow if it doesn't rain.

d Students read through sentences 1–6. Go through the first sentence to make sure they have understood how the first conditional works. Students complete the exercise. Students compare answers in pairs. Then check answers as a class.

> **Answers**
> 2 won't meet; don't go out
> 3 will come; says
> 4 doesn't want; will eat
> 5 will be; hears
> 6 buy; won't have

> **Language notes**
> 1 Remind students we don't use *will/won't* in the *If* clause. We say *If I work hard, ...* NOT ~~If I will work hard~~ ...
> 2 Students may find it useful to think about how this structure works in their own language. They may want to translate some of the sentences in Exercises 2c and d, to show this.

Grammar notebook

Students should copy the completed table into their notebooks and any translations of sentences for Exercises 2c or d, or examples of their own which may help them remember this structure.

3 Speak

With books closed, divide the class into Student As and Bs and put As and Bs together into pairs. Student As turn to page 43 and Student Bs turn to page 73. Students read through the questions on their cards and check any problems with you. Student As should ask their questions first and then Student Bs answer. Students then swap roles with Student Bs asking their questions and As answering. Students should note down their partner's answers and then some can report them back to the class. If there are any interesting answers, ask the student(s) to give the class more details.

4 Pronunciation

See notes on page 156.

5 Grammar

* *when* and *if*

a Read through the questions and sentences 1 and 2 with students. Elicit that sentence 1 uses *when* in the first conditional and sentence 2 uses *if*. Ask students if they see any difference in meaning, and ask them the second question in their book. (*Sentence 1 means the speaker is sure he/she will see John.*) Put another example of your own on the board at this point to check they have understood the difference clearly.

b Students read through sentences 1–4. Go through the first item with them as an example, making sure they are clear about the speaker's certainty. Students complete the exercise. Check answers.

> **Answers**
> 2 If 3 if 4 when

6 Vocabulary
✱ Adjectives of feeling

a With books closed, write the adjectives *frightening* and *frightened* on the board. Ask students: *How do you think the man in the text on page 42 felt when he fell on to the track?* Elicit *frightened*. Then say: *He was frightened because the situation was … .* Elicit *frightening*. Ask students: *Have you ever felt frightened or been in a frightening situation?* Elicit some examples from the class. Students now open their books on page 44 and read Exercises 6a and b instructions.

b In pairs, students go through the text and find examples of *-ed* adjectives. Check answers. You could ask some students to put the adjectives into sentences of their own.

> **Answers**
> terrified; shocked; amazed

> **Language note**
>
> It may be useful to remind students of the spelling rules for *-ed* adjectives at this point.
>
> Noun/Verb + *-y*: Change the *-y* to *-i* and add *-ed*.
>
> Noun/Verb + other consonant: Add *-ed*.
>
> Students may also find it useful to know that the pronunciation of *-ed* adjectives is the same as past simple regular endings.

c ▶ **CD3 T18** Read through the adjectives in the box with students. Check they understand them all. Do the first item with students as an example. Remind them to look carefully at each picture and think about how the person is feeling. Once students have completed the exercise, play the recording. Students check their answers. Play the recording again, for students to repeat each word.

TAPESCRIPT/ANSWERS

A excited
B frightened
C tired
D annoyed
E interested
F bored

d Students read through sentences 1–8. Go through the example with students, reminding them again of when *-ed* and *-ing* adjectives are used. Students complete the exercise. Check answers.

> **Answers**
> 2 terrifying
> 3 frightened
> 4 exciting
> 5 interesting

> 6 shocked
> 7 annoyed
> 8 tiring

✱ **OPTIONAL ACTIVITY**

Students copy and complete the following table.

Verb	-ed adjective	-ing adjective
worry	worried	
frighten		frightening
interest		
excite		
	annoyed	
tire		
exhaust		exhausting

> **Answers**
> worrying; frightened; interested; interesting; excited; exciting; annoy; annoying; tired; tiring; exhausted

Vocabulary bank

Refer students to the vocabulary bank on page 66. Read through the words and phrases in open class and check understanding. For further practice of this vocabulary, divide the class into pairs and ask them to test each other, e.g. *A: What do you do when you are bored? B: I yawn and daydream.*

Vocabulary notebook

Students note down the new adjectives from this unit and add any more of their own as they come across them.

7 Listen and speak

a Read through the words in the boxes with students and check understanding. Explain that students must label each picture with a word from each box. Go through the example with them, showing them how the words have come from each box. Students complete the exercise. In pairs, students compare answers. Stronger students could check answers in a dictionary. Check answers as a class.

> **Answers**
> 2 airline pilot 3 dog trainer 4 window cleaner
> 5 steel worker

b Read through the list of nouns and verbs with students and check they understand them all. Stronger students can check any words they don't know in a dictionary. Go through the example with students, explaining that there is one verb and two nouns for each picture. Students complete the exercise. In pairs, students compare answers. Check answers as a class.

✱ OPTIONAL ACTIVITY

Students can write first conditional sentences about each picture using the nouns and verbs from Exercise 7b, e.g. Picture 1: *If the rope breaks, he'll fall.*

c Students read the instructions. Discuss their views on picture 1 and elicit a score for this from the class. In pairs or small groups, students discuss the other pictures and give them a score. Groups can give feedback to the class. Are there similar results?

d ▶ CD3 T19 Explain to students that they will hear two people talking about the pictures in Exercise 7a. They should listen carefully and write in the first column of their table the number of the picture being talked about. Go through the example with students, playing the recording and pausing it after the first answer. Play the recording again for students to complete column 1. Check answers.

TAPESCRIPT

Radio host: Welcome to *Two Great Minds*. With me in the studio are Claudia and Tony. A minute ago, we showed them three pictures and asked them to think about the question: How brave do you think these people are? Tony, you start.

Tony: OK, Claudia – what about this picture? What score did you give her?

Claudia: I gave her two. She knows what she's doing, and she's good with animals. I don't think she has to be that brave.

Tony: But some dogs are really dangerous! Look at those teeth!

Claudia: Hmm. I'm not sure. How many points did you give her?

Tony: Four.

Claudia: OK, we don't agree here. No big deal!

Tony: What did you give the next picture?

Claudia: Well, he has to be very brave. Look how high up he is. I can't imagine going up there on my own in that little lift. It's just a rope, really. If it breaks, he'll fall and die. I gave him five. What about you?

Tony: I only gave him three.

Claudia: Really? Why?

Tony: Well, if he stays in the lift, there's no danger. I think it looks more dangerous than it really is. Yeah, three points. So what about the third picture? I gave her three.

Claudia: Yeah, me too. These modern X-ray machines aren't really dangerous any more. They won't make her ill if she's careful.

Tony: That's right.

Claudia: So we both agree on three for her.

Tony: Yeah.

Radio host: Good, OK, thanks. Well, as usual, we also want to know what you people think, so please have a look at the photos – you can find them on our website, www.twogreatminds ...

e ▶ CD3 T19 Play the recording again for students to note down the scores Tony and Claudia give to each picture. Pause after the first score is given and go through the example in column 2 of the table. Continue playing the recording for students to complete the scores. Check answers.

✱ OPTIONAL ACTIVITY

Ask students to get into small groups and discuss their own reactions to Tony and Claudia's scores. Do they agree or not? Why/why not?

f Ask students to look at the example dialogue, and then to work in new pairs and discuss their own choices for Exercise 7c. Ask several pairs to give feedback to the class.

Photostory: Chicken

8 Read and listen

Warm up

Write these questions on the board: *What are you afraid of? What makes you nervous?*

Ask students to ask and answer the questions in pairs. Elicit feedback from one or two pairs of students.

Ask students what they remember about the previous episode of the photostory in Unit 4 and what happened (Jess and Joel went running. Jess had a pain in her stomach and Joel got tired).

a ▶ CD3 T20 Students look at the pictures and answer the questions. Play the recording while students read and listen to check their answers. If students ask questions about vocabulary, write the words on the board, but do not explain the meaning at this stage.

TAPESCRIPT

See the text on page 46 of the Student's Book.

b Students read through sentences 1–8. Go through the first item with them as an example if necessary. In pairs, students complete the exercise. Remind them to provide evidence from the text to back up true answers and ask them to correct the false ones. Check answers.

> **Answers**
> 2 T 3 F 4 F 5 T 6 T 7 T 8 T

9 Everyday English

a Ask students to locate the expressions 1 to 6 in the text on page 46 and decide who says them. Ask students to translate the expressions into their own language. Check answers.

> **Answers**
> 1 Miss Bradley 2 Debbie 3 Jess 4 Debbie
> 5 Debbie 6 Jess

b Ask students to read through the dialogues and complete the sentences. Go through the first sentence with them as an example if necessary.

> **Answers**
> 2 after all 3 I beg your pardon? 4 Well done
> 5 not a big deal 6 Go on

Vocabulary notebook

Encourage students to add the expressions to the *Everyday English* section in their vocabulary notebooks and, if necessary, to add translations to help them remember the meanings.

✱ OPTIONAL ACTIVITY

Weaker classes: Students can act out the dialogues. Make sure they are saying them with the correct intonation and expression and in the right context.

Stronger classes: Students can write their own short dialogues using the expressions. They can then act them out in front of the class. Make sure they are saying them with the correct intonation and expression and in the right context.

Discussion box

Weaker classes: Students can choose one question to discuss.

Stronger classes: In pairs or small groups, students go through the questions in the box and discuss them.

Monitor and help as necessary, encouraging students to express themselves in English and to use any vocabulary they have learned from the text. Ask pairs or groups to feedback to the class and discuss any interesting points further.

10 Improvisation

Divide the class into pairs. Tell students they are going to create a role play between Debbie and Pete. Read through the instructions with students. Give students two minutes to plan their dialogue. Circulate and help with vocabulary as necessary. Encourage students to use expressions from Exercise 9. Students practise their conversation in pairs. Listen to some of the best conversations in open class.

11 Team Spirit ⊙ DVD 1 Episode 6

Warm up

Look at the photo with students and ask them to describe what is happening. Ask them if they have ever broken anything expensive and what happened. Listen to some of their ideas in open class.

a In pairs students match the words and phrases. Allow them to use a dictionary if necessary. Check answers.

> **Answers**
> 2 g 3 a 4 h 5 d 6 e 7 f 8 b

b Divide the class into pairs. Ask students to imagine how Joel feels. Students work together to make up a story to explain the situation. Circulate and help with vocabulary as necessary. Listen to some of the best stories in open class. Play Episode 6 of the DVD while students watch and discover what really happened.

12 Write

The planning for this exercise can be done in class and the writing can be set as homework.

Warm up

As an introduction to the topic of reading books, ask students how often they read and what the last book they read was. Divide the class into pairs and ask them to recommend a book to their partner. Listen to some of their ideas in open class as feedback.

a Tell students that they are going to read a text in which a girl describes a book she has read. Students read the text and answer the questions. Check answers.

> **Answers**
> 1 *A Picture to Remember* by Sarah Scott-Malden.
> 2 A girl called Christina.
> 3 Outside a bank.
> 4 Because she saw the face of two bank robbers and they were after her.

UNIT 6   139   B

5 She went to the gym, went into the street and went to visit her friend Philippe in hospital.
6 The robbers crashed their car and were caught by the police.

b Read through the instructions in open class. Ask students to take some time to think of a book or TV programme, then make notes of the main points they want to include and plan the order in which to include them. Emphasise the importance of using verbs, adjectives and adverbs to make their text more interesting.

In a subsequent lesson, encourage students to read each other's descriptions and decide which they think is the best report.

13 Last but not least: more speaking

a Give students five minutes to work individually and answer the questions. Circulate and help with vocabulary as required. Make sure they make some notes to refer to later.

b When students have some ideas, ask them to draw a simple picture of the situation. You may like to draw an example of your own on the board to stress the fact that the drawing doesn't need to be of a high standard!

c Use your drawing on the board as an example and elicit ten *Yes/No* questions from students. Pay attention to word order and intonation patterns. Divide the class into pairs. Students take it in turns to look at each other's drawings and ask their questions. The goal is to understand their partner's picture and be able to describe what happened in detail. If some students finish more quickly than others, allow them to change partners and repeat the exercise.

d If some students have not managed to understand the picture, ask students to describe it. You may like to ask students with difficult pictures to hold up their picture for the whole class to see and guess what is happening.

✱ OPTIONAL ACTIVITY ─────────

Ask students to write their names on the pictures. Collect students' pictures and stick them up around the room. In pairs, students circulate and discuss each picture, trying to guess what is happening. If they don't understand, they should ask the artist to describe what is in the picture or give them clues and let them use their imagination. Monitor and check students are on task. When students have had time to look at a variety of pictures, ask them to vote on the best and funniest pictures.

Check your progress

1 Grammar

a 2 's going to help 3 'm not going to watch 4 Are ... going to wear 5 are going to visit 6 's not going to ride 7 're going to dance

b 2 must 3 must 4 mustn't 5 mustn't 6 must 7 mustn't

c 1 'll buy 2 comes; will be 3 will complain; make 4 have; 'll get

2 Vocabulary

a 2 take up 3 look up 4 told off 5 work out 6 set up 7 check ... out

b 1 tiring 2 excited; boring 3 frightening; frightened 4 interesting; bored

How did you do?

Check that students are marking their scores. Collect these in and check them as necessary and discuss any further work needed with specific students.

Memo from Mario

What a brave person!

Three dictation techniques

1 Whisper dictation

- One way of presenting 'Subway hero' (page 42) is by dictating parts of the text.
- Tell the students to close their books.
- Whisper-dictate the first two paragraphs of the text down to ... *frightening moment*.
- Tell the students to open their books and check for any errors they have made.

> **RATIONALE**
>
> The range of voice used in language teaching is not always as broad as it could be. Whisper dictation is one way of remedying this.
>
> Technically the sounds of a language whispered are different from when the same words are spoken, e.g. If you say aloud: *He hurried down the hallway clutching his hat.* And then whisper the same phrase ... did you notice how much more prominent the aspirated *h* sounds were?

2 Dictogloss

- Ask a tall student to come to the board or the IWB and dictate to them the first three lines of the third paragraph of 'Subway hero'. Ask the student to write the lines at the top of the board or the IWB.
- Explain to the group that you are going to read them three short sentences (from the 'Subway hero' text).
- Tell them to listen very carefully.
- As soon as you stop speaking they are to jot down all the key words they heard.
- Tell them not to write while you are speaking.
- Read the next three sentences from the text, from *The train is going* ... to ... *be OK*.
- Give the students time to write down keywords and compare them with their neighbours'.
- Tell them you will give them a second reading. They are to jot down more of what they hear.
- Read a second time.
- They write and compare.
- Now ask them to reconstruct the three sentences as accurately as they can.
- If you feel a third reading is necessary, let them have one.
- Ask a confident student to come to the board or the IWB without his paper and to reconstruct the text with the help of the whole group. Give no help; let the group process take its course.

- Ask a student at the back of the class to read the three sentences slowly and clearly from the text in the Student's Book so that any mistakes on the board can be corrected.

> **RATIONALE**
>
> This is a student-centred exercise in which <u>they</u> work and <u>you</u> observe. To my mind, dictogloss is a mixture of auditory memorization and guided composition. A rich activity. For the time taken by the activity your students have been making the first conditional patterns on their own without realising what they are doing.
>
> Dictogloss is one of the best ways I know of presenting a new structure as it forces focus on the forms to be assimilated.

3 Dictating too fast

- Choose the next section of the text and warn the class that you will be reading fast and they will have to write very fast to keep up. Books should be closed.
- Dictate at a pace that allows the fastest writers in the group to just keep up. If you go <u>too</u> fast students will give up, which is not your aim.
- Ask the students to work in groups of three and help each other with words they skipped during the dictation. After the frustration of the dictation there should now be a buzz of relieved cooperation, as people help each other.
- Students open their books and check what they have written.

> **RATIONALE**
>
> There are students in any group who find the pace set by the teacher too slow for them and they suffer in most of their lessons. In this activity they are stretched and then they are in position to help slower paced students. They come into their own and maybe we need more exercises for them.

Travellers' tales

Unit overview

TOPIC: Customs around the world; advice

TEXTS
Reading and listening: about UK culture
Reading: about a charitable footballer
Writing: an email giving advice to a visitor
Listening: a song: Willie Nelson *On the Road Again*

SPEAKING AND FUNCTIONS
Talking about problems and giving advice
Asking and answering questions
Giving opinions on a text

LANGUAGE
Grammar: *should/shouldn't*; *What's it like?*
Vocabulary: personality adjectives; adjectives
for expressing opinions
Pronunciation: Silent consonants

1 Read and listen

Warm up

Write *United Kingdom* on the board and ask
students what they know about life there. Do
they know any famous places or people from the
UK? Listen to their ideas and write any interesting
vocabulary on the board.

a Read through the words 1–6 in open class and
check understanding. You may need to explain
queue and *bump into*. Students match the words
with the pictures. Check answers.

> **Answers**
> 1 C 2 F 3 E 4 A 5 B 6 D

b ▶ **CD3 T21** Tell students they are going to listen
to two people talking about mistakes they made
when meeting people from other countries. Play
the recording while students take notes. Encourage
them to write down key words rather than trying
to write whole sentences. You could pause as
necessary to check understanding and clarify any
difficulties. Students answer the questions and
compare answers with a partner before feedback.

TAPESCRIPT
Speaker 1: I was a teacher for a long time in London,
and one time I worked with a group of students
from Qatar. They were really nice and polite

and one evening they asked me to go for dinner.
The dinner was at one of the student's houses.
And they cooked this fantastic meal – meat and
rice and everything. It was delicious. And I ate
everything on my plate. And then one of the
students put more rice and meat on my plate! So
I ate it all. And then he put more rice and meat
on my plate! And I didn't know what to do, so
I said: 'Thanks a lot but I don't want any more
food!' And they laughed and explained that in
their culture, if you eat everything on your plate
it means 'More please!', so if you <u>don't</u> want more
food, you should leave something on the plate.

Speaker 2: When I was in England one time, I met
some friendly people and one day they said:
'Come to our place for dinner. Friday at 8 o'clock!'
I was pleased, so on Friday I went to their house
but in my country, if someone says 8 o'clock,
you shouldn't arrive before 8.30 – and anyway,
in my country, no one has dinner before about
nine in the evening! So I went to their house at
about quarter to nine, rang the bell and my friend
looked surprised when she saw me. I went in and
there were five or six people at the dinner table,
all eating their ice cream! The dinner was over! It
was a bit embarrassing.

> **Answers**
> Speaker 1 went to dinner with students from
> Qatar and didn't leave any food on the plate.
> Speaker 2 arrived too late for dinner with
> English friends.

c Divide the class into pairs. Ask students if they
have ever made a similar mistake and ask them to
describe it to their partner. Give an example of
your own to get them started. For feedback, ask
individuals to describe their mistake to the class.

d Read through the questions and check
understanding. In pairs, students decide whether
the sentences are true or false. Encourage them to
discuss reasons for their answers.

e ▶ **CD3 T22** Play the recording while students
complete the exercise. Tell them to listen for reasons
for the answers. Let students compare answers with
a partner before feedback in open class.

TAPESCRIPT/ANSWERS
1 True. It is polite to say sorry when you bump into
  someone. Most people in the UK say sorry in this
  kind of situation even if it is not their fault.

2 False. In Britain, people usually stand in queues at bus stops or at ticket offices, and if you go to the front of the queue, people will think you are very rude.

3 False. Some people do this but others don't.

4 False. In the past, not many people in the UK kissed others when they met them for the first time. These days, more and more people kiss each other, but it's OK if you don't.

5 True. You shouldn't arrive early, and most people arrive on time or just five minutes late.

6 True. It is not polite to talk with your mouth full of food. But of course many people like talking during a meal, especially with their friends and families.

7 False. You should cover your mouth with your hand when you yawn, but not when you laugh.

8 False. If you're hungry and someone offers you food, just say 'Yes, please!'

Grammar

✳ should/shouldn't

a Quickly read through the example sentences with the class.

Books closed. Write the example sentences on the board, but with the target language gapped (should/shouldn't). Can they remember which words go in the spaces and what they mean? Ask students to quickly find more examples of *should* and *shouldn't* in the quiz on page 50 and underline them.

> **Answers**
> You should say 'Sorry'
> You should always take your shoes off ...
> You should always kiss someone ...
> ... you shouldn't arrive early
> You should always cover your mouth ...
> ... you should always say 'No, thank you' ...

Read the rule with the class. Make sure students are clear that we usually use *should/shouldn't* when we are giving advice to someone.

b Students complete the grammar table. Point out that *should* is a modal verb and explain that we don't need to add *do* or *does* to make questions or negatives. Ask them what other modal verbs they can think of (*can, will, must, might*, etc.).

> **Answers**
> Negative: shouldn't
> Short answers: should; shouldn't

c Students read through the verbs in the box and items 1–6. Go through the example. In pairs, students complete the exercise. Check answers by asking pairs to read one of their dialogues to the class.

> **Answers**
> 2 should watch
> 3 Should; go; shouldn't watch
> 4 should go
> 5 Should; wear; should wear
> 6 shouldn't go

Speak

Divide students into pairs.

Weaker classes: It might be an idea to let all the Student As read Student A's role card together in pairs, so that they can discuss 'their problem' and possible solutions. Student Bs can work together and do the same with 'their' problem (see Student's Book pages 51 and 73).

Stronger classes: You can write examples of some other ways of giving advice on the board, and encourage students to use these structures as well, e.g. *If I were you, I'd ... . Why don't you (talk to your parents)? What about (talking to your parents)?*

Student A works with Student B and they tell each other about the problem on their role card and give each other advice, using *should/shouldn't*.

Ask several pairs to demonstrate their dialogues to the class. Find out what everyone thinks of the advice they were given.

Vocabulary

✳ Personality adjectives

a ▶ **CD3 T23** Students read through the adjectives in the box. Play the recording for students to listen and repeat each adjective. Make sure students are stressing the words in the correct place.

TAPESCRIPT
1 kind
2 hard-working
3 polite
4 honest
5 organised
6 cheerful
7 relaxed
8 friendly

b In pairs, students complete the sentences with the adjectives in the box in Exercise 4a.

Weaker classes: Do the first two or three examples with the whole class first. This exercise should help them work out the meaning of the adjectives, so don't worry if they are new to the students.

Encourage students to use their dictionaries, if they have them, and to help each other.

c ▶ **CD3 T24**   Write the adjectives from Exercise 4a on the board. Students read through the adjectives in the box. Ask them if they can see any words which are similar to the adjectives in Exercise 4a (*dishonest, unfriendly, unkind, disorganised*).

Elicit from students that by adding the prefixes *dis-* and *un-* these adjectives are the opposites of the ones in Exercise 4a. Go through the first item with students and then students match the other adjectives to the pictures. Students check answers in pairs. Then play the recording for students to check or change their answers. Play the recording again, for students to repeat.

TAPESCRIPT/ANSWERS

A unkind	E unfriendly
B miserable	F nervous
C dishonest	G lazy
D rude	H disorganised

d   Remind students of the opposite adjectives they matched in Exercise 4c. Ask them to put them into the table. Students now go through the other adjectives in Exercise 4c and try to match them too.

e   Students read the sentences and complete them using their own ideas. Remind them to use adjectives.

> **Language note**
> Check students put the correct stress on the adjectives when a negative prefix is added: *happy – unhappy*.

Vocabulary bank

Refer students to the vocabulary bank on page 67. Read through the words and phrases in open class and check understanding. For further practice of this vocabulary, divide the class into pairs and ask them to describe people they know using the adjectives.

Vocabulary notebook

Students should note down the table of adjectives from Exercise 4d and add any new adjectives when they come across them.

5 Pronunciation

See notes on page 156.

6 Grammar

✴ *What's it like?*

a   Ask students: *What's the weather like today?* (*It's sunny, cloudy,* etc.) Then ask them: *What was the weather like yesterday?* (*It was sunny, cloudy,* etc.) Elicit the difference between the two questions (one is present, one is past).

Students now read through questions 1–5 and answers a–e. Go through the first item with them as an example. Students complete the exercise. Check answers.

b   Read the instructions with students and students complete the table.

> **Language note**
> Explain that when we use this question in the present tense singular we normally use the short form *What's it like?* NOT ~~*What is*~~ .

c   Students read through the dialogues. Go through the example with them. Ask them why the verb is *was* to check understanding. Students complete the exercise and compare answers in pairs. Ask pairs to read out their dialogues to the class.

Grammar notebook

Students should copy the completed table into their grammar notebooks. If necessary, they can add some example sentences or translate some.

7 Vocabulary

✴ Adjectives for expressing opinions

a ▶ **CD3 T27**   Put the column headings + *(positive)* and – *(negative)* on the board. Give students an example of your own to show the meaning of *brilliant* and *boring*. Elicit that *brilliant* is a positive adjective and *boring* is a negative adjective and write them under the relevant heading on the board.

Stronger classes: They can now classify the other adjectives in the box under the relevant headings.

Weaker classes: They may need more help with the meaning of each adjective so elicit some example sentences to show the meaning.

They can then classify the adjectives under the headings.

Students can compare answers in pairs. Ask students to come out and write the adjectives under the headings on the board. Then play the recording for students to listen and check. Play the recording again, for students to repeat.

TAPESCRIPT
boring, brilliant, interesting, attractive, fantastic, awful, cool, dull, ugly, dreadful

Answers
+: interesting, attractive, fantastic, cool
–: awful, dull, ugly, dreadful

Language note
Cool is used to express a positive opinion, colloquially, especially by young people to mean 'very good', e.g. *Her new trainers are really cool.* Cool can also be used about the weather, e.g. *It's rather cool for July.*

[b] Do the first item as an example with students. In pairs, students discuss which adjectives apply to the other items. Check answers.

Answers
1 interesting, boring, brilliant, fantastic, awful, dull, dreadful
2 boring, interesting, attractive, awful, dull, ugly, cool
3 boring, brilliant, interesting, fantastic, awful, dull, ugly, dreadful
4 boring, brilliant, fantastic, awful, cool, dull, dreadful
5 brilliant, fantastic, awful, cool, dull, dreadful

8 Speak

[a] Students read through the items in the box. Go through the example dialogue with them, eliciting another adjective to complete the second sentence. In pairs, students now ask and answer questions about the things in the box.

[b] Students work in different pairs and read through the situation. Give them time to think of possible questions and answers. Then in pairs, students ask and answer. Remind student B that one of his/her answers must be false.

Culture in mind

9 Read and listen

If you set the background information as a homework research task ask students to tell the class what they have found out.

BACKGROUND INFORMATION

Ecuador is a country in South America bordered by Colombia on the north, by Peru on the east and south, and by the Pacific Ocean to the west.

The Galápagos Islands are a group of volcanic islands distributed around the equator, 972 km west of Ecuador in the Pacific Ocean.

Chota Valley is a valley which runs east-west between the two ranges of the Andes.

Warm up
Books closed. Ask students to think of famous footballers in their country or worldwide. Write some names on the board and then write the following list: *house, car, clothes, holidays, girlfriend, free time*. In pairs, students discuss the lifestyle of a top footballer and talk about each of the categories: *What type of house does he have?* etc. Circulate and help with vocabulary. Listen to some of their ideas in open class. Ask students if they think footballers have difficult lives.

[a] Books open. Look at the photos with students and ask them to read through the text quickly to find answers to questions 1–3. Tell them not to worry about every word, but to concentrate on the task. Check answers.

Answers
1 Ulises de la Cruz
2 He is a professional football player.
3 Piquiucho in Ecuador

[b] ▶ **CD3 T28** Students read the text and listen to the recording to check their answers.

[c] Read through the instructions with the class and check understanding. Students read the text again and compare answers with a partner before feedback.

Answers
1 border 2 village 3 barefoot 4 World Cup
5 abroad 6 poverty

10 Speak

Read the questions with the class. In small groups, students discuss their answers. Get feedback from some individuals and write the most interesting ideas on the board.

11 Write

The planning for this exercise can be done in class and the writing can be set as homework.

a Look at the text and tell students it is an email giving advice about life in Britain. Read through the instructions with students. Students read the email and match the topics with the paragraphs.

Answers
a 3 b 2 c 1

b Ask students to work in pairs and make a list of useful tips for British tourists visiting their country. Encourage them to make notes of their ideas and write sentences using *should* and *shouldn't*.

c Tell students they are going to write an email to an English-speaking e-pal giving advice. Give them time to plan the layout of the email, using the email in Exercise 11a as an example. In a subsequent lesson, students read each other's emails and decide which gives the best advice.

Memo from Mario

Travellers' tales

Shoulds and should nots in the family

- Once you have done the grammar work on *should* and *shouldn't* suggested by the authors, do a brainstorm on home exhortations.

- Ask the students what things they are told to do and not to do by their parents, grandparents and older brothers and sisters.

- Have a student come to the front and write all the *shoulds* and *shouldn'ts* the whole class has talked about on the board or the IWB.

- You may often have to help students translate their home exhortations and prohibitions.

- Some may be in the form of proverbs.

- Ask different students round the class about the situations in which these things were said to them and by whom.

- Put the students into groups of three. Ask them to think ahead to when they may be parents.

- Ask them to write a list of six or seven *shoulds* and *shouldn'ts* for their future children.

- Ask the groups to join with another two groups to compare 'parental' notes.

> **RATIONALE**
> By drawing on family situations the attempt here is to endow this modal with its full power in the students' second language by drawing on the power of its equivalent/s in the mother tongue. A question we need to ask in teaching English as well as *how much?* is the question *how deep?* The syllabus tends to deal more with extent than with affective depth. From being an 'over there' linguistic code, English needs to become a 'right here inside me' language.

Crazy records

Unit overview

TOPIC: Record holders; sleeping and dreaming

TEXTS
Reading and listening: extracts from the Guinness Book of Records
Listening: an interview with someone who wants to break a record
Reading: a text about a record breaker
Writing: a letter or email about Los Angeles

SPEAKING AND FUNCTIONS
Asking and answering about past experiences

LANGUAGE
Grammar: present perfect + *ever/never*
Vocabulary: verb and noun pairs; expressions about sleep
Pronunciation: *have* and *has* in the present perfect
Everyday English: *Careful!; for a while; Tell you what; such good fun; By the way; Wait and see!*

1 Read and listen

If you set the background information as a homework research task ask students to tell the class what they have found out. If you have a copy or can get hold of a copy of the Guinness Book of Records it may be useful to bring it in for this lesson.

BACKGROUND INFORMATION

The Guinness Book of Records was first published in 1955 and the idea came from the director of the Irish brewing company, Guinness. It has been published annually ever since and today it holds the all-time sales record for a copyrighted book. There is a museum featuring a lot of the records from the books in Tennessee, USA.

Dian Fossey (born 16 January 1932 in San Francisco, California, died 26 December 1985, Virunga Mountains, Rwanda) was an American zoologist who completed an extended study of gorilla groups over a period of 18 years. She observed them daily for years in the mountain forests of Rwanda.

Photographs showing the gorilla 'Peanuts' touching Fossey's hand depicted the first recorded peaceful contact between a human being and a wild gorilla.

Fossey's book *Gorillas in the Mist* was made into a film starring Sigourney Weaver.

Miniature Wonderland (German: *Miniatur-Wunderland*) is a model railway attraction in Hamburg, Germany and the largest of its kind in the world. As of January 2008, the railway consists of 11,000 metres (36,089 ft) of track, divided into five sections: southern Germany, Hamburg and the coast, America, Scandinavia and Switzerland.

The exhibit includes 900 trains made up of 12,000 carriages; 300,000 lights, 200,000 trees and 200,000 human figures.

Warm up

Ask students if they have ever seen the *Guinness Book of Records*. Perhaps they can tell you about an interesting record they know about, e.g. the tallest person in the world, etc.

a Students read through the texts quickly. Check any problems. If necessary, go through the first one with them as an example. Students then match each paragraph with a picture. Students can compare answers in pairs. Check answers.

> **Answers**
> A 3; B 4; C 1; D 2

b ▶ **CD3 T29** Explain that one of the records 1–4 in the text is NOT true. Play the recording for students to read and listen. In pairs or small groups, students give their ideas about which record is not true and give their reasons.

TAPESCRIPT
See the reading text on page 56 of the Student's Book.

> **Answer**
> 4 (the motorcycle is 3.4 m tall. 5 m long and weighs about 3 tons)

c Divide the class into small groups and ask them to discuss the records. Listen to some of their ideas in open class.

2 Grammar

✳ Present perfect + *ever/never*

a Read the sentences with students. Ask them what they notice about this tense (it uses *has/have*). Read through the Rule box with students and then ask them to complete it. Point out that the use of *ever* here means 'at any time in your life' and that *never* means 'at no time in your life'.

Students then look at the grammar table and complete it. Check answers. To check understanding at this point, ask a student a question of your own and elicit their response. The student can then choose another student and ask the question. Continue like this until you are sure students are confident using this structure, e.g.

T: *Alberto, have you ever seen a tiger?*
S1: *Yes, I have. / No, I haven't.*
S1: *Silvia, have you ever been to France?*
S2: *Yes, I have. / No, I haven't.*

Language notes

1 Explain that *ever* is used in questions and *never* is used in negative statements. Students should note their positions: *ever* is positioned between the subject pronoun and the past participle in questions and *never* is positioned after the *have/has* and before the past participle.

2 Remind students that *it's* can mean *it is* or *it has*. They should read the whole sentence and work out from the context which *it's* is being used.

b Put the headings *Base form* and *Past participle* on the board. Read through the list of base forms with students and go through the example with them. Elicit and write on the board any other irregular past participles students know. Using the Irregular verbs list on page 74, students complete the exercise. They can compare answers in pairs before a whole class check. To check students have understood the past participles, call out a few base forms (with irregular past participles) and ask students to give you the irregular past participles.

LOOK!

Students may be confused by the difference between *has gone* and *has been*. Look at the examples and explanations in the Look! box with students. Encourage them to translate the sentences, as they may express this differently in their own language.

c Students read through sentences 1–5. Go through the example with them, reminding them of the position of *never*. Students complete the exercise. Remind them to use short forms where possible. Students can compare answers in pairs, then check answers with the whole class.

Grammar notebook

Remind students to make a note of these irregular past participles and to note down any more as they come across them.

 ## 3 Pronunciation

See notes on page 156.

 ## 4 Speak

a Read through the prompts with students and explain that they have to make dialogues, using the prompts. Do the first one in open class as an example.

Divide students into pairs and ask them to take turns to ask and answer questions. Monitor them as they work. At the end of the activity, ask several pairs to demonstrate their dialogues to the class.

b In pairs or small groups, students make up more questions for each other with the verbs given. Ask them to demonstrate their questions to the class.

 ## 5 Vocabulary

✱ Verb and noun pairs

a Read through the example with students. Ask students to match the verbs with the nouns. Students compare answers in pairs. Check answers.

b Students read through sentences 1–5. Do the first item with them as an example, if necessary. Remind students to look at the context of each sentence and to check the verb form they need. Students complete the exercise. Check answers.

c Students read through sentences 1–6. Do the first item with them as an example, if necessary.

Answers

2 having a shower	4 make dinner
3 tells stories	5 spend time
6 taking an exam	

✳ OPTIONAL ACTIVITY

Stronger classes: They can think of their own gapped sentences using these verb and noun pairs and give them to a partner to fill in the gaps.

Vocabulary bank

Refer students to the vocabulary bank on page 67. Read through the words and phrases in open class and check understanding. For further practice of the vocabulary, divide the class into pairs and ask them to test each other by saying the second part of the phrase for their partner to complete, e.g. *A: a mess B: to make a mess.*

Vocabulary notebook

Remind students to copy down these expressions in their vocabulary notebooks. They can translate them into their own language if necessary or note down some examples to help them remember them.

6 Read

a Students read the instructions and match the pictures to the activities. Check answers.

Answers
A 3; B 4; C 1; D 5; E 2

✳ OPTIONAL ACTIVITY

Before asking students to read the text, ask them if they can do the activities in Exercise 6a and how long they think they could do them for.

b Tell students that they are going to read a text about a man called Furman who has broken an incredible number of records. Pre-teach *holder, raw, pogo stick.* Students read the text silently and answer the question. If you have a weak class, you may prefer to read the text aloud with the class.

Answer
Skipping

c Students read the text again and find answers to the questions.

Weaker classes: Read through the text with the class, pausing where necessary to check comprehension and help with any difficult vocabulary. Students answer the questions and compare answers with a partner before feedback.

Answers
1 203 2 103 kilometres 3 less than an hour

✳ OPTIONAL ACTIVITY

If you have a competitive class, divide them into small groups and ask them to compete against one another to break the following records. Write this list on the board:
Saying the alphabet in English Record: 45 seconds
Writing five words beginning with 'b' (this can be substituted with other letters) Record: 1 minute
Writing five words ending in 'g' Record: 1 minute

In their groups, students compete to see if they can break the records. When they have a champion, hold a competition in class. With strong classes, you could hold a competition for saying the alphabet backwards!

7 Listen

Warm up

Write the following questions on the board:
How often do you eat something?
How long do you sleep every day?
How much time do you spend sitting down every day?

In open class, listen to students' answers. You can find the class record holder for each activity.

a In pairs, students decide which of the activities would be the most difficult. Ask them to think of reasons why each one would be difficult. Listen to some of their ideas in open class.

b In open class, students discuss what they think the world record is for not sleeping.

c ▶ CD3 T31 Tell students they are going to listen to a conversation between two teenagers in which they discuss record-breaking. Play the recording while students check their answer to Exercise 7b. Encourage them not to worry about every difficult word, but to concentrate on the task.

TAPESCRIPT

Matthew: Hey Grace. Here's your magazine back – thanks.

Grace: Oh, thanks Matthew. Hey, did you read that thing about the man breaking records? What was his name? Furman or something?

Matthew: Yes, I did. Brilliant! 24 hours pushing a car! And three records in one day – incredible.

Grace: Incredible? I think he's mad.

Matthew: Yeah, well, perhaps he is – but he's in the *Guinness Book of World Records*, eh? And do you know, ... ?

Grace: What?

Matthew: Well, I'm thinking, if <u>he</u> can be in the *Book of World Records*, why not <u>me</u>?

Grace: You? Come on Matthew – you must be crazy.

Matthew: No, seriously.

Grace: OK then – tell me. What are you going to do? What record is the great Matthew Smith going to break?

Matthew: Well, I've given this some thought – and I think I want to break the record for not sleeping.

Grace: Not sleeping? Matthew, you fall asleep after 30 minutes at school.

Matthew: You <u>think</u> I'm asleep in the lessons, but I'm not. I'm awake.

Grace: And looking out the window, daydreaming.

Matthew: OK, <u>that's</u> true. I daydream a lot in lessons. And one of my daydreams is about being in *The Guinness Book of World Records*.

Grace: OK – you're going to break the record for staying awake. What's the world record now?

Matthew: Erm ... well, it's 11 days.

Grace: What?!?!

Matthew: Yeah, 11 days. An American guy. In 1965.

Grace: 1965!? You mean, no one has broken the record since 1965?

Matthew: That's right. The record is still 11 days. 11 days without going to sleep.

Grace: And this American guy in 1965 – how was he after 11 days?

Matthew: Well, after four days he thought he was a famous footballer ...

Grace: Uh huh ...

Matthew: ... and he started to forget things. But he went to sleep for 14 hours and then he was fine.

Grace: No, no, no – I can't believe that. I mean, if you don't go to sleep for 11 days, it must be bad for you. I mean, think about it. If you don't sleep for one night, how do you feel in the morning?

Matthew: Not very good. Well, awful, in fact.

Grace: So, after 12 days, how are you going to feel?

Matthew: Yeah, perhaps you're right. Perhaps I'll think of something else. Another record that I can break.

Grace: I know! How about breaking the world record for stupid ideas?

Matthew: Oh, thanks Grace – it's always good to talk to you ...

> **Answer**
> 11 days

d ▶ **CD3 T31** Read through the questions with students and check understanding. Play the recording while students listen and answer the questions. Pause as necessary to check comprehension and clarify difficult new vocabulary. Allow students to compare answers with a partner before feedback.

> **Answers**
> 1 An article about a man breaking records.
> 2 She thinks he is crazy.
> 3 He falls asleep.
> 4 He says he daydreams about being in *The Guinness Book of Records*.
> 5 In 1965
> 6 14 hours

8 Vocabulary

✳ Expressions about sleep

a ▶ **CD3 T32** Read the examples and instructions with the class. Go through the example, making sure students remember that it is the opposite they are looking for. Students match the opposites. Play the recording for students to listen and check their answers. Play the recording again for students to repeat the words.

TAPESCRIPT/ANSWERS

1	to go to bed	c	to get up
2	to go to sleep	a	to wake up
3	to be asleep	b	to be awake

b Students work in pairs to discuss the phrases, before giving their answers.

> **Answers**
> Dreaming: experiencing mental images while you are asleep.
> Daydreaming: having pleasant thoughts while you are awake.

c Students read through sentences 1–7. Go through the example with students, reminding them to look at the context of the sentence to help them work out which verb is needed and which form it is needed in. Students complete the sentences. Check answers.

> **Answers**
> 2 go to sleep 3 dreamed/dreamt 4 is asleep
> 5 was awake 6 woke up; got up
> 7 daydreams

Vocabulary notebook

This would be a good time to refer students to their vocabulary notebooks. Students can start a section called *Sleeping and waking* and note down any new expressions. They may find it useful to illustrate some of them or translate them into their own language.

9 Speak

a Read through the sentences with students. Students complete the sentences without looking back to the previous exercise if possible. Check answers.

b Students work in pairs and take turns to ask and answer the questions. Ask several pairs to report their answers to the rest of the class. Find out if anyone has the same answers.

Photostory: What's the next thing?

10 Read and listen

Warm up

Ask students what they remember about the previous episode of the photostory in Unit 6 and what happened (Jess and Pete called Debbie a chicken because she didn't want to give a talk at an old people's home. Debbie decided to give the talk after all).

a ▶ **CD3 T33** Ask students to read the questions and predict the answers but do not comment at this stage. Play the recording while students read and check their predictions. Tell students to underline the answers in the dialogue. Check answers in open class. If students ask questions about vocabulary, write the words on the board, but do not comment at this stage.

TAPESCRIPT

See the text on page 60 of the Student's Book.

b Read through the sentences. Students read the text again and match the beginning and endings. Students then work with a partner to put the sentences in the correct order. Check answers.

11 Everyday English

a Read through the expressions from the dialogue with students. Do the first item as an example. Ask students if they can remember (without looking back) who said this (Debbie). Students complete the exercise, only looking back at the dialogue if they need to. Ask students to translate the expressions into their own languages. Is the translation always

literal or do they use other words to express the same idea? Check answers.

b Students read the dialogues and then complete them with the expressions from Exercise 11a. Go through the first item as an example if necessary. Check answers.

★ OPTIONAL ACTIVITY

Weaker classes: Students can act out the dialogues. Make sure they are saying them with the correct intonation and expression and in the right context.

Stronger classes: Students can write their own short dialogues using the expressions. They can then act them out in front of the class. Make sure they are saying them with the correct intonation and expression and in the right context.

Discussion box

Weaker classes: Students can choose one question to discuss.

Stronger classes: In pairs or small groups, students go through the questions in the box and discuss them.

Monitor and help as necessary, encouraging students to express themselves in English and to use any vocabulary they have learned from the text. Ask pairs or groups to feedback to the class and discuss any interesting points further.

12 Improvisation

Divide the class into pairs. Tell students they are going to create a role play between Debbie and Joel. Read through the instructions with students. Give students two minutes to plan their dialogue. Circulate and help with vocabulary as necessary. Encourage students to use expressions from Exercise 11. Students practise their conversation in pairs. Listen to some of the best conversations in open class.

13 Team Spirit ⊙ DVD 1 Episode 7

Warm up

Give students your opinion on your abilities as a dancer. Tell them about the last time you danced and how you felt about it. In pairs ask students how often they dance and if they think they are good dancers or not. How many different dances do the class know how to do? Listen to some of their ideas in open class and encourage conversation on the topic.

a Look at the pictures with students and ask them what type of dancing they see in picture 1 (*line dancing*)

b Ask students to predict the answers to the questions.

c Play Episode 7 of the DVD while students check their predictions in 13b.

14 Write

a Students can do the preparation in class, and complete the writing at home.

Students read the letter and answer the question.

Answers

She asks:
- about the family her friend is staying with
- about things her friend has done in Los Angeles
- about people her friend has met
- if her friend has visited Hollywood
- if her friend has seen any film stars

---

b Remind students about the form for a personal letter or email. If students need help, ask them to look back through the book and find models of emails. Ask students to suggest ideas to answer the questions, and write them on the board.

Read through the suggested beginning for the letter or email. Students write their letters or emails at home. When they have finished, ask them to 'send' their work to a classmate to read.

15 Last but not least: more speaking

Warm up

Write the following jumbled sentence on the board: *been Paris, I've to never go but I want really to there go.*

Elicit the correct sentence from students (*I've never been to Paris, but I really want to go there.*). Refer students back to Exercise 2 and check their understanding of how the present perfect is used.

a Look at the pictures with students and ask them to describe what they see. Using the pictures to help with ideas, students complete sentences 1–4 so that they are true for them. You may like to give some examples of your own to get them started. Circulate and help with any difficulties.

b Read through the sample dialogue in open class. Pay attention to the way questions are asked to continue the conversation. Divide the class into pairs or small groups. Students tell each other about their sentences and ask each other to give reasons. Listen to some of the dialogues in open class and encourage other students to ask questions.

Check your progress

1 Grammar

a 2 should 3 should 4 should; shouldn't
5 shouldn't 6 Should

b 2 My brother has never studied a foreign language.
3 My parents have never flown in a plane.
4 I have never got 100% in a test.
5 Richard has never eaten frogs' legs.
6 Has your teacher ever shouted at you?
7 Have you ever spoken to a British person?
8 Have your parents ever won a competition?

2 Vocabulary

a 2 unkind 3 disorganised 4 miserable
5 unfriendly 6 impolite 7 lazy 8 nervous

b 2 raise 3 telling 4 build 5 have 6 spends 7 do

How did you do?

Check that students are marking their scores. Collect these in and check them as necessary and discuss any further work needed with specific students.

Memo from Mario

Crazy records

Two vocabulary revision techniques

▶ The two techniques proposed here will work well with any set of 20–30 words or collocations you want your students to revise. These could come from a given unit or from different parts of the book.

1 Categorisation

▶ Tell the students to work on their own and decide on categories into which they can fit these words.

▶ The categories can be of any sort apart from grammatical.

▶ There must be at least two categories and less categories than words.

▶ Four to six is often a good number.

▶ Tell the students to give each of their categories a category heading.

▶ Give the students an example, suppose the words are:

tiger

motor cycle

model train

raise money

toothpick

to swim

record book

▶ Possible categories might be:

Animal	vehicles	things people do	things people have
tiger	model train	swim	record book
	motor cycle	raise money	toothpick

▶ Give the students the set of words you want them to categorise and ask them to work on this in pairs.

▶ Go round helping them with words they have forgotten the meaning of.

▶ Go round helping them to find the category headings in English.

▶ Now, put the students into groups of six, three pairs together, so they share their, probably, quite different ways of categorising the words and phrases.

RATIONALE

In creating their categories, the students are thinking about, speaking and writing the words and thus enriching the connections in their brains that carry these words.

All this gives a boost to the students' long term memorisation process.

Acknowledgement

We owe this technique to Caleb Gattegno, originator of the Silent Way.

2 Placing words in my house

▶ Ask each student to draw a ground plan of their flat or of one floor of their house.

▶ Give them the words you want them to review.

▶ Tell them to place each in what they feel is an appropriate place in their house.

▶ Do the exercise yourself on a large poster-sized piece of paper or card.

▶ When the students have placed most of their words, put up your own ground plan on the board or wall and explain to them why you have put the words you have where you have.

▶ So you might have put *toothpick* on the kitchen table and *raise money* by the phone as you do a lot of phone charity work.

▶ Ask several students to explain to the class where they have put certain words and why.

▶ Put the students into groups of four to compare their placing of the words.

RATIONALE

Placing words in a familiar space is a memory technique that goes back to the Ancient Greeks. It strongly appeals to people with a good spatial intelligence.

When students have to revise vocabulary for a test or exam both the categorised words and the 'housed' words are much more stimulating to the mind than the normal bilingual lists.

The more students use these two activities the richer the result. These are not one-off techniques.

Pronunciation

Unit 2 Exercise 8

✱ /θ/ (think) and /ð/ (that)

a ▶ **CD2 T35** Write the words *think* and *that* on the board and drill the pronunciation of each a few times. Explain that one is voiced (*that*) and the other unvoiced (*think*), and elicit which is which. Divide the class into two and ask half the class to say *think* and the other *that*. Can they hear the difference? Students doing the voiced sound may find it useful to put their hand to their throat and feel the vibration. Swap sounds after a few minutes.

Students read through the words. Play the recording for students to listen and repeat.

TAPESCRIPT

1 think, three, month, something, toothache
2 that, those, with, brother, sunbathing

b ▶ **CD2 T36** Go through the first item as an example without the recording. Make sure students are clear about which sound to underline and which to circle.

Weaker classes: This can be done in two parts: first they listen for the /θ/ sound and underline it, then they listen for the /ð/ sound and circle it.

Play the recording for students to listen and underline/circle. Play the recording again, pausing for students to repeat.

TAPESCRIPT/ANSWERS

1 Give me (th)ose <u>th</u>ings.
2 (Th)ere's no<u>th</u>ing in my mou<u>th</u>.
3 I <u>th</u>ink it's <u>Th</u>ursday.

───── ✱ OPTIONAL ACTIVITY ─────

Stronger classes: They can think of more words themselves. Put them on the board and drill them.
Weaker classes: Give them a few more words to work out which sound it is and practise them. For example:
/ð/: *brother, this, those, these, sunbathing*
/θ/: *through, something*

Unit 3 Exercise 3

✱ 'll

▶ **CD2 T40** Ask students to read through sentences 1–4. Tell students that they are going to listen to the sentence pairs. Explain that in each sentence a there is a verb without 'll and in sentence b, the contraction of *will* ('ll) is heard. Read the first two sentences aloud yourself, if necessary, for students to hear the difference.

Play the recording. Students say whether they hear sentence a or b in each pair. Check answers.

TAPESCRIPT/ANSWERS

1 I'll ask the teacher.
2 They go to school early.
3 We'll have a lot of work to do.
4 I'll go to London by train.

Stronger classes: They can think of their own sentences in the style of Exercise 3 and work with a partner to guess which ones they are saying.

Unit 4 Exercise 6

✱ /əʊ/ (go)

a ▶ **CD3 T3** Drill the word *go* a few times and check students are clear how it is pronounced. If students have problems with this sound, show them how to make their lips very round as in the English exclamation *Oh!* and practise a few more times. Play the recording, for students to repeat each word.

TAPESCRIPT

show, no, homework, clothes, boat, snow

b ▶ **CD3 T4** Students read through sentences 1–4. Explain that they will listen to the recording and they must underline the /əʊ/ sound in each sentence where it occurs. Do the first item as an example aloud.

TAPESCRIPT/ANSWERS

1 She was the <u>o</u>nly person who survived.
2 She walked sl<u>o</u>wly along the river.
3 The plane expl<u>o</u>ded.
4 When she w<u>o</u>ke up, she was al<u>o</u>ne.

Unit 5 Exercise 8

✱ must and mustn't

a ▶ **CD3 T12** Read out the first sentence, making sure that the stress on *must* is clear. Ask students which word was stressed in the sentence (*must*). Read through the instructions and the other sentences with students. Play the recording. Play the recording again, for students to repeat.

TAPESCRIPT

1 I must go to the post office later.
2 You <u>must</u> work harder.
3 You <u>must</u> come to my party!

> **Answers**
> Sentences 2 and 3. Because it is important that these things are done.

b ▶ **CD3 T13** Drill the pronunciation of *mustn't* /mʌsənt/ a few times. Play the recording for students to listen and repeat.

TAPESCRIPT

1   You mustn't eat that!

2   We mustn't forget.

3   You mustn't drive too fast.

c In pairs, students take turns to read the sentences to each other and check their pronunciation. Monitor and drill *must/mustn't* if more practice is necessary. Play the recording again for students to listen and check their pronunciation.

Unit 6 Exercise 4

✱ **Stress in conditional sentences**

a ▶ **CD3 T17** Students read through sentences 1–5. Read the first sentence aloud as an example, putting extra stress on the underlined words. Check students can hear the stressed words and understand which parts of conditional sentences are stressed. Play the recording. Students mark the stressed words in the sentences. Check answers.

TAPESCRIPT

1   If it <u>rains</u>, I <u>won't go</u> to the <u>beach</u>.

2   We <u>won't pass</u> the <u>test</u> if we <u>don't work hard</u>.

3   I'll <u>give</u> him the <u>card</u> if I <u>see</u> him.

4   If you <u>decide</u> to <u>come</u>, I'll <u>meet</u> you at the <u>cinema</u>.

5   She <u>won't arrive</u> on <u>time</u> if she <u>misses</u> the <u>train</u>.

b Play the recording again, for students to listen and repeat.

✱ **OPTIONAL ACTIVITY**

Working in small groups (of three or four), students make a chain of first conditional sentences. Each group is given the start of a sentence and the first student completes it. Student 2 must then take the second part of Student 1's sentence and make a new first conditional sentence, e.g.

S1: If it rains this weekend, I'll go to my friend's house.

S2: If I go to my friend's house, I'll listen to some CDs.

S3: If I listen to some CDs, I'll dance.

S4: If I dance, I'll get tired.

S1: If I get tired, I'll go home and go to bed!

Unit 7 Exercise 5

✱ **Silent consonants**

a ▶ **CD3 T25** Students read through words 1–7. Do the example with them. Play the recording for students to listen and repeat. Students then underline the silent consonants in each word. Check answers.

TAPESCRIPT/ANSWERS

1 <u>h</u>onest   2 shoul<u>d</u>   3 sc<u>h</u>ool   4 <u>w</u>rite
5 clim<u>b</u>   6 <u>k</u>now   7 t<u>w</u>o

b ▶ **CD3 T26** **Stronger classes:** They can underline the silent consonant in words 1–6 without listening first.

Weaker classes: Play the recording, pausing after each word for them to underline the silent consonant.

Play the recording again for students to check their answers, then play it again for students to repeat.

TAPESCRIPT/ANSWERS

1 shoul<u>d</u>n't   2 w<u>r</u>ong   3 foreig<u>n</u>   4 lis<u>t</u>en
5 is<u>l</u>and   6 fas<u>c</u>inating

✱ **OPTIONAL ACTIVITY**

Ask students to think of as many more words as they can with silent letters.

Example answers
knife, autumn, often, hour, science

Unit 8 Exercise 3

✱ *have* and *has* in the present perfect

▶ **CD3 T30** Read through the example dialogues with students. Play the recording and ask students to listen carefully and note down what they think the difference is between the pronunciation of *have* and *has* in each exchange. Play the recording again for students to listen and repeat.

TAPESCRIPT

A: Have you <u>ever</u> <u>driven</u> a <u>car</u>?

B: <u>Yes</u>, I <u>have</u>.

A: Has she <u>ever</u> studied a <u>foreign</u> <u>language</u>?

B: <u>Yes</u>, she <u>has</u>.

Answer
In each dialogue, the first one is unstressed, the second one is stressed.

Project 1

A poster about the future

Divide the class into groups of about four or five.

1 Brainstorm

a Read through the instructions as a class and look at the example topics. Each group decides on a topic. Give them a few minutes to do this and monitor the discussions, making sure each student has a chance to voice their opinion.

b Students now take a few minutes to decide how far into the future they are going to look. Give them a few minutes to do this, making sure each member of the group is happy with the decision.

c Read through the instructions and example questions with students. It is a good idea here to encourage students to include open questions which will require more than a *yes/no* answer. If necessary, answer a few of the example questions to highlight this point. Students complete this part of the activity in class.

2 Make the poster

a This part of the project can be set for homework. As a class, brainstorm ideas for finding visuals, website addresses, magazines, comics, etc. Students should bring in their visuals to the next class.

b Students look at the pictures the groups have collected and select a few to illustrate their poster. The groups must agree on the visuals. Students work in their groups and write predictions about each picture. This should be done in their notebooks or on rough paper. When students are satisfied that their predictions are written correctly and grammatically, they can transfer them to the poster.

c Supply each group with a large sheet of paper, and sticky tape or glue for them to start making their posters. They should write the title at the top.

d Students now write their personal opinions of the predictions. If they have written e.g. *Robots will do the housework in most people's homes*, ask them to write their opinions of this. Will they miss doing the housework themselves? Students can check their texts in their groups before deciding on final versions and sticking them onto their poster.

3 Presentation

Each group should prepare a short presentation to explain their poster to the rest of the class. Encourage other groups to ask questions. Posters can then be displayed on the classroom walls.

Project 2

A talk on an event that happened this year

1 Listen

▶ **CD3 T34** Ask students to predict what one of the stories is about. Play the recording. Check answers.

TAPESCRIPT

Speaker 1: One really sad thing that happened this year was that my dog died. She was called Mitzi and I really miss her. She was 14 years old – that's old for a dog – and we got her when I was very young, so we sort of grew up together. She died in April this year. We knew she wasn't very well and then …

Speaker 2: I want to talk about the fire that broke out in our town earlier this year. It happened two months ago. The fire started in the shoe shop in Miller Street, early in the evening. We first realised something was wrong when my mother noticed a lot of smoke outside, and then we heard the fire engines …

Speaker 3: Football is the most important thing in my life, and the best thing that happened this year was when Chievo won the European Cup. The Flying Donkeys! It was brilliant. The final was on 26 May and they played against Manchester United at the Bernabeu Stadium in Madrid. My friends and I watched the match on television and …

> **Answers**
> 1 Someone's dog died.
> 2 A fire in a town.
> 3 The football team, Chievo, won the European Cup.

2 Choose a topic

Read through the instructions with the class. Give them some time to think about a topic.

3 Plan

a Read through the questions with the class.

b Students work on their own to make a list of important words for their topic. Students make notes on small cards they can look at as they speak.

c For homework, they should collect visuals or music, etc. to make their presentation really interesting.

d Using their cards and visuals, students quietly practise their talk in class. Monitor and help.

4 Give the talk

Divide the class into small groups. Students give their talk to the others in their group.

Get it right! key

Unit 2: Present continuous for future arrangements

2 's arriving   3 're staying   4 're going
5 are driving   6 're returning   7 we're going

Unit 3: *will/won't*

a 2 will be   3 'll pass   4 'll look   5 won't
remember   6 'll be   7 won't sleep
8 'll stay   9 will give   10 won't be
11 won't stay

b Students' own answers

Unit 4: *too* + adjective

2 too   3 very   4 too   5 too

Unit 4: Adverbs

2 good – well   3 normaly – normally
4 carefully – careful   5 finaly – finally

Unit 5: *must/mustn't* and *don't have to*

2 She doesn't have to study Latin every day.
3 She mustn't eat unhealthy food.
4 She mustn't go to bed very late.
5 She mustn't lose all her competitions.

Unit 6: Adjectives of feeling

2 interested   3 annoyed   4 confusing
5 annoying

Unit 8: Present perfect

2 speak – spoken – spoke
3 eat – eaten – ate
4 swim – swum – swam
5 take – taken – took

Unit 8: Present perfect or past simple?

2 a   3 b   4 a

Unit 8: Present perfect + *ever/never*

2 Have you ever lost anything important?
3 Have you ever found anything expensive?
4 Have you ever fallen in love?
5 Have you ever received a really good present?

Workbook key

1 Welcome

A At school

1
1 Maths
2 Chemistry
3 PE
4 Geography
5 Physics
6 French
7 Biology
8 ICT
9 History

2
1 doesn't like
2 know; do
3 read
4 works
5 Does; speak; she doesn't; speaks
6 don't like; love

3
1 don't have to
2 doesn't have to
3 have to
4 doesn't have to
5 don't have to
6 don't have to

B Work and free time

1
A 2 do the
B 3 tidy
C 7 do the; up
D 5 do the
E 4 do the
G 6 do the

2
2 isn't doing
3 is/'s doing
4 Are; tidying
5 is; doing
6 is/'s doing

3
2 'm/am playing
3 plays
4 's/is raining
5 's/is shining
6 's/is calling
7 don't think

4
1b   2e   3a   4d   5c

C At the school canteen

1

```
R V G Y T O R S A O F P
R E T A W X A E O R D L
S H G B A T S O S Q A S
A M S E L B A T E G E V
R P O E S N O A O T R S
S B P O E R C M N A B S
S G E L R H V O I E S U
D D G A E H J T O M P G
R I C E N S S H N P U A
J A S F Z S E U S M P R
N E T I U R F N M I W D
C H I C K E N J U I C E
```

2
a   2 are   3 is   4 is   5 is   6 are

b   1 some   2 a; some   3 an; some
4 some   5 some; a   6 an; some

3
2 some F
3 any C
4 some B
5 any E
6 some D

4
1 most delicious
2 best; most expensive
3 hotter; healthier

D What a story!

1
2 wanted; started
3 met
4 knew
5 finished
6 thought

2
2 How long did the trip take?
3 Did you enjoy the trip?
4 What was the most difficult thing about the trip?
5 How high were the highest waves?

3
2 Harry and Chuck weren't the two best
footballers in our class.
3 She didn't buy a pen and a notebook.
4 They didn't follow me all the way home.
5 Tom didn't phone you three times yesterday.
6 Her family didn't move to Mexico when she was 12.

4 Students' own answers

2 We're going on holiday

1 2 May 3 plane 4 Chiang Mai 5 elephants
6 fainted

2 **a** 1 is having 2 are paying 3 is going
4 aren't / are not flying 5 are travelling
6 am not going 7 are spending 8 are staying

b 2 Sorry, I'm having lunch with my Grandma on Saturday.
3 Sorry, I'm meeting Uncle Jack at the airport on Friday.
4 Sorry, my cousins are arriving from Germany on Sunday.
5 Sorry, Helen is coming to my place on Monday.
6 Sorry, I'm studying for my maths test on Wednesday.
7 Sorry, I'm going shopping with Dad on Tuesday.

c 1 Is Peter coming
2 he isn't
3 Are Ann and Paul coming
4 they are
5 Are you and your family going
6 we are
7 Are you travelling
8 we aren't
9 Is your sister going
10 she is

d 1 F 2 N 3 N 4 F 5 F 6 F 7 F 8 F
9 N

3 **a** 2 the day after tomorrow 3 in three hours' time 4 next year 5 in three weeks' time

b 2 canoeing 3 windsurfing 4 camping
5 snorkelling 6 sailing 7 sunbathing
8 sightseeing

c

stay ...	travel ...	hire ...	spend ...	buy ...
at home	by plane	a boat	a week	a postcard
on a farm	to London	a car	some time	presents
in a hotel	by car	canoes	three days	

d 2 They spent some time / a week / three days
3 hired a car
4 travelled by plane
5 stayed in a hotel

e 1 try 2 visiting 3 looking 4 buy 5 meet
6 learn 7 go

4 **a** ► CD3 T35 TAPESCRIPT/ANSWERS
/θ/ think; Maths; thousand; thirteen; athlete; throw

/ð/ that; clothes; those; father; brother; these

b ► CD3 T36 TAPESCRIPT/ANSWERS
1 It's my sixteenth birthday next month.
2 They're sunbathing together on the beach.
3 Her grandfather is healthy, but he's very thin.
4 My brother can throw this ball further than me.

5 2 don't worry 3 then 4 your fault 5 at all
6 Hang on

6 **a** 2 verb 3 adjective 4 preposition
5 singular 6 plural

b 1 e 2 c 3 d 4 a 5 b

c 2 We no longer have a room at the hotel.

7 Possible answers:
2 On Saturday night in a big room in a hotel in town.
3 Her aunt and uncle.
4 On Friday.
5 Their flat is very small.
6 Her grandfather because he's still in hospital.
7 They are going to buy some new clothes.

8 ► CD3 T37 TAPESCRIPT

Girl: Hello.

Boy: Hi Emma. It's Adam.

Girl: Oh, Adam, hi!

Boy: How are you? How was the party on Saturday?

Girl: Oh, it was really good. Well, most things were good, anyway. The room looked fantastic – the decorations were lovely and the flowers looked really beautiful.

Boy: And the food?

Girl: Great – delicious. Everyone really enjoyed the food. The only thing was, the birthday cake was a bit of a disaster. Mum cooked it too long, so it was black on the bottom and it was very dry. Mum wasn't very happy about it.

Boy: Oh, that's a shame.

Girl: The other problem was the jazz band. Two of the musicians didn't come! They went to the wrong address.

Boy: Oh no!

Girl: Yeah, can you believe that? My brother had to run home and get a CD player and some CDs. But it didn't seem to matter. Everyone danced and had a good time. And there were loads of presents for Dad and he loved them. I think he had a very good night.

Answers:

1 ✓ 2 ✓ 3 ✗ 4 ✗ 5 ✓

Unit check

1 1 coach 2 breakfast 3 sailing 4 sunbathing
5 hiring 6 aren't 7 campsites 8 youth 9 is

2 2 c 3 b 4 a 5 b 6 b 7 c 8 a 9 b

3 2 windsurfing 3 camping 4 going to a market
5 climbing 6 snorkelling 7 buying souvenirs
8 sailing 9 horse riding

3 It'll never happen

1 2 won't work 3 they'll never be 4 will want
5 will buy 6 will only weigh 7 won't buy
8 it will be

2 **a** 2 D 3 H 4 G 5 A 6 C 7 F 8 B

b 2 won't be 3 won't win 4 will help
5 will find 6 won't wear 7 won't hurt
8 will see

c 2 Will; come 3 Jenny go 4 Will; be
5 will; finish 6 will; see

d 2 You'll win a lot of money, but you won't become famous.
3 You won't live in a big house, but you will have a big car.
4 You'll get married, but you won't have a baby.

e Students' own answers

3 **a** ▶ **CD3 T38** TAPESCRIPT
1 I'll go now.
2 She'll help you.
3 They'll be here on Monday.
4 You'll find I'm right.
5 The information will be on the internet.
6 The universe will continue to get bigger.

b ▶ **CD3 T39** TAPESCRIPT/ANSWERS
1 Don't worry. I'**ll** do this for you.
2 We **do** our homework after lunch.
3 Ask Julia – she'**ll** know the answer.
4 The film **will** start soon.
5 During a flight, the flight attendants **work** very hard.

6 Go to university. I'm sure you'**ll** see how important it is for your future.
7 I doubt they'**ll** be here in half an hour.
8 They say that in the future, people **will** take holidays on the moon.

4 **a** 2 I think the baby will wake up.
3 I don't think he'll give it back.
4 I think he'll know how to do it.
5 I don't think they'll be late.
6 I think / don't think I'll finish before 9 o'clock.

b 2 doubt 3 not sure 4 maybe 5 hope
6 sure

5

Astrology	Palmistry	Fortune cookies	Reading tea leaves
newspaper	lines	biscuits	cup
stars	hand	paper	pot
		restaurant	

6 **a** 1 n 2 v 3 n

b 1 b 2 d 3 c 4 a

7 2 5–6 3 27–28 4 25–26 5 18–21 6 3–4
7 16–17 8 7–10

8 Students' own answer

Unit check

1 1 think 2 abroad 3 probably 4 to find
5 don't 6 sure 7 nonsense 8 maybe 9 she'll

2 2 c 3 c 4 c 5 b 6 b 7 a 8 a 9 c

3 2 century 3 fortune 4 leaves 5 predict
6 nonsense 7 reliable 8 palmistry 9 astrology

4 Don't give up

1 B3; C5; D6; E2; F4

2 **a** 2 a 3 e 4 f 5 b 6 c

b 2 too 3 too 4 very 5 very 6 too

c 2 're too difficult.
3 's too cold.
4 's too small.
5 's too far.
6 's too young.
7 's too easy.
8 're too expensive.

3 **a** 1 sun 2 hot 3 wind 4 thunder
5 lightning

b 2 strong 3 thick 4 bright 5 dark
6 heavy 7 gentle 8 violent

4 **a** 1 safely 2 noisy 3 early 4 hard
5 brilliantly 6 good 7 fast 8 easily
9 late

b 2 stupid 3 slowly 4 dangerously 5 usual
6 healthy

c 2 She's working hard
3 He's playing badly
4 The dogs are running quickly
5 She's smiling happily
6 They're shouting loudly
7 She won easily
8 He's got up late

5 **a** ▶ CD3 T40 TAPESCRIPT/ANSWERS

j<u>o</u>b what w<u>a</u>nt f<u>o</u>ggy be<u>lo</u>ng pr<u>o</u>bably
r<u>o</u>pe w<u>o</u>n't j<u>o</u>ke k<u>i</u>lo g<u>o</u>ing n<u>o</u>se

b ▶ CD3 T41 TAPESCRIPT/ANSWERS

1 Our dog has got a cold nose.
2 <u>Bob</u> and <u>Tom</u> don't (go) to the (coast).
3 The f<u>o</u>reign politician <u>told</u> a <u>lot of</u> (jokes).
4 <u>John</u> <u>want</u>s to (own) a (mo)bile(phone).
5 (Those) tomat(oes) are <u>old</u>.
6 (So) <u>what</u>? (Throw) them in the <u>pot</u>!

6 2 In fact 3 the best thing to do 4 Are you sure?
5 in a minute 6 in a way

7 **a** o: potato; hello
ow: tomorrow; window; follow
oa: boat; soap
o + consonant + e: nose; joke; hope

b Students' own answers

8 Students' own answers

9 Students' own answers

Unit check

1 1 too 2 heavily 3 windy 4 really 5 snowed
6 weather 7 happily 8 sunny 9 angry

2 2 c 3 a 4 a 5 a 6 b 7 c 8 a 9 a

3 2 sun 3 shower 4 lightning 5 thunder
6 thick fog 7 bright sunshine 8 heavy snow
9 violent storm

5 Promises, promises

1 4 midnight 5 December 12 strike 7 cheer
6 world 2 goodbye 11 old 1 resolutions
13 easy 9 break

2 **a** 2 e 3 b 4 f 5 a 6 c

b 2 check out 3 take up 4 work out
5 give up 6 tell; off

c 2 away 3 up 4 up 5 off

3 **a** 2 F 3 T 4 T 5 F 6 T

b 2 's 3 Are 4 aren't 5 isn't 6 are 7 'm
8 Is

c 2 A: Is; going to learn
B: she is
3 A: Is; going to move
B: he isn't
4 A: Are; going to wear
B: I'm not
5 A: Are; going to do
B: they are
6 A: Are; going to hire a houseboat?
B: we are

d 2 I'm not going to enjoy
3 are going to have
4 are not going to see
5 are going to miss

e Students' own answers

f 2 must do 3 mustn't use 4 must wear
5 mustn't bring 6 must be

4 ▶ CD3 T42 TAPESCRIPT/ANSWERS

1 You **mustn't** do that.
2 You **mustn't** sit here.
3 She **must** speak to him.
4 We **must** give her the letter.
5 I **mustn't** stay here.
6 You **mustn't** forget me.

5 2 rock 3 heart beat 4 Jamaica 5 equal
6 charts 7 Wailers 8 style 9 lyrics

Mystery name: Bob Marley

6 Students' own answers

7 2 B 3 A 4 C 5 C

▶ CD3 T43 TAPESCRIPT

Denise: Hi Robbie! Happy New Year!

Robbie: Denise! Happy New Year! Good to hear
from you! How are you? What's happening in
your life?

Denise: Oh, big news. My father's got a new job
and that's going to mean a huge change for
my family. It means we're going to move from
London to Newcastle.

Robbie: Newcastle – is that close to London?

Denise: No, it's miles away, in the north of England.
We're moving out in five weeks' time.

Robbie: Wow! Have you got a new place to live?

Denise: Yes, we're going to move into a house in Newcastle. My parents say it's a nice house and it's bigger than our flat here in London – it's got four bedrooms and a garden. I'm going up there next weekend to check it out.

Robbie: So what's happening with the flat in London?

Denise: We're going to sell it. That's OK with me, it isn't a very nice flat and it's too small. But still, it's going to be very hard to leave London. I'm really going to miss my friends here and it's going to be difficult starting in a new school. I'm not looking forward to it, really.

Robbie: What about your mother?

Denise: Mum? She can't wait. She's going to give up her job and she's really happy about that. And she wants to take up painting again – she was a good artist, you know, before she got married.

Robbie: Well, I'm sure it'll be a big change. I hope it all goes well ...

8 Students' own answers

Unit check

1 1 resolutions 2 must 3 going 4 isn't 5 to
6 tell 7 give 8 take 9 healthy

2 2 a 3 a 4 a 5 b 6 b 7 c 8 b 9 a

3 2 Check 3 charts 4 from 5 hit 6 up
7 lyrics 8 work 9 equal

6 What a brave person!

1 1 small 2 ground 3 shocked 4 hospital
5 serious 6 dirty 7 brave 8 help 9 right

2 **a** 2 don't 3 he'll have to 4 you'll be
5 she'll send

b 2 If the train doesn't come soon, we'll walk home.
3 You won't get wet if you wear a raincoat.
4 I won't sing well at the concert if I'm too nervous.
5 If my friends see me, they won't recognise me.

c 1 will go for a ride on her bike.
2 rains, Christine will read her book.
3 wakes up early, he'll go shopping.
4 doesn't wake up early, he'll listen to music.

d Students' own answers

e 1 the rope will break
2 the dog will attack her
3 they won't find us
4 they'll/will have a crash
5 you'll/will feel better
6 the plane won't take off

f 2 when 3 if 4 If 5 if 6 when

3 **a** ▶ CD3 T44 TAPESCRIPT/ANSWERS
1 If he <u>tries</u> to <u>get</u> up, the <u>train</u> will <u>kill</u> him.
2 If he <u>doesn't</u> <u>move</u>, he'll <u>be</u> <u>OK</u>.
3 If <u>I</u> don't <u>help</u> him, the <u>man</u> will <u>die</u>.

b ▶ CD3 T45 TAPESCRIPT/ANSWERS
1 <u>Neil</u> will <u>look</u> for a <u>job</u> when the summer holidays <u>begin</u>.
2 I'll do my <u>homework</u> when I <u>get</u> <u>home</u> tonight.
3 We'll <u>take</u> a <u>taxi</u> if <u>Dad</u> <u>can't</u> meet us at the <u>station</u>.
4 <u>If</u> you <u>waste</u> <u>time</u>, you <u>won't</u> <u>finish</u> your <u>work</u>.
5 It'll be <u>great</u> if I <u>win</u> this <u>competition</u>!
6 We'll have a <u>big</u> cele<u>bration</u> when it's your <u>twenty</u> first <u>birth</u>day.

4 **a** 2 e 3 d 4 f 5 a 6 b

b 2 terrified 3 worried
4 annoyed 5 exciting 6 frightening

c 1 jump 2 scratch 3 red 5 daydream
6 nails 7 forehead 8 yawn

5 2 Well done 3 that's that 4 after all
5 big deal 6 beg

6 Students' own answers

7 **a** B 2 E 3 A 4 C 5

b 2 Sharon threw stones at the dog.
3 The dog turned and went towards Sharon.
4 Because the dog's owner arrived.

8 Students' own answers

Unit check

1 1 bored 2 exciting 3 annoying 4 tired
5 when 6 interested 7 I'll 8 arrives 9 I'm

2 2 b 3 c 4 b 5 a 6 a 7 b 8 c 9 b

3 2 worried 3 excited 4 tired 5 passengers
6 terrified 7 temperature 8 exciting
9 annoyed

7 Travellers' tales

1 **a** 2 should, picture B
3 shouldn't, picture A
4 should, picture D

b 2 shouldn't eat a lot of sweets.
3 should get a weekend job.
4 should have music lessons.
5 shouldn't go to bed late.
6 should talk to his teacher about it.

c 2 Should students stand up
3 Should you take a present
4 When should you use
5 Should people take off
6 What should a person say
and students' own answers

d Students' own answers

2 **a** 2 cheerful 3 lazy 4 polite 5 miserable
6 hard-working 7 organised 8 rude
9 nervous

b James: b Sally: a Cathy: a Joanne: b
Max: b

▶ CD3 T46 TAPESCRIPT

James is usually very happy. He smiles a lot and you often hear him laughing.

I like Sally because she always tells you what she thinks. Sometimes you don't like what you hear but you know she's telling you the truth.

Cathy's great. She doesn't worry a lot about problems. And she never gets angry, even when people are unfriendly or unhelpful.

Joanne doesn't usually do her homework and she never makes her bed or tidies her room. She sleeps until 11 o'clock at the weekend and she watches TV all the time.

Max is a strange guy. He doesn't like talking to people and he doesn't speak when he sees you. He always works alone and he never invites people to go to his place.

c 2 arrogant 3 thoughtful 4 outgoing
5 modest 6 unsympathetic 7 sympathetic
8 bad-tempered 9 shy 10 thoughtless

3 **a** ▶ CD3 T47 TAPESCRIPT/ANSWERS
1 ans(w)er, twenty
2 kind, (k)nife
3 of(t)en, faster
4 autum(n), station
5 clim(b)er, robber
6 horse, (h)our
7 went, (w)rong
8 hold, shou(l)d
9 S(c)ience, disco

b ▶ CD3 T48 1 lam(b) 2 cou(l)d
3 cas(t)le 4 colum(n) 5 (w)rap

4 2 What are your new sunglasses like?
3 What's the weather like?
4 What were Helen's friends like?
5 What was the party like?
6 What's your neighbour like?

5 **a** 2 d 3 a 4 b

b 2 cool 3 ugly 4 interesting

6 2 centre 3 huts 4 village
5 residents 6 poverty 7 water

7 **a**

dis-	un-	different adjective
orderly – disorderly	healthy – unhealthy	quiet – noisy
obedient – disobedient	usual – unusual	beautiful – ugly
	lucky – unlucky	stupid – clever

b possible – impossible; perfect – imperfect; useful – useless; careful – careless

8 3 F 4 F 5 F 6 T 7 T 8 F

9 Students' own answers

Unit check

1 1 cheerful 2 miserable 3 lazy 4 shouldn't
5 dishonest 6 like 7 disorganised 8 kind
9 should

2 2 c 3 c 4 b 5 a 6 c 7 a 8 b 9 b

3 2 disorganised 3 dishonest 4 rude
5 hard-working 6 relaxed 7 ugly 8 shy
9 thoughtless

8 Crazy records

1 **a** 2 In 2005, 637 people dressed in gorilla suits and ran in a race.
3 The Miniature Wunderland train measures 110 metres.
5 Gregory Dunham's motorcycle weighs about a ton.

b 2 measures 3 weighs

2 **a** 2 worked 3 driven 4 learned/learnt
5 eaten 6 written 7 listened 8 done

b 2 has been
3 have never
4 spoken
5 We have never been
6 Have you travelled

B 164 WORKBOOK KEY

c 2 A: Has a snake ever bitten you?
  B: No, I've never seen a snake.
3 A: Have you ever flown to the USA?
  B: No, I've never been in a plane.
4 A: Have your friends swum in this pool?
  B: No, they've never learned to swim.

d 2 Have you ever met a pop star?
3 Have you ever eaten Mexican food?
4 Have you ever tried windsurfing?
5 Have you ever been in hospital?

e 1 've/have never had
2 Have; had
3 've/have never been
4 have driven
5 've/have never cycled
6 has never killed
7 Have; eaten

3 ▶ **CD3 T49** TAPESCRIPT/ANSWERS

1 I cut my finger.
2 Have you seen the parrot?
3 He's told the teacher.
4 They've won lots of prizes.
5 He's seeing the doctor.
6 She's eaten the chocolate.

4 **a** 2 took a risk 3 raise money
    4 break the record 5 told a joke
    6 build a house

b do your best
give a hand / a presentation
have an accident / an argument
make a mess / an effort
take a break / an exam
tell the time / the truth

c 2 did 3 take 4 had 5 tell 6 giving

d 2 Joe went to sleep at work and his boss
    wasn't very happy.
3 The baby is asleep so please be quiet –
    I don't want her to wake up.
4 Maria had a dream about flying.
5 The baby is awake so you don't have to
    be quiet.
6 I went to bed at midnight but I read until
    two in the morning.

5 2 → what 2 ↓ wait 3 fun
4 → white 4 ↓ way

6 No change: cut – cut – cut
Same past simple and past participle: make –
made – made, meet – met – met
Different past participle: write – wrote – written,
fly – flew – flown, drive – drove – driven, go –
went – gone
No change: cut – cut – cut

7 1 mushrooms 2 do you want 3 please 4 cut
5 four 6 six 7 can eat six pieces 8 mine
9 decide 10 red 11 blue 12 rains
13 black horse 14 bigger than 15 brown one

▶ **CD3 T50** TAPESCRIPT

Boy: This is one of my favourite jokes. Listen.

A man goes into a pizza place and asks for a pizza.
The girl asks him what he wants on it.

'Oh, ham and mushrooms and olives, please.'

'Fine,' says the girl. 'And what size pizza do you
want?'

'What sizes have you got?' asks the man.

'Well, you can have small, medium or large.'

'Oh,' says the man. 'Um … medium, please.'

The girl says: 'OK. And do you want me to cut it
into four pieces or six pieces?'

The man thinks about it and says, 'Just four pieces,
please. I'm not really very hungry. I don't think I
can eat six pieces!'

Girl: Yeah, that's a good joke. But I think this one's
good too.

Two farmers go out one day and they buy two
horses, one each. They put the two horses in
a field.

'Wait a minute,' says one farmer. 'How will we know
which horse is yours and which horse is mine?'

So the two farmers sit down and think about it.
They decide to paint the horses' tails – one tail
will be red and the other tail will be blue.

But that night, it rains, and the paint comes off.
So the two farmers think about it again. Then
one of them says, 'Oh, what stupid farmers we
are! Look, it's easy. Your black horse is bigger
than my brown one!'

8 Students' own answers

Unit check

1 1 snake 2 never 3 risk 4 truth 5 spoken
6 was 7 ever 8 been 9 haven't

2 2 c 3 b 4 b 5 b 6 a 7 c 8 b 9 c

3 1 best 2 argument 3 daydreaming 4 asleep
5 awake 6 take 7 mess 8 truth

Teaching notes for communication activities and grammar practice

Unit 2

Communication activity

Areas practised

Present continuous for future arrangements
Future time expressions; Holiday activities

- Divide the class into student A and B pairs. Copy and cut up the text items for each pair and the student A/B parts.

- Give students a few minutes to read through the information. Check any problems.

- Go through the example as a class, drawing students' attention to the use of the present continuous.

- Students then complete their own holiday table and ask their partner about their holiday.

- Monitor and check students are using the present continuous question forms correctly and that they are taking turns to ask and answer. Note down any errors to go through as a class after the activity.

- Ask pairs to feedback to the class.

Grammar practice key

1
2 At 12.30 on Saturday she's having lunch with Marta.

3 At 7.00 on Saturday she's seeing a film.

4 At 9.00 on Sunday she's studying for a test.

5 At 1.00 on Sunday she's having lunch with her grandparents.

6 At 8.00 on Sunday she's meeting Ana.

2
2 My father isn't seeing the bank manager today. He's seeing him tomorrow.

3 We aren't having a party on Friday. We're having one on Saturday.

4 You aren't spending a day on a canal boat. You're spending a week.

5 Linda isn't having lunch at 12.30. She's having lunch at 1.00.

6 My brother isn't having a driving lesson today. He's having one tomorrow.

3
2 ✓

3 ✗ She is seeing the dentist in two days' time.

4 ✓

5 ✗ Are you going camping next summer?

6 ✓

7 ✗ My brother is flying to Paris in September.

4
2 are driving   3 are taking   4 are planning
5 are staying   6 are crossing   7 are
spending   8 am going   9 are (you) doing

Unit 3

Communication activity

Areas practised

will/won't
Expressions to talk about the future

- Divide the class into student A and B pairs. Copy and cut up one sheet for each pair.

- Explain the concept of fortune tellers (people who predict the future, often using a crystal ball or reading people's palms, using cards, etc.), if necessary.

- Go through an example as a class. Students now make questions from the prompts. Remind them to write their questions, using *will* or *won't*.

- Students then take turns to be the fortune teller. They should look at the picture clues and use them to answer their partner's questions.

- Monitor and check students are taking turns to ask and answer and that they are using the question and answer forms correctly. Make a note of any repeated errors to go through as a class after the activity.

- Ask several pairs to demonstrate some of their questions and answers to the class.

Grammar practice key

1
2 won't do   3 will take place   4 will stay
5 will ask   6 will go   7 will buy

(2)

2 Martina won't be a famous footballer. Cesare will be a famous footballer.

3 Martina will live abroad. Cesare will live abroad.

4 Martina will learn to drive. Cesare will learn to drive.

5 Martina will buy a house. Cesare will buy a house.

6 Martina will go to university. Cesare won't go to university.

7 Martina won't learn to speak Russian. Cesare won't learn to speak Russian.

(3)

2 ✗ I won't go to the park at the weekend.

3 ✓

4 ✓

5 ✗ You won't have a lot of work to do.

6 ✓

7 ✓

(4)

2 a   3 b   4 a   5 a   6 b   7 b

Unit 4

Communication activity

Areas practised

too + adjective; Adverbs
The weather

- Divide the class into pairs. Copy and cut up one sheet for each pair.

- Students spread out all the cards face down on their table.

- Explain to students that they must turn over one picture card and one sentence card and see if they match. If they match, the student keeps them and has another turn. If they don't match, the student must turn the cards back over in exactly the same place.

- Ask a stronger pair to demonstrate and ask them to read out the sentence they turn over. Ask the whole class if they think it matches the picture card which was turned over.

- The game continues like this until students have matched all the picture cards and sentences, using their memory and the picture content to help them.

- Monitor and check students are taking turns to turn the cards over and they are helping each other find the pairs. Check that they are reading the sentences and not merely turning the cards over.

- Ask pairs to feedback to the class and read out or come and stick their matching pairs on the board.

Alternatively, this could be done in small groups.

Grammar practice key

(1)

2 badly   3 slowly   4 hard   5 quickly
6 quietly   7 late   8 well   9 early

(2)

2 ✓

3 ✓

4 ✗ Paco and Juana play the clarinet badly.

5 ✗ My father speaks Chinese well.

6 ✓

7 ✗ He fell off his bike but luckily, he didn't break his leg.

8 ✓

9 ✗ Did you answer all the exam questions easily?

(3)

2 too dangerous   3 too expensive   4 too hot   5 too dark   6 too difficult   7 too big   8 too young   9 too cold

(4)

2 sunny   3 temperatures   4 cloudy   5 cool
6 rain   7 sun   8 warm

Unit 5

Communication activity

Areas practised

be going to: intentions and predictions
Phrasal verbs

- Copy and cut up one sheet for each student. Only give out the quiz questions initially. Do not give out the score sheets.

- Students read the quiz. Check any problems.

- Explain that students have to answer the questions.

- Once they have completed the quiz, give out one score sheet to each student. Students can add up their scores and compare results.

- Ask pairs to feedback to the class. Were there any surprising results?

    Note: This is meant to be light-hearted and fun and students should not take it seriously.

Grammar practice key

2 My dad is going to work less.

3 My brother is going to give up listening to loud music.

4 My sister is going to take up German classes.

5 My brother is going to read a book a week.

6 My grandmother is going to learn to drive a car.

7 My grandfather is going to go on holiday every two months.

2 ✗ John isn't going to visit his brother in London.

3 ✓

4 ✓

5 ✓

6 ✗ We're going to learn to dance salsa.

7 ✓

8 ✗ She's not going to do the washing.

9 ✗ Are we going to travel to Scotland in September?

2 mustn't eat   3 must throw (it) away
4 must go   5 mustn't move
6 must do   7 mustn't walk

2 must   3 must   4 mustn't   5 mustn't
6 mustn't   7 mustn't   8 must   9 must

Unit 6
Communication activity

Areas practised
First conditional; *when* and *if*

- Divide the class into groups of four. Copy and cut up one sheet per group.

- Each student chooses a topic sentence.

- Explain to students that they must finish off the first sentence, using the correct tense for the first conditional. Then they must start the second sentence with the end of their first sentence. Demonstrate this with one of the sentences.

- Students then fold their first sentence under so that all that can be seen is the first half of the new conditional sentence. Then they pass their sheet to the next student in the group.

- The next student continues that sentence and then writes the start of the next one.

- Encourage students to use some adjectives of feeling from the unit.

- The activity continues in this way until all the students in each group have written sentences in all the columns.

- Monitor and check students are using the first conditional correctly and make a note of any repeated errors.

- Once students have written all their sentences, the papers are unfolded and a group member reads out the whole sequence of sentences.

- The class can vote for the most interesting/ sensible or the funniest/silliest series of sentences.

Grammar practice key

2 If it rains, we won't go to the football match.

3 Will you come to my party if I invite you?

4 I'll watch television when I finish my homework.

5 Will Mike retire when he's 65?

6 If it's too hot, they won't go to the zoo.

7 If I buy a cake, will you eat half?

8 Will you meet me at the airport when I arrive?

2 ✓

3 ✗ If you are hard-working, you'll pass your exams.

4 ✓

5 ✗ When I feel tired, I'll go to bed.

6 ✓

7 ✗ You'll see lots of fish if you swim under water.

2 see   3 stays   4 won't watch   5 will invite
6 will (we) eat   7 grows

2 interested   3 boring   4 frightened
5 frightening   6 tired   7 annoying
8 bored   9 tiring

Unit 7
Communication activity

Areas practised
should/shouldn't; *What's it like? / What are they like?*
Personality adjectives

- Divide the class into teams of four to six. Copy and cut up one sheet for each team.

- Put the cards in a pile face down on each team's table.
- Explain to students that they must each turn over a card and look at the adjective. The other team members must not see the card.
- They must describe this adjective to the rest of their team without using the adjective and the other words on the card.
- The rest of the team have to guess what the adjective is.
- If a student guesses a word correctly, he/she wins a point.
- If the student describing the adjective uses words they cannot say, he/she must tell the group the word and the next student has a turn.
- Monitor and check students are describing the adjectives without using the words they cannot say.

Grammar practice key

1
2 shouldn't 3 should 4 should
5 shouldn't 6 should 7 shouldn't
8 should 9 shouldn't

2
2 Do you think I should wear the green dress?
3 John shouldn't talk to his teacher like that!
4 You shouldn't eat so much chocolate.
5 Do you think we should go to the cinema?
6 He shouldn't be rude to his parents.
7 Helen should be polite to the customers.
8 You should take your umbrella.
9 Should they take a present?

3
2 ✓
3 ✗ Should she travel alone in Brazil?
4 ✗ You shouldn't kiss your neighbour in England.
5 ✓
6 ✗ You should look after your suitcase.
7 ✓
8 ✓
9 ✗ She shouldn't speak English in Spain.

4
2 What is the food like?
3 What are the houses like?
4 What is London like?
5 What are the shops like?
6 What are the clothes like?

Unit 8
Communication activity

Areas practised
Present perfect + *ever/never*
Animals
Verb and noun pairs: *raise money, win a prize, break a record, build a house, tell a joke, take a risk*
Revision of past simple questions

- Divide the class into student A and B pairs. Copy and cut up one sheet per pair.
- Students read through their questions.
- Demonstrate a question and answer with a stronger pair. Draw students' attention to the present perfect question but remind them they will have to answer the follow up questions in the past simple.
- Students ask and answer their questions.
- Monitor and check students are taking turns to ask and answer and that students are making a note of their partner's replies.
- Once students have asked and answered all their questions, ask pairs to feedback to the class. If they have a cross in a box, encourage them to answer using 'X has never …'.
- If there are any interesting answers, encourage students to tell the class more about them.

Grammar practice key

1
2 has lost 3 has cleaned 4 has rained
5 have eaten 6 have travelled 7 have met
8 has built 9 has won

2
2 Have they ever owned an unusual pet?
3 Have you received the letter?
4 Has she seen a parrot?
5 Have we ever eaten potatoes?
6 Have you ever touched a snake?
7 Have they ever written a book?
8 Has she been to Paris?
9 Has he milked a cow?

3
2 ✓
3 ✗ She has eaten too much today.
4 ✗ Ow! I've cut my finger!
5 ✗ I'm hungry. I haven't eaten since yesterday!
6 ✓
7 ✗ He has built all the houses in this street.
8 ✓
9 ✗ He hasn't got any Elvis CDs.

4
2 ever 3 never 4 never 5 ever 6 ever
7 never 8 ever 9 ever

Communication activity 2

Places

Honolulu, Hawaii; New York City, USA; Florence, Italy; Edinburgh, Scotland; Madrid, Spain; the New Forest, England; Lisbon, Portugal; Ankara, Turkey; the Greek Islands

How to get there

fly; drive; sail; by bus

Things to do

windsurfing, camping, horse-riding, sightseeing, snorkelling, canoeing, sailing, rock climbing, hiking

When you can go

next weekend; next Monday; the week after next; next month; the day after tomorrow

Student A

Look at the list of places, how to get there, things to do and when you can go on holiday. Choose a place, a way to get there, three things to do there and one date when you can go. Complete your chart below with the information.

Place?	
How to get there?	
Things to do?			
When?	

Now ask student B questions and find out where they are going, how they are getting there, what they are doing and when they are going.

A: *Are you going to Honolulu?*   A: *How are you getting there?*
B: *No, I'm not.*   B: *I'm flying.*
A: *Are you going to Edinburgh?*
B: *Yes, I am.*

Now listen to student B and answer their questions about your holiday.

Student B

Look at the list of places, how to get there, things to do and when you can go on holiday. Choose a place, a way to get there, three things to do there and one date when you can go. Complete your chart below with the information.

Place?	
How to get there?	
Things to do?			
When?	

Now listen to student A and answer their questions about your holiday. Then ask student A questions to find out where they are going, how they are getting there, what they are doing and when they are going.

B: *Are you going to Honolulu?*   B: *How are you getting there?*
A: *No, I'm not.*   A: *I'm flying.*
B: *Are you going to Edinburgh?*
A: *Yes, I am.*

Grammar practice 2

1 Write sentences about what Juana is doing next weekend. Use the information in the table and the present continuous tense.

Saturday	Sunday
9.00: swimming lesson	9.00: study for test
12.30: lunch with Marta	1.00: lunch with grandparents
7.00: see film	8.00: meet Ana

1 *At 9.00 on Saturday she's having a swimming lesson.*

2 ....

3 ....

4 ....

5 ....

6 ....

2 Complete the sentences. Use the present continuous form of the verbs. Use the clues to help you.

1 She / travel by plane to France (✗) / by boat (✓)

   She isn't travelling by plane to France. She's travelling by boat.

2 My father / see the bank manager today (✗) / tomorrow (✓)

   ....

   ....

3 We / having a party / on Friday (✗) / on Saturday (✓)

   ....

   ....

4 You / spend a day / on a canal boat (✗) / a week (✓)

   ....

   ....

5 Linda / have lunch at 12.30 (✗) / 1.00 (✓)

   ....

   ....

6 My brother / have a driving lesson today (✗) / tomorrow (✓)

   ....

   ....

3 Right (✓) or wrong (✗)? Correct the wrong sentences.

1 I is going sailing tomorrow. [✗]

   I am going sailing tomorrow.

2 We're going to Edinburgh by train. [ ]

   ....

3 She are seeing the dentist in two days' time. [ ]

   ....

4 They are visiting Venice next week. [ ]

   ....

5 Is you going camping next summer? [ ]

   ....

6 He's taking his driving test next week. [ ]

   ....

7 My brother are flying to Paris in September. [ ]

   ....

4 Complete the email. Use the present continuous form of the verbs in the box.

> go   stay   ~~plan~~   plan   spend
> drive   cross   take   do

Hi Emily,

This summer my family and I (1) *are planning* to travel through France and Spain by car. We (2) .... to the south coast and then we (3) .... the ferry to the north of France. We (4) .... to stay in the north of France for a few days and then drive through France to Spain. We (5) .... in Bilbao for one night and then we're driving to the south of Spain. After that, we (6) .... the Straits of Gibraltar and we (7) .... one night in Gibraltar. I (8) .... sailing when we're there. I can't wait! What (9) .... you .... this summer?

Email me and let me know.
See you soon,
Carolina

Communication activity 3

Student A

You are going to visit a fortune teller. You want to ask the following questions. First, write the questions. Then write your own predictions. Use *will* or *won't* in your questions and predictions.

(your favourite sports team) / win / the competition?

I / pass / my exams?

What / present / my parents / buy / me?

Our class / go / on a school trip / this year?

I / be / famous / one day?

I / win / the lottery?

I / get married?

How many / children / I / have?

I / have / hamburger and chips / dinner / tonight?

Ask your partner the questions. Were any of your predictions correct?

Now change roles. You are the fortune teller. Use the clues in the crystal ball to answer your partner's questions. Use *Yes, ... will* or *No, ... won't* or *I think you'll, You'll probably, Maybe you'll, I'm sure you'll, I doubt you'll.*

A: *Will I pass my exams?*

B: *Yes, you will. / No, you won't.*

Student B

You are going to visit a fortune teller. You want to ask the following questions. First, write the questions. Then write your own predictions. Use *will* or *won't* in your questions and predictions.

(your favourite singer) / win / the competition?

I / pass / my exams?

What / present / (your friend) / buy / me / for my birthday?

Our family / travel / abroad / this year?

I / become / a doctor / one day?

I / be / rich / one day?

I / marry / a pop star?

How many / children / I / have?

What I / have / for dinner / tonight?

You are the fortune teller. Use the clues in the crystal ball to answer your partner's questions. Use *Yes, ... will* or *No, ... won't* or *I think you'll, You'll probably, Maybe you'll, I'm sure you'll, I doubt you'll.*

Now change roles. Ask your partner your questions. Were any of your predictions correct?

A: *Will I pass my exams?*

B: *Yes, you will. / No, you won't.*

Grammar practice 3

1 Complete the sentences. Use *will* or *won't* with the verbs.

1 I ___won't be___ (be) there until 5.00 pm.

2 I _____ (do) well in my tests tomorrow. I didn't study enough.

3 The next space launch _____ (take place) in June 2012.

4 He feels very ill. He thinks he _____ (stay) in bed today.

5 I don't understand this question. I _____ (ask) the teacher to help me.

6 My parents think they _____ (go) to the country this weekend.

7 We think we _____ (buy) a new car next year, but we're not sure.

2 Look at the information below. Write sentences about Martina and Cesare. Use *will* or *won't*.

	Martina	Cesare
1 Get married	✓	✗
2 Be a famous footballer	✗	✓
3 Live abroad	✓	✓
4 Learn to drive	✓	✓
5 Buy a house	✓	✓
6 Go to university	✓	✗
7 Learn to speak Russian	✗	✗

1 *Martina will get married. Cesare won't get married.*

2 _____

3 _____

4 _____

5 _____

6 _____

7 _____

3 Right (✓) or wrong (✗)? Correct the wrong sentences.

1 He will studies Italian at university. ☒

   He will study Italian at university.

2 I willn't go to the park at the weekend. ☐

   _____

3 They'll pass their exams next week. ☐

_____

4 We think we won't go to Paris this summer. ☐

_____

5 You willn't have a lot of work to do. ☐

_____

6 She'll ask the teacher about the problem tomorrow. ☐

_____

7 The doctor will see all patients today. ☐

_____

4 What will each person say? Circle the correct answer.

1 A student who doesn't understand a question in his homework.
   (a) 'I'll ask the teacher.'
   b 'I ask the teacher.'

2 A business person who travels to London by train every day.
   a 'I travel to London by train.'
   b 'I'll travel to London by train.'

3 A woman who wants to travel by train but the train has been cancelled.
   a 'I travel by bus.'
   b 'I'll travel by bus.'

4 A couple who can't go to Greece on holiday.
   a 'We'll go to Portugal.'
   b 'We go to Portugal.'

5 A man who trains with a football team every day.
   a 'I play football.'
   b 'I'll play football.'

6 A girl has an exam and wants to be at school early.
   a 'I get up early.'
   b 'I'll get up early.'

7 A dentist who has to see a woman with toothache.
   a 'I see her now.'
   b 'I'll see her now.'

RESOURCES UNIT 3

Communication activity 4

What are they saying? Find the picture and sentence to match.

It's too foggy. I can't see well.	It's snowing. It's too cold. I can't go out now.
It's too cloudy. I can't land safely.	It's too windy. We have to walk home slowly and carefully.
It's raining. It's too wet to go out and play. Luckily, I've got a game here we can play.	Listen to that! They're playing very badly.
They're playing the music very loudly.	What's he saying? I can't hear him. He's talking very quietly.
Come on! We've got to run fast to catch that train!	You're too tired! You have to go to bed early tonight.
Come on! It's too hot. I burn easily.	Jones, you're late again! What happened this morning?

RESOURCES   UNIT 4

Grammar practice 4

1 Complete the sentences with the correct adverb. Use the adjectives to form the adverbs.

1 They won the match _____easily_____ . (easy)

2 Listen to that! He plays the piano very
_____ . (bad)

3 I don't understand. Can you explain that
more _____ please? (slow)

4 You won't pass your exam. You need to
study _____ . (hard)

5 My brother always eats _____ . (quick)

6 You'll have to talk _____ because the
baby is asleep. (quiet)

7 They always arrive _____ for school.
(late)

8 My parents can dance very _____
but they can't sing. (good)

9 I have to get up _____ tomorrow
because I've got an exam. (early)

2 Right (✓) or wrong (✗)? Correct the wrong sentences.

1 Do you eat quick? ☒
   Do you eat quickly? _____

2 I can't speak quietly. ☐
   _____

3 Does your brother study hard for his
   exams? ☐
   _____

4 Paco and Juana play the clarinet bad. ☐
   _____

5 My father speaks Chinese good. ☐
   _____

6 Do you get up late at the weekends? ☐
   _____

7 He fell off his bike but lucky, he didn't
   break his leg. ☐
   _____

8 My teacher speaks English slowly. ☐
   _____

9 Did you answer all the exam
   questions easy? ☐
   _____

3 Complete the sentences. Use an adjective from the box with *too*.

> hot big young expensive ~~heavy~~
> cold dark difficult dangerous

1 I can't carry this bag. It's __too heavy__ .

2 Look at the weather. We can't reach
   the summit now. It's _____ .

3 She can't afford to buy those trainers.
   They're _____ .

4 Look at the temperature! It's
   _____ to be outside.

5 I can't see a thing. It's _____ .

6 They couldn't answer the last question.
   It was _____ .

7 Do you think these trousers are
   _____ for me?

8 You can't see that film. You're
   _____ .

9 Let's go to the indoor pool. It's
   _____ to swim in the river today.

4 Complete the weather report with the words from the box.

> warm sunny rain ~~hot~~ cloudy
> cool sun temperatures

Today will be a (1) _____hot_____ and (2)
_____ morning, with (3) _____
rising to 35 °C.
This afternoon the weather will change.
It will become (4) _____ with a (5)
_____ wind from the east.
Tomorrow morning it will (6) _____ but in
the afternoon the (7) _____ will come out
again. It will be a (8) _____ day.

RESOURCES   UNIT 4

Communication activity 5

What are you going to do?

Answer the quiz questions and then compare your answers with a partner. What does the quiz say about you?

1 You find 100 euros on the pavement. What are you going to do?

You are going to:

a keep the money because you want to buy some new CDs.

b give the money to a local charity.

c go immediately to the local police station and give the money to them.

2 You are walking to work and see an accident between a car and a bicycle. What are you going to do?

You are going to:

a continue walking but phone for an ambulance.

b continue walking and ignore the accident.

c stop and check the person is OK and phone for an ambulance.

3 You win a million euros on the lottery. What are you going to do?

You are going to:

a give it all to charity.

b save some, spend some and give some to the rest of your family.

c spend it all immediately on a new house, new car and lots of computer games.

4 You see your friend's girlfriend with another boy. What are you going to do?

You are going to:

a talk to your friend's girlfriend and find out what is going on.

b phone your friend immediately and tell him to finish with his girlfriend.

c talk to your friend and his girlfriend together and help them work out their problems.

5 You see the person next to you cheating in an exam. What are you going to do?

You are going to:

a talk to the person after the exam and tell them to tell your teacher.

b tell your teacher immediately.

c ignore it.

6 Your friend has eaten too much during the holidays and has put on some weight. What are you going to do?

You are going to:

a tell him not to worry and offer to buy him more chocolate.

b not say anything.

c tell him to give up chocolate and to take up a sport he likes.

- -

1	a	(0)	2	a	(3)	3	a	(5)	4	a	(3)	5	a	(3)	6	a	(0)
	b	(5)		b	(0)		b	(3)		b	(0)		b	(5)		b	(3)
	c	(3)		c	(5)		c	(0)		c	(5)		c	(0)		c	(5)

What does your score mean?

0 – 10   You don't like working out problems. You like an easy life!

11 – 20   You like helping people. You are a good friend.

21 – 30   You are very generous. You will never have very much money because you always give it away!

Grammar practice 5

1 In January, you and your family made some resolutions. Put the words in the correct order to find out what they were.

1 I'm / to / chocolate / give / going / eating / up

I'm going to give up eating chocolate.

2 is / dad / work / my / going / less / to

....

3 music / going / give / my / to / up / is / listening / to / loud / brother

....

4 going / take / up / is / to / German / my / sister / classes

....

5 is / brother / to / a / read / book / going / week / a / my

....

6 car / drive / going / learn / grandmother / to / a / is / to / my

....

7 is / go / holiday / two / months / on / going / every / my / to / grandfather

....

2 Right (✓) or wrong (✗)? Correct the wrong sentences.

1 Are you going to go to the concert tomorrow? ☑

....

2 John isn't go to visit his brother in London. ☐

....

3 They say it isn't going to rain today. ☐

....

4 Are they going to play tennis this afternoon? ☐

....

5 I'm not going to go on holiday. ☐

....

6 We're going to learning to dance salsa. ☐

....

7 Is he going to clean the house? ☐

....

8 She's not going do the washing. ☐

....

9 Are we go travel to Scotland in September? ☐

....

3 Complete the sentences. Use *must* or *mustn't* and a verb from the box.

go   ~~stop~~   do   eat   move
walk   throw away

1 The traffic light is red. *You must stop* .

2 You are very fat. You .... so much.

3 The rubbish smells. You .... it ....

4 My tooth hurts! I .... to the dentist.

5 You have broken your leg. You .... it.

6 You are unfit! You .... more exercise.

7 The grass is wet. You .... on it.

4 Complete the text with *must* or *mustn't*.

John went to the doctor because he didn't feel well. The doctor gave him some medicine and said: 'You (1) *must* take the medicine three times a day. You (2) .... stay in bed and you (3) .... rest. You (4) .... get up for anything! You (5) .... do any exercise. You (6) .... drink alcohol and you (7) .... smoke. You (8) .... drink lots of water and you (9) .... sleep all you can!'

Communication activity 6

You are offered a job in Madrid next year.	You are offered a place in the top football team in your country.	You are offered a free round-the-world travel ticket.	You are offered a job as a top fashion model.
1 If I go to Spain next year, ...	1 If I play for (Juve), ...	1 If I travel round the world, ...	1 If I work as a top fashion model, ...
2	2	2	2
3	3	3	3
4	4	4	4

© Cambridge University Press 2010   **Resources Unit 6**

UNIT 6

RESOURCES

Grammar practice 6

1 Put the words in order to make sentences.

1 you / I / home / get / call / I / when / 'll
When I get home, I'll call you.

2 the / to / won't / go / rains / we / match / if / it / football
....

3 party / come / will / you / to / if / invite / my / I / you / ?
....

4 when / finish / watch / I / television / my / 'll / homework / I
....

5 Mike / when / 's / will / retire / he / 65 / ?
....

6 go / zoo / 's / won't / it / the / if / hot / they / too / to
....

7 buy / will / if / you / a / half / I / eat / cake / ?
....

8 the / at / when / meet / I / you / me / will / arrive / airport / ?
....

2 Right (✓) or wrong (✗)? Correct the wrong sentences.

1 When you see the gorilla you scream! ☒
When you see the gorilla, you'll scream!

2 You'll feel cold when you jump into the water. ☐
....

3 If you'll be hard-working, you'll pass your exams. ☐
....

4 When you go on holiday to Spain, you'll speak Spanish. ☐
....

5 When I'll feel tired, I go to bed. ☐
....

6 When you jump from the aeroplane, your parachute will open. ☐
....

7 You see lots of fish if you'll swim underwater. ☐
....

3 Complete the sentences. Use the correct tense of the verbs in the box.

> see ~~speak~~ invite watch eat
> stay grow

1 When he goes to Lisbon he *won't speak* any English.

2 Will you tell him I'm here if you .... him?

3 If Diana .... in a hotel, will you go and see her?

4 I .... the television if you don't want me to.

5 Susanna and David .... Cristina to the party if she brings Pedro.

6 When Dad comes home, ... we .... dinner?

7 If the apple tree .... well, we'll have lots of fruit.

4 Complete the sentences. Use the correct form of the words in brackets.

1 It's very *exciting* (excite) being a pop star.

2 He's really .... (interest) in American Football.

3 History is such a .... (bore) subject!

4 Paul was really .... (fright) of the spider.

5 I had a .... (fright) experience yesterday.

6 I didn't sleep last night. I'm really .... (tire).

7 Their dog is really .... (annoy). It jumps on top of you.

8 She was so .... (bore), she nearly fell asleep.

9 It was a very .... (tire) day.

RESOURCES   UNIT 6

✱ Communication activity 7

kind
You can't say:
* ✱ helps people and thinks about other people's feelings
* ✱ is the opposite of unkind

unfriendly
You can't say:
* ✱ is unpleasant to people and not polite
* ✱ is the opposite of friendly

hard-working
You can't say:
* ✱ works a lot
* ✱ is the opposite of lazy

dishonest
You can't say:
* ✱ does not tell the truth
* ✱ is the opposite of honest

polite
You can't say:
* ✱ always says *please* and *thank you*
* ✱ is the opposite of impolite/rude

unkind
You can't say:
* ✱ is not pleasant
* ✱ is the opposite of kind

honest
You can't say:
* ✱ tells you what he/she really thinks
* ✱ is the opposite of dishonest

lazy
You can't say:
* ✱ does not want to work
* ✱ is the opposite of hard-working

organised
You can't say:
* ✱ is always tidy and keeps things in order
* ✱ is the opposite of disorganised

miserable
You can't say:
* ✱ is very unhappy
* ✱ is the opposite of cheerful

cheerful
You can't say:
* ✱ is usually happy and smiles a lot
* ✱ is the opposite of miserable

nervous
You can't say:
* ✱ is worried all the time
* ✱ is the opposite of relaxed

relaxed
You can't say:
* ✱ doesn't worry about things
* ✱ is the opposite of nervous

rude
You can't say:
* ✱ is unpleasant
* ✱ is the opposite of polite

friendly
You can't say:
* ✱ is easy to talk to and makes friends easily
* ✱ is the opposite of unfriendly

disorganised
You can't say:
* ✱ is untidy
* ✱ is the opposite of organised

Grammar practice 7

1 Complete the sentences with *should* or *shouldn't*.

1 I've got toothache. I *should* go to the dentist.

2 You've just won the lottery. You _____ be miserable!

3 He studies very hard. He _____ pass the exam.

4 It's very late. We _____ go home now.

5 There's so much to do. You _____ be so relaxed!

6 I've lost my keys. You _____ try to help me find them.

7 We're going to the beach. We _____ sit in the sun for too long.

8 I feel ill. I _____ go to the doctor.

9 He's got no money in the bank. He _____ buy a new car!

2 Put the words in order to make sentences.

1 walk / grass / you / on / shouldn't / the / !

   You shouldn't walk on the grass!

2 I / think / the / wear / you / dress / green / do / should / ?

   ----

3 John / his / like / that / talk / to / teacher / shouldn't / !

   ----

4 chocolate / so / shouldn't / much / you / eat

   ----

5 go / do / think / should / cinema / the / you / we / to / ?

   ----

6 be / he / his / parents / to / shouldn't / rude

   ----

7 customers / to / be / the / should / polite / Helen

   ----

8 should / you / your / take / umbrella

   ----

9 a / should / present / they / take / ?

   ----

3 Right (✓) or wrong (✗)? Correct the wrong sentences.

1 Shouldn't you speak to strangers.   ✗

   You shouldn't speak to strangers.

2 Should you kiss people in France when you meet them?   ☐

   ----

3 Should she travels alone in Brazil?   ☐

   ----

4 You shouldn't to kiss your neighbour in England.   ☐

   ----

5 My brother shouldn't drive so fast.   ☐

   ----

6 You should looks after your suitcase.   ☐

   ----

7 Jenny should give up smoking.   ☐

   ----

8 Should they learn Chinese before going to China?   ☐

   ----

9 She shouldn't speaks English in Spain.   ☐

   ----

4 Write questions about England. Use *What ... like?*

1 the people

   What are the people like?

2 the food

   ----

3 the houses

   ----

4 London

   ----

5 the shops

   ----

6 the clothes

RESOURCES   UNIT 7

Communication activity 8

Student A

Work in pairs. Ask student B the questions below. If B answers *Yes*, tick (✓) the box. Then ask the other questions and note down the answers. Then think of one more question to ask him/her.

If B answers *No*, put a cross (✗) in the box.

You ask the first question. Then student B will ask you his/her first question.

1 **Has anyone in your family ever raised money for a charity?** ☐
Which charity?
What did they do?
(Your own question)

2 **Have you ever held a tarantula?** ☐
How did you feel?
What did it feel like?
(Your own question)

3 **Have you ever touched a snake?** ☐
When did you touch it?
What did it feel like?
(Your own question)

4 **Have you ever taken a risk?** ☐
What was the risk?
Why did you take it?
(Your own question)

5 **Have you ever seen a tiger?** ☐
Where did you see it?
How did you feel?
(Your own question)

✂ -

Student B

Work in pairs. Ask student A the questions below. If A answers *Yes*, tick (✓) the box. Then ask the other questions and note down the answers. Then think of one more question to ask him/her.

If A answers *No*, put a cross (✗) in the box.

Student A asks the first question. Then you ask student A your first question.

1 **Have you ever won a prize?** ☐
What was the prize for?
What was the prize?
(Your own question)

2 **Have you ever held a frog in your hand?** ☐
What was it like?
When did you hold it?
(Your own question)

3 **Has anyone you know ever broken a record?** ☐
What was the record?
When did they break it?
(Your own question)

4 **Have you ever ridden a horse?** ☐
When did you ride a horse?
What was it like?
(Your own question)

5 **Have you ever heard a parrot talking?** ☐
Whose parrot was it?
What did it say?
(Your own question)

Grammar practice 8

1 Complete the sentences. Use the present perfect form of the verbs in the box.

> clean ~~read~~ eat build meet lose
> win travel rain

1 I _have read_ the book.
2 He .... his keys.
3 She .... the kitchen.
4 It .... all day.
5 We .... our dinner.
6 They .... all over the world.
7 Maria and Alejo .... the Pope.
8 Simon .... his own house.
9 David .... the lottery.

2 Write questions about the sentences. Use the clues to help you.

1 I have never broken my leg. (you)
   Have you ever broken your leg?
2 I have never owned an unusual pet. (they)
   ....
3 We haven't received the letter. (you)
   ....
4 He hasn't seen a parrot. (she)
   ....
5 They have never eaten potatoes. (we)
   ....
6 He has never touched a snake. (you)
   ....
7 She has never written a book. (they)
   ....
8 We haven't been to Paris. (she)
   ....
9 We haven't milked a cow. (he)
   ....

3 Right (✓) or wrong (✗)? Correct the wrong sentences.

1 She has lived here for ten years. ✓
   ....
2 Have you heard the news? ☐
   ....
3 She has eat too much today. ☐
   ....
4 Ow! I've cutted my finger! ☐
   ....
5 I'm hungry. I hasn't eaten since yesterday! ☐
   ....
6 I haven't learnt very much English this year. ☐
   ....
7 He has build all the houses in this street. ☐
   ....
8 Have you seen his pet snake? ☐
   ....
9 He haven't got any Elvis CDs. ☐
   ....

4 Ever or never? Circle the correct word.

1 I haven't (ever) / never been to America.
2 Have you ever / never seen an alligator?
3 He's ever / never seen the Queen.
4 She's ever / never told a joke!
5 They haven't ever / never watched that programme.
6 Have you ever / never owned an unusual pet?
7 I have ever / never won a prize.
8 Have his parents ever / never seen his teacher?
9 Has Peter ever / never climbed a mountain?

RESOURCES

UNIT 8

Acknowledgements

The publishers are grateful to the following contributors:
Annie Cornford and Ruth Bell-Pellegrini: editorial work
Claire Thacker: initial script writing
Pentacor Book design: text design and layouts

The publishers are grateful to the following illustrators:
Dylan Gibson 76, 87, 91, 93, 95, 174
Mark Watkinson (Illustration) 75, 77, 172